T0302100

Business and Public Policy

It is increasingly common for businesses to face public policies and government regulation that demand some form of environmental or social protection. These protective public policies have grown in number, complexity, and stringency over the last few decades, not only in industrialized countries but also in the developing world. In this book, Jorge E. Rivera presents a new theoretical framework for understanding the relationship between protective public policies and business compliance. This framework explains different levels of business compliance in terms of three distinct factors: the link between the stages of the protective public policy process and different levels of business resistance, the moderating effects of country context, and firm-level characteristics. The second part of the book supports and elaborates on this framework by presenting empirical studies that examine two voluntary environmental programs: the US ski industry's Sustainable Slopes Program and the Certification for Sustainable Tourism in Costa Rica.

JORGE E. RIVERA is Associate Professor of Strategic Management and Public Policy at The George Washington University School of Business, Washington DC. He is also an associate editor of the journals *Policy Sciences* and *Business & Society.*

Business, Value Creation, and Society

Series editors
R. Edward Freeman, *University of Virginia*
Stuart L. Hart, *Cornell University* and *University of North Carolina*
David Wheeler, *Dalhousie University, Halifax*

The purpose of this innovative series is to examine, from an international standpoint, the interaction of business and capitalism with society. In the twenty-first century it is more important than ever that business and capitalism come to be seen as social institutions that have a great impact on the welfare of human society around the world. Issues such as globalization, environmentalism, information technology, the triumph of liberalism, corporate governance, and business ethics all have the potential to have major effects on our current models of the corporation and the methods by which value is created, distributed, and sustained among all stakeholders – customers, suppliers, employees, communities, and financiers.

Published titles in this series:
Fort *Business, Integrity, and Peace*
Gomez and Korine *Entrepreneurs and Democracy*
Crane, Matten, and Moon *Corporations and Citizenship*
Painter-Morland *Business Ethics as Practice*
Yaziji and Doh *NGOs and Corporations*

Forthcoming titles:
Sachs, Rühli, and Kern *Stakeholders Matter*
Maak and Pless *Responsible Leadership*

Business and Public Policy

Responses to Environmental and Social Protection Processes

JORGE E. RIVERA
The George Washington University

CAMBRIDGE UNIVERSITY PRESS
Cambridge, New York, Melbourne, Madrid, Cape Town,
Singapore, São Paulo, Delhi, Mexico City

Cambridge University Press
The Edinburgh Building, Cambridge CB2 8RU, UK

Published in the United States of America by Cambridge University Press, New York

www.cambridge.org
Information on this title: www.cambridge.org/9781107406285

First published 2010
First paperback edition (with corrections) 2012

A catalogue record for this publication is available from the British Library

Library of Congress Cataloguing in Publication data
Rivera, Jorge E.
Business and public policy : responses to environmental and social protection processes / Jorge E. Rivera.
p. cm. – (Business, value creation, and society)
Includes bibliographical references.
ISBN 978-0-521-89781-5
1. Business. 2. Industries – Social aspects. 3. Industries – Environmental aspects. 4. Political planning. I. Title. II. Series.
HF1008.R58 2010
658.4′083–dc22 2010014628

ISBN 978-0-521-89781-5 Hardback
ISBN 978-1-107-40628-5 Paperback

To my parents, Jorge and Leonor, and my wife Jennifer, with love

Contents

Figures

Tables

Foreword

In this book, Jorge Rivera makes a very important contribution to our emerging knowledge about how private strategies and public policies interact to advance the cause of sustainability. By looking across theories (e.g., institutional theory and policy sciences) and country contexts (developed and developing) he is able to generate important new insights that should help inform future action.

First, he clearly documents and illustrates the "dance" that exists between business and government when it comes to the policy process. Rivera shows that companies both influence and are influenced by the policy process. He posits an inverted U-shaped relationship, with increasing resistance from business as the process moves from initiation to selection, and thereafter, declining resistance that turns into growing cooperation in implementation. Corporate behavior is not the simple result of a one-way flow of isomorphic pressure as the neo-institutionalists might have us believe.

Even more importantly, Professor Rivera proposes that country matters when it comes to business resistance to environmental and social policies, with countries with lower levels of democracy and income per capita evincing more business resistance to environmental and social policy. Other things being equal, this would tend to suggest that "developing" countries would show more business resistance to such policies than "developed" countries, the result being poorer environmental and social performance. However, Rivera also shows us that the actual *design* of the policy might be more important than the country characteristics. Indeed, through close examination of two voluntary environmental programs – the US ski industry's Sustainable Slopes Program and Costa Rica's Certification for Sustainable Tourism – he shows that the opposite behavior can result: Costa Rica's program results in beyond-compliance behavior whereas the US ski industry program actually attracts players with lower environmental performance ratings. This counter-intuitive result stems from fundamental differences in program design: the Costa Rican program is run by the government and includes third-party, performance-based certification, which provides certified hotels with a price premium and sales benefits not available to uncertified hotels. The US ski industry's program, in contrast, lacks third-party certification, involves no specific environmental standards, and has no sanctions for poor performance. The result is that superior performers steer clear, leaving only the laggards to participate, perhaps for the "public relations" benefit.

Finally, Professor Rivera shows that company characteristics also influence the likelihood of engaging in the private–public "dance" described above: chief executive officers' level of formal education and environmental expertise are associated with higher corporate participation and also with higher beyond-compliance environmental performance ratings.

We are very pleased indeed to publish this book in the series on *Business, Value Creation, and Society*. The purpose of the series is to stimulate thinking about new ways to combine economic value creation with social contribution and environmental sustainability. Professor Rivera has made an important contribution toward this end.

Stuart L. Hart
S. C. Johnson Chair in Sustainable Global Enterprise
Johnson School of Management
Cornell University
Ithaca, NY, USA

Acknowledgments

I owe much gratitude to many individuals and organizations that helped make this book possible. The support from The George Washington University and my colleagues in the Strategic Management and Public Policy Department was instrumental in all my efforts. Tim Fort's help, advice, encouragement, and example planted the seed for me to start thinking about the possibility of writing a book-long manuscript. He also opened the door that gave me initial access to multiple university presses. Mark Starik's friendship and advice have been invaluable in helping me survive my initial journey as Professor. At GW, the grants from the Center for International Business Research, the School of Business' Dean Research Fellowship, and the Institutes for Corporate Responsibility and Latin American Studies were particularly instrumental in allowing me to dedicate the extra time required to finish this book. Rochelle Rediang, Aditi Vira, Prathima Parthasarathi, and Resmi Jacob deserve much appreciation for their support in editing the book's citations and references.

My writing would not be legible without the immense help and patience of Brian Oetzel. His thorough reviewing of the multiple drafts of my journal articles and book chapters has been critical for improving the clarity of my work. Many thanks Brian for your excellent and always prompt support! In Costa Rica, I am indebted to the help of many friends, colleagues, and organizations. In the mid-1990s the Instituto Centroamericano de Administración de Empresas (INCAE) Business School provided me with financial support and valuable assistance for the early research of the hotel industry in that country. In particular, INCAE's Professor Alvaro Umaña's advice and mentorship was instrumental in allowing me to follow my dreams to do research and pursue a doctoral education. Rodolfo Lizano, the creator of the Certification for Sustainable Tourism at the Costa Rican

Institute of Tourism, provided me with access to unique data and was also very generous in responding to my many questions and requests for additional information. In early 2009, I had the privilege of spending my sabbatical at the Centro Agronómico Tropical de Investigación y Enseñanza (CATIE; the Tropical Agricultural Research and Higher Education Center) as a research associate of the Environment for Development Center in Central America. The time, freedom, and ideas from my great friends Francisco Alpizar, Juan Robalino, and Allen Blackman gave me the energy to finish this book when exhaustion made it seem an impossible task. Additionally, I want to thank my editor, R. Edward Freeman, for his trust and comments, and the great people at Cambridge University Press: Paula Parish, Thomas O'Reilly, and Jennifer Davis who patiently guided me through the production process for the book.

I am also thankful for the mentorship, ideas, and inspiration that I received from many professors: in college, Thelma de Gallardo, Willy Knedel, Janet Willer, and Raymundo Zea; at Duke University, Robert Healy, William Ascher, and Stuart Hart. Robert Healy, my dissertation chair, was particularly influential in shaping my research while giving me the freedom to pursue my own interests. Equally inspirational have been the ideas and enthusiasm of Peter deLeon, my co-author and great friend. Of course, my deepest gratitude goes to Jennifer, my wife, and my parents, Jorge and Leonor, whose unconditional love and support fill my daily life with the hope and energy to try to make a difference.

Publication acknowledgments

This book compiles research work that I have conducted over the last ten years. Previous versions of this work have been published in academic journal articles and they are reproduced with the kind permission of the co-authors and publishers. I am deeply thankful to my co-authors for their help, ideas, encouragement, criticism, and companionship during this long journey of discovery. Portions of Chapters 1, 2, 3, and 10 appeared in an article published in *Policy Sciences*: Rivera, J., Oetzel, J., deLeon, P., and Starik, M. 2009. "Business responses to environmental and social protection policies: towards a framework for analysis," *Policy Sciences* **42**: 3–42.

The analysis of the US ski industry's Sustainable Slopes Program presented in Chapters 5 and 6 was originally published in two *Policy Studies Journal* articles: first, Rivera, J. and deLeon, P. 2004. "Is greener whiter? The Sustainable Slopes Program and the voluntary environmental performance of western ski areas," *Policy Studies Journal* **32** (3): 417–37; and second, Rivera, J., deLeon, P., and Koerber, C. 2006. "Is greener whiter yet? The Sustainable Slopes Program after five years," *Policy Studies Journal* **34** (2): 195–224.

The studies of the Costa Rican Certification for Sustainable Tourism discussed in Chapters 7, 8, and 9 were respectively published in the following three journal articles: Rivera, J. 2004. "Institutional pressures and voluntary environmental behavior in developing countries: evidence from Costa Rica," *Society and Natural Resources* **17**: 779–97.

Rivera, J. and deLeon, P. 2005. "Chief executive officers and voluntary environmental performance: Costa Rica's Certification for Sustainable Tourism," *Policy Sciences* **38** (2–3): 107–27.

Rivera, J. 2002. "Assessing a voluntary environmental initiative in the developing world: the Costa Rican Certification for Sustainable Tourism," *Policy Sciences* **35**: 333–60.

1 *Introduction*[1]

In the early 1990s when "green" businesses were seldom observed in the US and the very idea of "green and competitive" was considered on the cutting edge of management practices, "eco-lodges" were already very popular in Costa Rica. Indeed, at that time the symbiosis between hotels and Costa Rica's world-class national parks was yielding one of the most impressive examples of hotel industry prosperity directly linked to proactive business environmental protection. Conversely, in the late 1990s and early 2000s, the US ski resort industry was showing strong resistance to new environmental regulation demands and to the protection of biodiversity in US national forest lands. At first glance, this dynamic may seem paradoxical: higher beyond-compliance environmental protection by businesses in a developing country much poorer than the US. To understand this apparent paradox, this book provides a framework of analysis and empirical studies developed over a period of more that ten years in collaboration with several outstanding colleagues. More generally, in this book I contribute towards providing answers to three broad research questions that continue to attract the attention of a large number of scholars, policymakers, and managers interested in environmental and social protection issues:

(1) How are the stages of the environmental and social protection policy process linked to different levels of business resistance?
(2) How does country context affect the level of resistance shown by business to environmental and social protection policy demands?
(3) How do firm-level characteristics affect the environmental and social protection policy process–business response relationship?

Main book ideas and propositions

Public policies and regulations that demand increased environmental and social protection (hereafter called protective public policies) by business have been growing in number, complexity, and stringency over the last few decades not only in industrialized countries but also in developing nations (Baron, 2005; O'Rourke, 2004; Vig and Kraft, 2006). Neo-institutional scholars interested in organizations have contributed significantly to our understanding of the logic that shapes business' responses to government laws and other socially enacted values, beliefs, norms, and routines. Although some scholars have begun to stress a wide array of legitimate organizational responses to multiple and sometimes conflicting institutional pressures (Hoffman, 1999; Oliver, 1991), most neo-institutional research continues to highlight compliance as the most legitimate and expected response to coercive regulatory pressures (Dacin *et al.*, 2002; Hirsch, 1997).

Thus, a relatively limited view has emerged that portrays public policies and regulations as followed by business (Friedland and Alford, 1991; Hirsch, 1997; Hoffman, 1999; Suchman and Edelman, 1997). To be sure, compliance with environmental and social protection public policies and their regulations is certainly the prevalent response of firms in the US but not of those in developing countries. Yet it is important to highlight that in the US it has taken decades to enact and implement these protective policies and for them to reach the point of being internalized by business managers and other influential social groups. This long US public policy process is affected by intense advocacy and/or opposition by multiple social, government, and business actors. Additionally, it requires massive public expenditure to create and institutionalize new government agencies with strong monitoring–enforcement capacity and political clout. Hence, in the first part of this book (Chapters 2–4), I seek to contribute to the neo-institutional literature by focusing on developing a conceptual understanding of the protective policy process–business response relationship. Specifically, my first goal is to discuss, in Chapter 2, the underlying logic explaining the protective public policy process dynamic in the context of the US to elucidate how its stages are associated with business' political strategies involving different degrees of resistance and/or cooperation. To do this, I integrate neo-institutional scholarship with ideas from the policy sciences literature that has for a long time emphasized the importance of taking a process perspective to understand policymaking (Clark, 2002; Lasswell, 1971).

I see business as both influenced by protective public policies and actively involved in the intensely adversarial socio-political process of contesting, remaking, and redefining them (Fligstein and McAdam, 1993; Hoffman, 1997; Oliver, 1991; Seo and Creed, 2002). That is, during the policy process businesses and their stakeholders are not just bystanders constrained by the coercive force of regulations; they are also strategic actors trying to shape them (Oliver, 1991; Steinmo *et al.*, 1992). Specifically, I posit that other things being equal – such as firm characteristics and in-country regional conditions – business responses are likely to have an inverted U-shaped relationship with the protective policy process dynamic in the US, showing increasing resistance as the process moves from initiation to selection and thereafter declining resistance that turns into growing cooperation in mid-implementation.

Another important gap in the neo-institutional literature on organizational analysis is its focus on studying business behaviors in industrialized countries such as the US, those in Europe, and other developed nations. Except for studying how business behavior is affected by variations in different styles of democracy and state control, organizational neo-institutional scholars have paid little attention to significant contrasts in other key country contextual characteristics such as: level of democracy, system of interest representation, regulatory approach, and national economic income. Thus, another goal of this book is to contribute towards filling this gap by developing, in Chapter 3, a conceptual framework of analysis clarifying how these additional country contextual variables may intervene to moderate the protective policy process–business response relationship described for the context of the US in Chapter 2 of the book.

In general terms, my propositions suggest, other things being equal, higher levels of business resistance to different stages of the protective policy process in countries with:

(1) Lower levels of democracy,
(2) A predominant reliance on command-and-control regulatory instruments (as opposed to incentive-based ones), and/or
(3) Lower economic income per capita,
(4) I also posit that a country's system of interest representation moderates the inverted U-shaped relationship between the protective policy process and firms' responses in such a way that firms operating in pluralistic countries are more likely to offer: (i) higher political resistance during the different stages of the policy process

than firms operating in neo-corporatist countries; and (ii) lower political resistance during the different stages of the policy process than firms operating in state-corporatist countries.[2]

In Chapter 4, I relax the assumption that holds firm-level characteristics constant to discuss their moderating effect on the protective policy process–business response relationship. Firm-level characteristics may also affect how different firms are socialized into distinct country political and economic traditions (George *et al.*, 2006) thus affecting how they may respond to the pressures and demands exerted by policy process stages. To be sure, there are extensive literatures on corporate political strategy and corporate social and environmental management that have identified how a large array of company characteristics is respectively associated with differences in corporate political practices and environmental/social protection practices (Berchicci and King, 2007; Cavazos, 2005). Building upon these literatures, I develop a set of propositions that focus only on a few of the firm characteristics that have more prominently and consistently been identified to affect these practices. In general terms, the propositions suggest lower resistance and higher environmental/social performance during the different stages of the protective policy process for firms with:

(1) Higher financial performance,
(2) Larger size,
(3) Higher export orientation,
(4) Chief executive officers with higher levels of formal education,
(5) Multinational corporation ownership,
(6) Public ownership, and
(7) Membership in industry associations.

When considering these propositions it is important to keep in mind a critical caveat: the moderating effect of firm-level characteristics on firm responses to protective policy demands is particularly important during the enactment and early implementation stages of the protective policy process when regulatory demands are not yet fully institutionalized (Tolbert and Zucker, 1983). As regulations and standards become fully institutionalized, this moderating influence that firm characteristics have on business responses to the policy process may decline to the point of showing no significant effect (Baron *et al.*, 1986; Friedland and Alford, 1991; Tolbert and Zucker, 1983).

In delineating the boundaries of the first part of the book (Chapters 2–4), it is important to stress first that this part is focused exclusively on conceptual development. I do not provide empirical evidence testing the logic and propositions advanced. The few examples included in these chapters are illustrative only and not offered as empirical evidence. Also, while in my theorizing I recognize the importance that country regional conditions may have on determining firms' responses to government demands, their effect on the policy process–business response relationship proposed is explicitly not considered. Although holding country regional conditions constant in my analysis precludes me from developing a more general framework of the policy process–business response relationship, it allows me to take a first step towards exploring a central component of this framework; explaining how business-level and country-level contextual characteristics moderate the policy process–business response relationship above and beyond the effect of regional in-country conditions. This approach is, of course, the traditional science-based method for the initial analysis of specific relationships of interest while acknowledging that other variables may have an effect on such relationships (Kuhn, 1962; Popper, 2002; Rowley, 1997). I also do not consider economic policies and regulations that, in contrast to protective policies usually opposed by firms, tend to be traditionally supported by existing businesses.[3]

Empirical studies

In the second part of the book (Chapters 5–9), I present empirical studies that examine business environmental protection behavior in the US and Costa Rica. The significant differences in the contexts of these two countries suggested some of the ideas proposed by the conceptual framework developed in the first part of the book. They involve the evaluation of two voluntary environmental programs: the US ski industry's Sustainable Slopes Program and the Certification for Sustainable Tourism in Costa Rica. For more than a decade now, having had the luck of working together with outstanding co-authors, my empirical research and refereed academic journal publications have been focused on the study of these two voluntary environmental programs (VEPs) both in the US and developing countries (in the acknowledgments section I thank these co-authors whose gifted insights have at all times improved my research and ideas. Also, the journal articles from which the book chapters were developed are specified in the initial endnote of each chapter). Studying VEPs also helped with the initial examination of the conceptual framework developed in this book because VEPs tend to attract participants displaying a wide range of responses to protective policy demands: from highly cooperative firms, seeking to adopt the most proactive environmental management strategies, to highly resistant firms that follow a manipulative free-riding approach.

Chapter 5 analyzes the initial implementation of the Sustainable Slopes Program (SSP), a voluntary environmental initiative established by the US National Ski Areas Association in partnership with federal and state government agencies. The findings from this study indicate that participation of western ski areas in the SSP is related to institutional pressures in the form of enhanced federal oversight and higher state environmental demands exerted by state agencies, local environmental groups, and public opinion. The analysis also suggests that, despite these institutional pressures, participant ski areas appear to be correlated with lower third-party environmental performance ratings. This behavior seems to reflect the lack of specific institutional mechanisms to prevent opportunism in the current design of the SSP. That is, the program does not involve specific environmental standards, lacks third-party oversight, and does not have sanctions for poor performance.

In Chapter 6, I focus on two basic questions: are voluntary programs effective in promoting higher environmental performance by participant firms? If so, which distinct areas of environmental performance are more likely to be improved by firms joining a voluntary environmental program? These questions are addressed by assessing the environmental effectiveness of the ski industry's SSP in the western United States between 2001 and 2005. I found no evidence in this five-year analysis to conclude that ski areas adopting the SSP displayed superior performance levels than nonparticipants for the following areas of environmental protection: overall environmental performance, expansion management, pollution management, and wildlife and habitat management. SSP participants appear to show a statistically significant correlation only with higher natural resource conservation performance rates.

Changing country context and the program examined, the study discussed in Chapter 7 aims to identify how institutional forces, such as regulatory and stakeholder pressures, are related to proactive environmental behavior by hotel facilities participating in the Certification for Sustainable Tourism (CST), a voluntary environmental program established by the Costa Rican government. This program is among the first third-party performance-based environmental certification initiatives implemented in the developing world. Findings suggest that voluntary environmental programs that include performance-based standards and third-party monitoring may be effective in promoting beyond-compliance environmental behavior when they are complemented by isomorphic institutional pressures exerted by government environmental monitoring and trade association membership. Surprisingly, findings also indicate that compared to locally owned hotels, foreign-owned and multinational subsidiary facilities do not seem to be significantly correlated with higher participation and superior environmental performance in the CST.

In Chapter 8, I evaluate whether the education, environmental expertise, and nationality of firms' chief executive officers (CEOs) are associated with greater participation and environmental performance in the CST. The findings suggest that CEOs' level of formal education and environmental expertise appear to be significantly associated with higher corporate participation in voluntary programs and also with higher beyond-compliance environmental performance ratings. Contrary to conventional expectations, CEOs from industrialized countries (as opposed to developing countries) do not appear to show a statistically significant association with participation in the CST program and with higher beyond-compliance environmental performance.

Chapter 9 evaluates the ability of voluntary environmental programs to generate economic benefits for firms. Given their voluntary nature, provision of economic benefits to firms is a necessary condition for these programs to become effective environmental policy instruments. Specifically, the paper focuses on assessing the price premium and sales benefits for hotels participating in the CST program. Results indicate that hotels with certified superior environmental performance show a positive relationship with differentiation advantages that yield price premiums. Participation in the CST program alone is not significantly related to higher prices and higher sales.

Finally, in Chapter 10, I wrap up the book by outlining a few concluding remarks and suggest a future research agenda.

Notes

1. This chapter includes slightly modified portions of: Rivera *et al.* (2009), reproduced with kind permission of Springer Science and Business Media.
2. See definitions of pluralistic, neo-corporatist, and state-corporatist countries in Chapter 3, pages 58–9.
3. Economic policies are regulations that establish prices, subsidies, trade tariffs, accounting practices, etc., and tend to be demanded by existing businesses which are their main beneficiaries (Hawkins and Thomas, 1984; Kagan, 1984; Stigler, 1971; Winston, 1993). Tax-increasing policies are exceptions to this generalization about the tendency for businesses to support economic policies and regulations (Stigler, 1971).

2 *Business responses to the protective policy process in the US*[1]

The conceptual ideas discussed in this chapter build on policy scientists' work that has long emphasized the importance of taking a process perspective to understand policymaking (Clark, 2002; Lasswell, 1971). This chapter also follows sociology's neo-institutional scholars in drawing from Berger and Luckmann's (1967) phenomenological approach to understanding institutions and institutional processes (DiMaggio and Powell, 1983; Scott, 1991, 2001; Tolbert and Zucker, 1996). In particular, I borrow from Andrew Hoffman's seminal work (1997, 1999) studying the evolution of corporate environmentalism in the US chemical and oil industries between 1960 and 1993. His work illustrates the predominant pattern of business responses to the institutional dynamic associated with evolving environmental protection demands in the US: initially chemical and oil firms show high levels of resistance that over a couple of decades turns into cooperation and even proactive beyond-compliance. This change from resistance to cooperation arises from new understandings, metaphors, norms, and regulations redefining appropriate business protective practices that gradually become taken for granted. Important elements in this redefinition of legitimate business behavior include: stakeholders' demands, new environmental protection paradigms, external environmental crises, and industry-generated accidents (Hoffman, 1997, 1999).

I advance this work by detailing the specific nature of the protective policy process–business response relationship in the US. Most importantly, this book contributes to previous work by integrating the policy sciences and organizational sociology's neo-institutional literatures to outline an underlying phenomenological logic explicating changes in business responses to different stages of the protective policy process in the US. This expanded focus on a socially constructed legitimacy-seeking rationality as opposed to exclusively self-interest maximization rationality, also differentiates this book from work by economists such as Tom Lyon and John Maxwell (2004). Assuming self-interest maximization and using a policy process perspective, they propose a framework that explains corporate resistance to environmental policy demands in the US. Their basic view is that firms' resistance to public policies increases as the cost of these policies climbs (Lyon and Maxwell, 2004: 36). In this book, this perspective is not rejected but it is made part of an expanded view of rationality as not only profit-seeking but also legitimacy-seeking.

Neo-institutional theory and public policies

Sharing an open systems perspective with other social science theories, sociology's neo-institutional theory gives the external context a central role in determining organizations' strategies (Katz and Kahn, 1966; Scott, 2001). Accordingly, managers' behavior is seen as restricted and shaped by the social and cultural environment in which they are embedded (Granovetter, 1985; Meyer and Rowan, 1977). Institutions are seen as the most important element of this external context and they are understood as: formal state organizations, policies and regulations, informal shared schemas, routines, norms, symbols, and ceremonial traditions that are highly stable and facilitate and constrain the behavior of social actors (DiMaggio and Powell, 1983; Hall, 1986; Meyer and Rowan, 1977; Powell and DiMaggio, 1991).

Neo-institutional scholars also challenge the traditional notion that businesses and their managers are exclusively rational profit-maximizers and emphasize the importance of also achieving social legitimacy for long-term business survival and competitiveness (Meyer and Rowan, 1977; Powell and DiMaggio, 1991; Scott, 2001). Legitimate businesses are those whose actions are seen as, or presumed to be, "desirable, proper, or appropriate within some socially constructed system of norms, values, beliefs, and definitions" (Suchman, 1995: 574). Because legitimacy is context specific, what is "rational" varies across countries, industries, and individuals experiencing different socialization processes. In other words, business preferences, interests, and values are often modified by their operation in different contexts and by their interaction with actors possessing different understandings of reality and appropriateness (Fligstein and McAdam, 1993). Additionally, neo-institutionalists highlight that it is not rare for decisionmakers to hold contradictory preferences and values, making it difficult to pursue single goals and strategies (Steinmo *et al.*, 1992).

Organizational scholars have contributed significantly to the neo-institutional literature. Their research strongly suggests that institutions determining social legitimacy exert coercive, normative, and cognitive pressures that have an isomorphic effect, through diffusion and imitation, leading businesses that operate in the same organizational field to adopt similar structures and strategies (Powell and DiMaggio, 1991; Scott, 2001).

Early neo-institutional scholars have highlighted compliance as the typical isomorphic response to institutional pressures arising from state policies and regulations. Yet, more recent work that revisits social science's structure versus agency dilemma has begun to stress a wider array of legitimate organizational responses to these pressures (Hirsch and Lounsbury, 1997; Hoffman, 1997; Oliver, 1991). Borrowing from this more recent scholarship and drawing on insights from the policy sciences and public policy literature, I view the enactment, adoption and implementation of protective policies as an inherently political process customarily entailing advocacy and/or opposition by multiple social, state, and business actors engaged in an intense power struggle (Brewer and deLeon, 1983; Kingdon, 1995). Indeed, except for the late implementation part of the protective policy process, lack of severe conflict among these groups is very rare in the US (Pressman and Wildavsky, 1984). Business is less passive in its resistance to state demands than originally proposed by early neo-institutionalists (Meyer and Rowan, 1977; Oliver, 1991). In this book the state and its policies are not understood as exclusively authoritative exogenous factors that determine business behavior. In other words, institutionalized public policies and their regulations are not as permanent and inflexible as they seem at first sight. Policy change may often be incremental, nonetheless it is pervasive in most polities. This dynamic perspective on policymaking, involving time and change, is critical for clarifying early neo-institutional arguments that seem to require circular evidence by portraying organizational choices as significantly determined by institutions and simultaneously shaping them (Peters and Pierre, 1998).

I see business as both influenced by public policies and actively involved in the intensively adversarial socio-political process of contesting, remaking, and redefining them (Fligstein and McAdam, 1993;

Hoffman, 1997; Oliver, 1991; Seo and Creed, 2002). That is, during the policy process businesses and their stakeholders are not just bystanders constrained by the coercive force of regulations; they are also strategic actors trying to shape them (Oliver, 1991; Steinmo *et al.*, 1992).

This highly political and fiercely contested public policy dynamic is particularly evident in the creation and implementation of protective public policies and regulations that are intended to coerce firms to adopt measures that safeguard, among others, the environment, consumers, workers' health and safety, and civil rights (Kagan, 1984; Milstein *et al.*, 2002; Vig and Kraft, 2006). Yet, until recently the neo-institutional literature predominantly relied on a more limited perspective deemphasizing the socio-political process through which protective policies are enacted, contested, diffused, and reproduced; depicting them as exogenous constraints that are effectively enforced by a powerful state capable of coercing firms to comply (Barley and Tolbert, 1997; Hirsch, 1997; Seo and Creed, 2002; Tolbert and Zucker, 1996). In fact, as long suggested by public policy scholars, business facing government demands adopts multiple political strategies that can range widely from strong opposition to proactive cooperation (Lindblom and Woodhouse, 1993; Lowi, 1964). In this book, business political strategies are understood as the concerted pattern of actions taken by firms to favorably shape public policies and demands arising from the commands, appeals, influence, and/or opposition of government agencies, social and environmental activists, and other stakeholders (Baron, 2005; Baysinger, 1984; Mahon, 1993).

Classification of business responses to policy process demands

The wide variety of strategies adopted by businesses is associated with different and often conflicting claims of power from the various actors involved in the stages of the policy process. The exercise of power during the policy process may take different forms, which have been classified in four basic "faces" or dimensions. First, power can consist of direct coercion, relying on the use of physical force, formal authority, possession of crucial skills, and/or the control of critical-scarce resources (Clegg *et al.*, 2006; Dahl, 1973). The second face of power involves the ability to manipulate dominant political procedures and institutions to limit discussion of issues deemed important and worthy of inclusion into the decision-making agenda (Bacharach and Baratz, 1962; Fleming and Spicer, 2007). Third, power can involve domination of others through imposing an ideology that shapes the values, preferences, and understandings that determine legitimate behaviors. By imposing an ideology so that all actors have a "shared" understanding conflict is thus pre-empted. These legitimized values, preferences, and understandings may even be against the interest of those being dominated (Clegg *et al.*, 2006; Lukes, 1974). Finally, the fourth face of power shapes the process of subjectification determining how the internal and external reality as a whole is perceived. Subjectification takes place when one actor is able to control the entire self-definition of other agents and thus produces self-monitoring that advances the interests of the powerful (Fleming and Spicer, 2007).

Beginning with Dahl's seminal work in conceptualizing political opposition, the patterns of resistance through cooperation to the exercise of power during the policy process have been classified using multiple criteria such as their levels of collective organization or their reliance on formal political channels (Blondel, 1997; Boddewyn and Brewer, 1994: 122; Dahl, 1971; 1973). In this book we follow management scholars by characterizing business responses according to the levels of active agency employed to resist policy process pressures and demands (Fischer, 1983; Oliver, 1991; Pfeffer and Salancik, 1978; Rowley, 1997). We conceptualize *resistance* here as the range of opposition acts and behaviors to claims of power or initiatives by others (Fleming and Spicer, 2007: 30; Jermier *et al.*, 1994: 9). *Cooperation,* at the other end of the spectrum of firm responses, is understood as conscious or unconscious assistance to the claims of power or initiatives by others (Fleming and Spicer, 2007; Oliver, 1991).

In developing these categories of business responses, I rely on Christine Oliver's (1991) proposed typology of strategic responses to institutional processes. She includes the following generic strategy categories listed in decreasing order of active resistance towards demands for conformity: manipulation, defiance, avoidance, compromise, acquiescence, and beyond-compliance (Oliver, 1991). Each of these generic strategy categories involves specific associated tactics described here in order of decreasing active resistance (see Table 2.1).

Table 2.1 *Example of business political strategies in response to environmental policy process demands*

Political strategy	Tactics (examples)

1. **Manipulation** (highest resistance)	a. **Control**
	• Seek dominance over environmental activists, policymakers, and government inspectors by:
	  • initiating bogus lawsuits against them
	  • covertly threatening violence and other illegal retaliation
	  • aggressively funding friendly politicians, "environmental" groups, and scientists involved in the environmental policy process
	  • using bogus means to convince government officials to commit activists and whistle-blowers to psychiatric hospitals.
	b. **Influence**
	• Actively lobby policymakers to diminish the importance of and/or need for environmental protection by:
	  • exaggerating high cost and technological challenges imposed by the adoption or enforcement of possible environmental regulations
	  • rejecting scientific evidence and environmentalists' claims about the causes and severity of environmental problems
	  • seeking to change the evaluation criteria used to assess environmental regulations and business environmental performance.
	c. **Co-opt**
	• Seek to neutralize different government officials and interest groups by using "legal incentives" such as donations, consulting jobs, board of director positions, etc.
	• Bribe politicians, government officials, and/or environmental activists.

Table 2.1 *(cont.)*

Political strategy	Tactics (examples)
2. Defiance	**a. Attack** • Characterize environmentalists and government officials as radical left-wing irrational alarmists. • Aggressively condemn environmental regulations as communist-type laws that are anti-economic growth. • Covertly assault environmental activists and government inspectors. **b. Challenge** • Actively refuse responsibility over environmental problems. • Dispute the legitimacy of regulators' enforcement activities with top government officials. • Question the authority of environmental inspectors during on-site visits. **c. Dismiss** • Deliberately ignore environmental problems created by business activities. • Disregard as illegitimate the environmental protection requests and demands from government agencies, environmentalists, and other stakeholders.
3. Avoidance	**a. Escape** • Moving polluting activities to locations with less stringent regulations and/or monitoring. • Phasing out products or processes perceived as too environmentally controversial. **b. Buffer** • Outsourcing highly polluting activities to independent sub-contractors. • Using the "rogue executive" pretext as an excuse to justify problematic behavior as an anomaly. **c. Conceal** • Symbolic adoption of end-of-pipe technology. • Stopping or reducing highly polluting production processes at visible times and during inspections.

Table 2.1 *(cont.)*

Political strategy	Tactics (examples)
	• Opportunistic participation in non-third-party voluntary environmental schemes. • Disposing of waste and pollution in isolated and distant locations.
4. Compromise	**a. Bargain** • Actively negotiate the stringency of environmental regulations with government and other stakeholders. **b. Pacify** • Limited adoption of visible and minimal environmental protection efforts to avoid conflict with influential stakeholders and preempt regulations. **c. Balance** • Seek less stringent environmental standards by directly involving economic growth interest groups in the environmental policy process.
5. Acquiescence	**a. Comply** • Deliberately conform to environmental regulations. • Intentionally adhere to key community and industry environmental protection expectations. **b. Imitate** • Emulate environmental compliance practices adopted by industry leaders. **c. Habit** • Unconsciously follow given environmental regulations.
6. Beyond-compliance (highest cooperation)	**a. Self-regulation** • Participate in independent performance-based environmental certification programs. • Follow uniform beyond-compliance standards globally.

Table 2.1 *(cont.)*

Political strategy	Tactics (examples)
	b. Leadership • Promote more stringent regulations and voluntary environmental protection standards through lobbying and public campaigns. • Supply chain greening: require global suppliers to obtain credible third-party environmental certification. • Green-partnering with government and other environmental stakeholders to develop and share with other industry competitors new environmental technologies and management systems.

Manipulation, the most active form of resistance, is conceptualized as the deliberate and opportunistic effort to "actively change or exert power over the content of the [external] expectations or the sources that seek to express or enforce them" (Oliver, 1991: 157). It includes control, influence and co-opt tactics (Oliver, 1991; Pfeffer and Salancik, 1978). *Defiance*, a less active form of resistance than manipulation that nevertheless is intentionally contemptuous of external demands, involves attack, challenge, and dismiss tactics (Oliver, 1991). *Avoidance* is defined as "seeking to preclude the necessity of conformity" through escape, buffer, and conceal tactics (Meyer and Rowan, 1977; Oliver, 1991: 154). *Compromise* involves relatively milder levels of active resistance that seek to reduce the need for unqualified compliance with external demands and entails bargain, pacify, and balance tactics (Oliver, 1991; Pfeffer and Salancik, 1978).

Acquiescence is understood here as conscious or unconscious cooperation with external demands and it involves compliance, imitation, and habit tactics (DiMaggio and Powell, 1983; Oliver, 1991). Additionally, following corporate environmental and social responsibility scholars (Cashore and Vertinsky, 2000; Hart, 1995; Roome, 1992), we build upon Oliver's initial set of categories by adding "*beyond-compliance*" to reflect the strategy adopted by a very small number of companies seeking to gain competitive advantage by consciously surpassing environmental and social protection regulatory requirements. Besides these categories of resistance to cooperation, it is important to notice that business can also show *unconscious unawareness*. In this category there is lack of resistance or cooperation, just plain unwitting ignorance. Here firms or individuals, because of lack of knowledge, are not resisting or cooperating but just oblivious of emerging policy issues.

Measuring resistance

Researchers have identified and measured a variety of strategies and tactics that firms employ to resist the public policy process (Birnbaum, 1985; Hillman *et al.*, 2004; Meznar and Nigh, 1995). Some of the commonly used tactics perceived to be effective at proactively reducing government regulation of business include making campaign contributions, lobbying policymakers, preparing technical reports, engaging in letter writing and media campaigns, and providing expert testimony, among others (Aplin and Hegarty, 1980; Baron, 2005; Birnbaum, 1985; Kraft and Kaminiecki, 2007). More recently, establishing environmental and social protection self-regulation initiatives has become a common tactic that may be used by business seeking to pre-empt the adoption of new more stringent protective policies and regulations (Darnall and Sides, 2008; Gibson, 1999). Business argues that compared to mandatory protective regulations, voluntary programs, such as the chemical industry's Responsible Care and forestry industry's Sustainable Forestry Initiative, are more cost-efficient and encourage innovating approaches that result in the adoption of beyond-compliance environmental and social protection practices. Yet, most empirical work in this area has found that voluntary programs that lack performance-based standards and third-party certification – strictly voluntary programs – have not been able to effectively promote higher corporate social and environmental performance (Darnall and Sides, 2008; King and Lenox, 2000). This suggests that strictly voluntary programs may be part of an avoidance strategy (see Table 2.1) seeking to resist the new protective regulations.

In the corporate political activity literature, scholars have measured resistance to the public policy process in terms of the frequency and level of intensity of opposition actions and tactics offered by business. For example, indicators of business resistance may include: (1) annual expenses on lobbying directed at opposing protective policy adoption and implementation; (2) the level of campaign donations given to politicians opposing protective policies; (3) the number of lawsuits challenging existing protective policy laws; and (4) the number and type of opposition statements provided during the public comment periods for regulatory and standard proposals (Cavazos, 2005; Hillman *et al.*, 2004; Meznar and Nigh, 1995).

The protective public policy process in the US

In the US, environmental and social protection policies and regulations are enacted and implemented in a context marked by strong pluralistic democratic traditions, a predominant reliance on command-and-control regulatory instruments, relatively strong government enforcement capacity, and a high per capita income. Accordingly, protective policies are the result of a process that is highly contested by multiple organized interest groups and often yields complex, ambiguous, fragmented, and conflicting regulations (Brewer and deLeon, 1983; Lindblom and Woodhouse, 1993; March and Olsen, 1989). It is also important to highlight that the pluralistic democratic traditions predominant in the US make it very difficult for business or any other group or coalition to sustainably capture protective policymaking (Kraft and Kaminiecki, 2007; Marcus, 1984; Smith, 2000).[2]

The policy process perspective has long dominated the study of public policy. First proposed by Harold D. Lasswell in the late 1940s (Lasswell, 1956; 1971), his delineation of the policy stages has provided a framework for scholars investigating the manner in which policy is substantively determined, assessed, and executed. For Lasswell, the policy process was most effectively rendered by a stages approach, which he subsequently described as the decision process.[3] This stages approach was later modified by Garry D. Brewer and others (Brewer and deLeon, 1983) to include a greater realization of the "political" and "cultural" aspects of the policy stages.[4] Building on these seminal works, there is an extensive literature that examines in detail the different policymaking stages, and its analysis falls outside of the scope of this chapter (see, for example, Brewer and deLeon,

1983; Sabatier, 2007). In this paper we disaggregate protective policy-making into three basic stages – initiation, formulation-selection, and implementation – that together may last for periods of at least ten years and typically may entail two decades or more (Baumgartner and Jones, 1993; Brewer and deLeon, 1983; Sabatier, 1999).

These stages have more or less defined the development of the policy process framework over the last thirty-five years, as a wealth of authors have written about them. Additionally, empirical studies have offered evidence suggesting that the policy process perspective offers insights as to which institutions, issues, individuals, and elements constitute the formation, adoption, and implementation of public policy (Sabatier, 1999). Yet, it is important to recognize the limitations of this perspective. As stressed above, public policymaking is often a complex, unstructured, and ambiguous endeavor affected by multiple issues and actors in which different stages tend to overlap and seldom follow a linear path. Yet, reliance on Lasswell's policy process model can help to disaggregate and simplify for study an otherwise muddled web of public policy transactions (Lindblom and Woodhouse, 1993; Lyon and Maxwell, 2004). Following, we discuss the basic stages of the policy process and firms' responses to them in the context of the US.

Protective policy process–business response in the US: an inverted U relationship

My basic proposition about the protective policy process–business response relationship suggests that:

Proposition 1: Other things being equal – such as firm characteristics and in country regional conditions – business responses are likely to have an inverted U-shaped relationship with the protective policy process dynamic in the US, showing increasing resistance as the process moves from initiation to selection and thereafter declining resistance that turns into growing cooperation in mid-implementation.

Besides drawing from Hoffman's work (1997, 1999), it is important to highlight that the resistance to cooperation dynamic suggested by Proposition 1 also follows the traditional western culture understanding of progress that portrays societies as struggling from barbarism

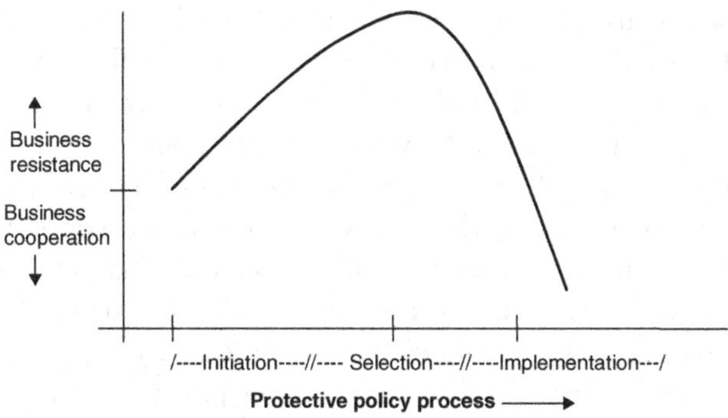

Figure 2.1 Protective policy process–business response relationship: US context (rudimentary illustration)

to institutionalized civilization. The *Oresteia*, the Greek trilogy produced by Aeschylus in 458 BC, is perhaps one of the earliest classic plays that immortalizes this "mythology" of progress dominant in western culture. In this "progress" dynamic, behavior and/or ideas initially seen as deviant may become, over time, accepted as norms, or as famously put by Thomas Huxley (1880) while analyzing Darwin's theory of evolution: "It is the customary fate of new truths to begin as heresies and to end as superstitions." In the remaining sections of this chapter, I develop arguments providing support for this core proposition (see Figure 2.1 for a rudimentary illustration of the proposed relationship).

Before doing this, it is important to stress the "other things being equal" condition established for Proposition 1. It delimits the relationship proposed and this chapter's arguments to the general US country context, known for its highly institutionalized pluralistic democratic traditions, high levels of wealth, predominant reliance on stringent command-and-control regulations, and strong government capacity to enforce the law (Hillman and Keim, 1995; Vasudeva, 2005; Vig and Kraft, 2006). Of course, businesses operating in other countries experience different societal fields that significantly shape the local policy process dynamic and its associated business responses (Bourdieu and Wacquant, 1992; Giddens, 1984; Jennings and Zandbergen, 1995). Hence, the next chapter of the book focuses on discussing the underlying logic explaining how country contextual characteristics moderate the policy process–business response relationship. Similarly,

Proposition 1 also assumes homogeneous firm-level characteristics. Firms' characteristics may also affect how different firms are socialized into distinct country political and economic traditions (George *et al.*, 2006) thus affecting how they may respond to the pressures and demands exerted by policy process stages. In Chapter 4, we relax this assumption to review the extensive literature on corporate political strategy that has already identified how firms' characteristics are associated with differences in corporate political activity (Cavazos, 2005). Holding these factors constant in the analysis precludes me from developing a more general theory of the policy process–business response relationship. Nevertheless, it allows me to take a first step towards exploring a central component of this relationship: explaining how business response changes across different stages of the US policy process above and beyond the effect of other variables such as different country contextual characteristics, firm-level features, and in-country regional conditions, among others.[5]

Initiation stage

Policy initiation in the US involves the identification of emerging social and environmental problems that are framed in disparate ways by competing interest groups. Specialized interest groups, scientists, and a few industry experts may seek to identify specific information required to increase/decrease the public salience of the problem and advance their preferred definition (Kingdon, 1995; Sabatier, 1999; 2007). Awareness of the emerging problems tends to be salient among a few specialists and passionate activists but almost nonexistent among the general public and top officials in government and industry (Kingdon, 1995). For example, the need to require safety seat belts to reduce the very high incidence of deaths in car accidents received widespread public attention in the US in the early 1970s but it was already evident to expert physicians and automobile engineers in the 1930s (Arnould and Grabowski, 1981; Cohen and Einav, 2003; Robertson, 1975; 1976).[6]

A few emerging environmental or social problems may gain the sustained attention of the media and support by a wider coalition of powerful interest groups and/or policymakers and thus become part of the public policy agenda (Barley and Tolbert, 1997; Baumgartner and Jones, 1993; Kingdon, 1995). This depends on the combination of political pressures exerted by firms and their stakeholders, the generation of less conflicting evidence, the occurrence of a significant contextual change or shock (e.g., a political or economic crisis, natural disaster, new government leadership, etc.) and/or the consistency of the problem definition with the ideology of top decisionmakers. Of course, the large majority of environmental and social protection issues do not enjoy high enough levels of attention and political support to become part of the policy agenda and advance to the next stages of the policy process (Kingdon, 1995).

During initiation, business in the US is more likely to show lower levels of resistance than in the formulation-selection and early implementation stages because most firms are unaware of the existence of nascent conditions that may erode the legitimacy of institutionalized governmental policies and regulations and thus highlight contradictions with the socio-political order (Hoffman, 1997; Jepperson, 1991; Seo and Creed, 2002). From a neo-institutional perspective, business nescience towards these emerging conditions arises from structures, norms, traditions, and values that historically have become ingredients of the policymaking order in the US (Hoffman, 1997; Scott, 2001; Tolbert and Zucker, 1996). They include a highly divided government structure with strong checks and balances at both the federal and state level where the different branches of government have multiple policymaking veto and override opportunities that make the approval and implementation of protective policies very difficult and usually slow. This institutionalized policymaking order also involves individualistic values and market-based traditions that require business profit maximization and favor protection of individual rights and private property over the collective goods and values promoted by protective policies (e.g., clean environment, safer roads, etc.).

Additionally, at the initiation stage, the inherent complexity and ambiguity of environmental or social phenomena make it very difficult to understand the causes and trends linked to perceived emerging problems that may not receive the attention of policymakers. Accordingly, business managers tend to rely on cognitive simplification processes to focus on narrower problems that are more immediate, simpler, and consistent with already institutionalized expectations in the US (Schwenk, 1984; Tversky and Kahneman, 1974). During initiation, managers are more likely to exhibit prior hypothesis bias that makes them pay selective attention to information and groups that validate their initial perceptions and assumptions (Schwenk, 1984; Tversky and Kahneman, 1974). Thus, they tend to show an inclination to perceive environmental and social protection problems as unimportant and assume a lack of responsibility even in the face of increasing evidence to the contrary (Bazerman *et al.*, 1997; Schwenk, 1984).

Business managers also tend to have a skewed idea of the importance and legitimacy of nonprofit organizations; often considering only a small number of major environmental and social protection groups as politically influential and/or legitimate policy process actors (Fligstein and McAdam, 1993; others). Thus, other things being equal, at this very early point of the policy process, scientific studies and demands from activist groups are respectively more likely to be seen by firm managers as inscrutable or fringe claims that illegitimately challenge protective policies' institutionalized regulatory order (Hart and Sharma, 2004; March and Olsen, 1989; Tolbert and Zucker, 1996). For example, since 1987 the Montreal Protocol has successfully phased out the global production and use of chlorofluorocarbon compounds (CFCs), known to be the major cause of the destruction of the atmosphere's ozone layer (Brack, 1996; Vig and Kraft, 2006). Yet, in the early 1970s most chemical firms manufacturing CFCs showed no concern for their environmental effects and were unaware of the initial emerging scientific model and laboratory evidence linking these chemicals to the destruction of the atmosphere's ozone layer (Brack, 1996; Hoffman, 2000; Reinhardt and Vietor, 1989, 1996; Vig and Kraft, 2006).

Usually, only a very small number of firms such as those confronted with more stringent protective public policies in other countries, or those focused on experimentation and technology innovation, or those with top managers holding enhanced social and environmental protection beliefs – e.g., multinational corporations (MNCs) or start-up companies – may be purposely cognizant of the emerging social problems and involved in beyond-compliance practices and early lobbying efforts (Bonardi *et al.*, 2005; Christmann and Taylor, 2001; Dowell *et al.*, 2000). Still, even these more informed firms tend to assume – often correctly – that most emerging issues seldom gain enough attention from the media, activist organizations, and the public to become part of the policy agenda. Yet, following this assumption, top business managers show illusion of control biases that result in a tendency to consider their firms to be "incumbent" organizations with relatively higher power and resources to derail the adoption of new protective policies that seek to deal with the small number of problems salient enough to be included in the policy agenda (Fligstein and McAdam, 1993; Kingdon, 1995; Schwenk, 1984).[7] However, given that the US context makes it very difficult to sustainably capture the policymaking process (see note 2 for a discussion of policy capture), business tends to overestimate its ability to derail enactment of protective policies. For example, despite strong and sustained business opposition, a large body of environmental policies has been enacted and implemented in the US since the 1970s (Kamieniecki, 2006; Smith, 2000).

Formulation-selection stage

The formulation-selection stage of the public policy process involves at first the development/identification and assessment of a few preferred alternative prescriptions to deal with the very few problems that have become increasingly germane to the public policy agenda (Kingdon, 1995; Moldan *et al.*, 2006). This is currently the case in the US regarding the use of voluntary versus mandatory measures to slow climate change by limiting the emission of harmful global warming gases (Levy and Kolk, 2002). It is important to note that despite objectivity claims by most interest groups and businesses, these activities seldom follow a "scientific" approach (Kingdon, 1995; Lindblom and Woodhouse, 1993). Most actors, including firms, focus on developing alternatives, gathering information, and producing political, technical and economic assessments that would help them prevail in the intense political struggle and bargaining involved in narrowing down or eliminating from consideration policy alternatives to be considered (Kingdon, 1995).

In the rare cases that enough support exists to overcome opposition from multiple sources, the selection of a preferred public policy typically involves a few top government officials from the legislative and executive branches of government (Brewer and deLeon, 1983; Kingdon, 1995). Here, political concerns take precedence over scientific data and assessments (Lindblom and Woodhouse, 1993). Most relevant are ideology and the small array of powerful special interests (e.g., environmentalists, social activists, and/or businesses) that tend to dominate the political battle of the moment (Kingdon, 1995;

Sabatier and Jenkins-Smith, 1999). In the end, instead of selecting the "optimal" policy, it becomes more important for policymakers to find, through negotiation, a satisfactory option that can gain consensual approval of the most influential actors (Janis, 1982; Lindblom and Woodhouse, 1993). Yet, it is important to stress that in most cases in the US no new policies are adopted and stalemate is very likely, often in the form of more studies and the appointment of symbolic commissions. Impasse is typical when issues – like global warming – are too controversial or when well-organized interest groups, like business coalitions, strongly oppose new government demands (Brewer and deLeon, 1983; Kingdon, 1995; Levy and Kolk, 2002; Moldan *et al.*, 2006).

During formulation-selection, most firms tend to display the highest levels of resistance compared to other stages of the policy process. The probability of new governmental demands is the greatest in this stage of the policy process because of the persistent, high-profile challenges made by multiple interest groups to existing protective policies and regulations. Most firms, given their managers' extensive socialization and internalization of the pre-existing protective public policy order, are spurred to actively defend its shared logic, values, and symbols, as well as its prescribed structures, routines, regulations, and standards (Barley and Tolbert, 1997; Pettigrew, 1987; Scott, 2001).

Business' utmost resistance arises for multiple reasons. First, potential changes to already institutionalized protective policies and norms challenge the issue-specific political accommodation that favors the interests of (powerful) incumbent groups and individuals such as business and top policymakers (Brewer and deLeon 1983; Fligstein, 1996). Second, managers usually have a strong preference for stable government policies and regulations that reduce risks and allow them to maintain legitimacy and a sense of control over the regulatory environment (Fligstein, 1996; George *et al.*, 2006). Third, business managers rely on multiple decisionmaking simplifications that are likely to bias their perception of the appropriateness and financial implications of possible protective policy alternatives. Typically, new policies and their associated regulations and practices are dismissed based on little to no evidence as too costly, too difficult to adopt, too unreliable, and/or not important to the mission of business.

These heuristics arise from extensive internalization of assumptions that: (1) establish profit making as the primordial social responsibility of business in the US; and (2) portray environmental and social protection as costly endeavors with little to no competitive benefits (Friedman, 1970). They are also reinforced by a lack of market prices for environmental and social protection goods that are generally assumed to be of little short-term value (Berchicci and King, 2007).

Thus managers are, for instance, prevented from identifying favorable social protection alternatives because of a failure to consider their long-term benefits (over-discounting of the future) and a tendency to ignore other political and legitimacy related implications (Bazerman and Hoffman, 1999). Anchoring biases that strongly favor initial judgments and previous experience also prevent individuals from using new positive information to modify their current practices and initial opposition to new protective policy alternatives (Schwenk, 1984; Tversky and Kahneman, 1974). Escalating commitment tendencies may also thwart adoption of more cooperative strategies by individuals committed to an adversarial approach even when they are aware that confrontation is not working (Schwenk, 1984). Escalating commitment is reinforced by business managers' assumption that government and activists groups are adversaries unwilling to negotiate in good faith to develop mutually beneficial policies (Bazerman and Hoffman, 1999).[8] Illusion of control biases also contribute to generate strong resistance to protective policies because they lead managers to overestimate their companies' abilities and effectiveness to self-resolve environmental and social protection problems (Bazerman *et al.*, 1997; Schwenk, 1984).

Business resistance may involve avoidance tactics as firms begin to try to actively influence policymakers and interest groups, and seek to shape the criteria involved in the assessment of social-environmental problems and the advocated public policies under consideration (Bonardi and Keim, 2005; Oliver, 1991). Their goal is usually to pre-empt the adoption of new protective policies, or if this is unavoidable, business is likely to bargain for policies and regulations with limited scope and lower stringency (Bonardi and Keim, 2005). A common tactic involves highlighting enhanced use of environmental and social protection practices that have been previously accepted as legitimate (Bonardi and Keim, 2005; Fligstein and McAdam, 1993; Lyon and Maxwell, 2004). Often, firms also seek to conceal poor performance by participating in strictly voluntary environmental programs lacking performance standards, third-party oversight, and sanctions/rewards for low/high performance respectively (Rivera *et al.*, 2006). Despite their lack of strong mechanisms to prevent opportunistic behavior by low-performing firms, strictly voluntary environmental programs are widely promoted by sponsoring industries as mandatory regulation substitutes that can effectively promote beyond-compliance practices (Steelman and Rivera, 2006).

As the probability of new protective policies increases, business tends to rely on more aggressive resistance strategies such as defiance and manipulation that seek to shape the expectations of policymakers, activists, and the media. One of the more publicized examples of companies aggressively fighting against protective regulations is the case of the US tobacco industry. In the early 1990s, the Food and Drug Administration (FDA) sought to regulate the sale of cigarettes as drug-delivery devices under the authority of the Federal Food, Drug, and Cosmetic Act (Baron, 2005; Kessler *et al.*, 1996; Steiner and Steiner, 2006). As the FDA's efforts intensified, the tobacco companies used multiple resistance tactics – including lobbying, political donations, marketing campaigns, and lawsuits – to successfully forestall FDA regulation. Their efforts included the now famously controversial sworn testimony before congress of the chief executive officers (CEOs) of all the major US tobacco firms. These CEOs testified in 1994 that "nicotine is not manipulated in cigarettes and that it is not addictive" (Kessler *et al.*, 1996; Steiner and Steiner, 2006).

Resistance by business may also involve taking advantage of highly influential appointments within environmental and social protection non-governmental organizations (NGOs) to try to influence, co-opt, and/or even control them. This is possible thanks to the growing number of top business executives taking positions on the board of directors/trustees at some of the most well-known environmental organizations in the US. For example, in 2008 top corporate executives constituted 63 percent of the board members at Conservation International (CI; see Table 2.2 for a full list of CI board members), 56 percent at Environmental Defense, and 52 percent at The Nature Conservancy (Conservation International, 2008; Environmental Defense, 2008; The Nature Conservancy, 2008).[9] Moreover, top corporate executives chaired the board at Environmental Defense and

Table 2.2 *Conservation International board of directors*

1. Board members from the business sector			
1. Henry H. Arnhold, Chairman, Arnhold and S. Bleichroeder	2. Lewis W. Coleman, President, DreamWorks Animation	3. Paula H. Crown, Principal, Henry Crown and Company	4. Barry Diller, Chairman and CEO, InterActiveCorp (IAC)
5. André Esteves, Chairman and CEO, UBS Bank, Latin America	6. Mark L. Feldman, President and CEO, L&L Manufacturing Company	7. Robert J. Fisher, Chairman, Gap Inc.	8. Jeff Gale, Founder, Gale Force Studios
9. Judson Green, CEO, NAVTEQ Corporation	10. William Harrison, Jr., former CEO, J P Morgan Chase and Company	11. H. Fisk Johnson, CEO, S C Johnson & Son	12. Frederico R. Lopez, CEO, First Gen Corporation, Philippines
13. Gordon Moore, Co-Founder, Intel Corporation	14. Nicholas J. Pritzker, Vice Chairman, Hyatt Corporation	15. Stewart A. Resnick, Chairman, Roll International Corporation	16. Kenneth F. Siebel, Chairman, Private Wealth Partners LLC
17. Orin Smith, former CEO, Starbucks Coffee Company	18. Dr. Enki Tan, Executive Director, GITI Group	19. Ray R. Thurston, CEO, Edgewood, LLC	20. Rob Walton, Chairman, Wal-Mart Stores, Inc.
21. James D. Wolfensohn, Chairman, Wolfensohn and Company	22. Marjorie Yang, Chairman and CEO, Esquel Group	23. Tamsen Ann Ziff, Ziff Brothers Investment	

Table 2.2 *(cont.)*

2. Board members from law firms			
24. Skip Brittenham, Senior Partner, Ziffren, Brittenham, & Partners LLP			
3. Board members from other sectors			
25. Meredith A. Brokaw, Conservationist	26. Harrison Ford, Actor	27. Jared Diamond, Professor of Geography, University of California, Los Angeles	28. Ann Friedman, Teacher, Bethesda, Maryland
29. S. K. I Khama,Vice President, Republic of Botswana	30. Kris Moore, Conservationist (Relative of Gordon Moore, Intel Founder)	31. Her Majesty Queen Noor of Jordan	32. Claire Perry, Curator of American Art, Stanford University
33. Story Clark Resor, Conservationist	34. Peter A. Seligmann, Chairman and CEO, Conservation International	35. John F. Swift, Conservationist, Cayucos, California	36. Megaron Txucarramae, Kayapó Grand Chief, Colider, Brazil

Source: Conservation International website accessed on February 11, 2008: www.conservation.org/discover/about_us/team/bod/Pages/default.aspx.

The Nature Conservancy.[10] To be sure, the proportion of corporate executives holding board of directors' positions is significantly lower among more combative environmental groups such as the Natural Resources Defense Council, where they comprise 36 percent of the board members (12 percent are from major law firm partners) (Natural Resources Defense Council, 2008).

Implementation stage

During policy implementation, government agencies are in charge of developing regulations and deploying monitoring and enforcement efforts to execute protective policies. Yet, as public policy scholars have long recognized and documented, implementation in the US remains highly contested by business and other interest groups and seldom resembles the precise intentions of the public policies adopted by elected officials (Bardach, 1977; deLeon and deLeon, 2002; Pressman and Wildavsky, 1984). This political struggle is particularly intense during early implementation when specific regulations and standards are initially developed, and budget and administrative resources begin to be allocated for monitoring and enforcement (Bardach, 1977; deLeon and deLeon, 2002; Pressman and Wildavsky, 1984). Besides significant changes and delays, lawsuits and, in some cases, complete obstruction, are often common (deLeon and deLeon, 2002; Pressman and Wildavsky, 1984; Tolbert and Zucker, 1983).

The pressures faced by firms as implementation unfolds change in character from being mostly political in nature, to increasingly more institutional (Berger and Luckmann, 1967; March and Olsen, 1989; Tolbert and Zucker, 1996). Political pressures, typical of early implementation, rely more on the exercise of coercion and incentives (the first and second faces of power) in the struggle to modify business behavior. On the other hand, institutional pressures associated with the small number of policies that survive and reach late-implementation, shape behavior by relying more on taken-for-granted socially shared understandings that not only delimit appropriate business behavior but also define the legitimacy of the systems of values, preferences and goals held by business managers – respectively the third and fourth faces of power. Thus, we posit that firms' resistance gradually changes from high levels of resistance in early implementation to cooperation with policies and regulations that over the years becomes institutionalized.

In early implementation most companies in the US are still likely to offer high levels of resistance, although probably not as high as during the formulation-adoption stage as they try to shape, challenge, and/or altogether stop the regulations, enforcement styles, standards, and budgets adopted to implement new protective policies (Hoffman, 1997). Despite the adoption of new policies, old institutionalized business practices and forms consistent with previous environmental and social protection policies are pervasive among most firms. Business managers are likely for a long time to continue exhibiting anchoring biases (Schwenk, 1984; Tversky and Kahneman, 1974) that favor the legitimacy and instrumentality of these old practices, organizational forms, norms, and routines supported by the old institutional order.[11] Accordingly, business resistance during early implementation seeks to minimize the additional requirements introduced by new regulations and standards so that they can avoid significant changes in management practices, technology, and firm structure.

Business relies on a combination of multiple strategies and tactics to exert resistance during early implementation. Traditionally, this involves active participation and lobbying during the public comment periods required of all regulatory agencies in the US. Industry may also try to exert control or co-opt expert panel members appointed to evaluate potential environmental and social regulations and standards. Of course, the purpose of tactics can be interpreted in multiple ways and they are not necessarily linked to manipulation. For instance, on numerous occasions after 2005, the American Chemistry Council and some chemical industry companies (e.g., ExxonMobil, Dow Agro, American Cyanamid, CYTEC Industries, Lyondell Chemical) were able to get scientists that they employed and/or funded, at the time, to be appointed onto the Environmental Protection Agency (EPA) and Food and Drug Administration (FDA) expert review panels responsible for establishing the safety levels of their chemical products (Dingell and Stupak, 2008a; 2008b; Layton, 2008). Simultaneously, the US chemical industry's American Chemistry Council was also seeking – and succeeding in the case of one prominent toxicologist – to remove renowned independent scientists from these panels (Dingell and Stupak, 2008a; 2008b; Layton, 2008).[12, 13] In fact, the aggressiveness of these industry tactics prompted, in 2008, an investigation by the House's Energy and Commerce Committee to examine questionable influence on the EPA and FDA by the chemical industry (Dingell and Stupak, 2008a; 2008b). Congressional investigators singled out nine cases with "evident conflicts of interest" (Dingell and Stupak, 2008a; 2008b). In these cases, expert panel members were employed and/or had received significant funding by the manufacturers of the chemical compounds under review by the panels (Dingell and Stupak, 2008a; 2008b; Layton, 2008).[14]

The most controversial of the cases under congressional investigation involved apparent conflict of interest in the safety evaluation of Bisphenol A (BPA), a chemical substance prevalent in myriad everyday consumer products – most notably many used by infants – containing polycarbonate plastics (e.g., baby bottles, sippy cups, infant formula containers, plastic food utensils, soda plastic bottles, CDs, and DVDs).[15] BPA has been strictly regulated in other industrialized countries (banned for baby bottles in Canada[16]) because of an extensive scientific literature associating it with detrimental endocrine-disruption effects in laboratory animals such as early female puberty and other diseases like breast and prostate cancers, and diabetes (Dingell and Stupak, 2008a; 2008b; National Institute of Health, 2008).[17] However, as of early 2008 the US Food and Drug Administration, based on two studies paid for by the American Chemistry Council,[18] continued claiming a lack of a "safety concern" at current levels of BPA exposure to adults and infants in the US (Mason, 2008; Layton, 2008).[19] At this time, despite the FDA assurances, even major retail stores in the US such as Wal-Mart announced their intention to follow Canadian government safety guidelines and stop selling baby products containing BPA (Mui, 2008).

Additionally, if the recently adopted protective policies are seen as highly unsatisfactory, business may rely on more aggressive resistance strategies by initiating lawsuits that challenge the legality of the policies and/or their regulations. Legal challenges, even when they fail, may result in long implementation delays – spanning years or, in a few cases, decades – that significantly extend the prevalence of previously institutionalized protective practices used by business. For business, the issue is not simply to try to save money by delaying the implementation of new protective policies. Lawsuits are also very expensive for all parties involved. Also at stake is the legitimacy of new protective policies and the credibility of the business, government, and NGO communities arguing for the appropriateness of new versus old protective practices, management systems, and technologies. Lawsuits may also be launched by government agencies and NGOs to compel business to improve compliance with protective policies and regulations (Vig and Kraft, 2006). Environmental NGOs also rely on the courts to try to force government agencies to improve enforcement and monitoring practices established by protective policies (Vig and Kraft, 2006). For instance, between 1960–93, of the 3,572 environmental protection cases litigated in US federal courts, 88 percent involved business, industry associations, government agencies, and NGOs as either plaintiffs or defendants (Hoffman, 1999).

In **mid-implementation** as government monitoring and coercion begin, business cooperation with the politically contested regulatory standards and enforcement practices is likely to increase because they progressively become part of the accepted patterns and knowledge shared by business managers, policymakers, and stakeholders (Berger and Luckmann, 1967; Tolbert and Zucker, 1996). The gradual increase of business cooperation is also spurred by the actions of other companies that seek to become "corporate social responsibility (CSR)/green leaders" in the industry directly affected by the new regulations or by other corporations outside the regulated industry. For instance, in the case of Bisphenol A, Wal-Mart's decision to stop selling baby products containing BPA makes it imperative for its suppliers to stop resisting the science questioning the safety of this chemical.

Insurance companies and banks may also play a role in promoting increased cooperation by firms affected by specific protective regulations (Hoffman, 1997). These pressures are exerted in multiple ways by insurers and banks. Firms with poor compliance with protective regulations may face: (1) reduced availability of insurance coverage and credit lines; (2) increased insurance policy premiums and high interest rates; (3) refusal of liability coverage even when an insurance policy has been placed; and (4) lawsuits by insurers and creditors seeking to avoid shared liability with noncompliant businesses.

Initially, cooperation may still be symbolic with the language and narratives used by business managers evolving gradually to adopt the terms and meanings of the protective regulations being institutionalized to provide "legitimated accounts" of the new environmental and social protection practices required. For instance, business begins pouring resources into corporate social and environmental plans and reports whose goals, terminology, and ideas are frequently recited by managers even if they are not implemented and their financial value is not clear. This decoupling of managers' narratives and actual implementation signals the practices that may be adopted later if the protective regulations attain high levels of institutionalization (Hoffman, 1997; Meyer and Rowan, 1977).

In mid-implementation it is also likely that new managerial positions and, in some cases, new departments are created to coordinate and establish the new environmental or social protection practices required to comply with new regulations. These new personnel often play the role of institutional entrepreneurs whose specific technical expertise and connections to other professionals, environmental/social protection advocates, and public officials contribute to accelerate the adoption of language, plans, and reports consistent with the new protective regulations and standards (Kim *et al.*, 2007).[20] Most importantly, the new personnel/departments can take advantage of windows of opportunity produced by increasing regulatory pressures, media stories, anti-industry demonstrations by activists, and conflict among top managers to build and organize internal coalitions.

These internal coalitions may over time allow the new managers and departments to obtain larger budgets to move beyond initial symbolic gestures adopted in early implementation and to actually establish innovative environmental and social protection practices (Kim *et al.*, 2007). Internal coalitions forged by environmental and social responsibility (E&SR) managers or their departments may also allow them to accrue enough influence to persuade top decisionmakers who are mildly reluctant to accept the value and legitimacy of new environmental and social protection practices, routines, and norms (Kim *et al.*, 2007). These coalitions are also critical to battle and/or bargain with other organizational members showing outright hostility to the adoption of enhanced environmental/social responsibility practices. Hostile internal opponents can rely on retaliatory measures and/or intimidation rituals that are very difficult to avoid/confront by E&SR managers acting alone. Typical retaliatory actions include, for example, salary reductions, undesirable working conditions, and layoffs. Less aggressive intimidation rituals, which are nonetheless very effective in controlling and/or discouraging reform-minded E&SR colleagues, include nullification, mocking, isolation, and defamation (Kim *et al.*, 2007; O'Day, 1974).[21]

Of course, in most cases, environmental and social responsibility managers find it very difficult to form strong coalitions because their ideas and initiatives are usually seen by top managers as idealistic, radical, threatening, and/or too expensive. Accordingly, these ideas and initiatives often receive marginal support, preventing institutionalization of new protective practices. Most businesses adopt the very minimum practices that allow them to avoid regulatory inspections and sanctions.

The small number of corporate environmental/social protection standards that become institutionalized do so over long periods of time through initial coercion and persistent political pressures, and later through habitualization[22] and objectification[23] processes that turn the standards and their practices into taken-for-granted routines, organizational structures, and conventions that evolve to become an integral part of collective understandings internalized by business managers and their stakeholders (Berger and Luckmann, 1967; Hoffman, 1997; March and Olsen, 1989). If the process of institutionalization persists over a long period of time, in late implementation the highest levels of business cooperation are likely to be observed as the collective internalized understanding of appropriate social and environmental responsibility becomes part of the objective reality of business (Berger and Luckmann, 1967; Tolbert and Zucker, 1996).

For example, despite a trend towards reduced inspections by the Occupational Safety and Health Administration (OSHA), most manufacturing firms in the US have demonstrated high levels of compliance with institutionalized occupational health and safety standards in the 1980s and 1990s (Bartel and Thomas, 1985; Gray and Jones, 1991; Weil, 1996). However, when initially established in the early 1970s these standards were seen as costly and highly controversial, and received strong opposition by business (Weidenbaum and DeFina, 1978; Weil, 1996).

Resistance to sedimented taken-for-granted practices is seen as highly illegitimate not only by policymakers and stakeholders but also by other members of industry and peer managers (Hoffman, 1997; Tolbert and Zucker, 1996). During late implementation, aggressive coercion is seldom required and most businesses, independently of their characteristics, have adopted institutionalized social and environmental protection practices and structures prescribed by politically bargained protective public policies and regulations (Hawkins and Thomas, 1984; Tolbert and Zucker, 1996). Indeed, at this point, informal pressures and sanctions in the form of ridicule, shame, and ostracism by peers and others are more pervasive than state coercion in reducing business behavior and practices perceived as deviant/ taboo – not only by the government and environmental and social protection activists, but also by other firms and industry organizations (Berger and Luckmann, 1966; Hoffman, 1997).

Late implementation has been the focus of most neo-institutional scholarship analyzing organizational responses to governmental requirements (Edelman, 1992; Suchman, 1995). Hence, it is only natural after the tensions and dynamics of the formulation-selection stage that compliance is seen as the expected isomorphic response to governmental pressures (Hirsch, 1997; Scott, 2001; Suchman and Edelman, 1997). Additionally, it is important to highlight that adopting institutionalized practices and structures during late implementation requires significantly reduced analytical efforts by business managers, freeing time and resources that may be used by a small number of them (usually at multinational corporations or other large businesses) to experiment with innovative beyond-compliance social and environmental protection practices (Christensen *et al.*, 2001; Hart, 1995; Porter and van der Linde, 1995). These beyond-compliance innovations, combined with political pressures and external shocks, contribute to the policy change feedback loop that further informs the implementation process and perhaps triggers a new initiation stage of the policy process (Hart, 1995; Porter and van der Linde, 1995; Tolbert and Zucker, 1996).

This feedback loop occurs not only during late implementation but it is also ubiquitous across all stages of the policy process. Change of institutionalized protective policies is more likely when their implementation results in significant contradictions between dominant collective values advocated by influential groups/actors and the actual environmental social practices adopted by business in response to these institutionalized protective policies (Peters and Pierre, 1998). These contradictions are pervasive because protective policy implementation rarely meets the expectations of environmental and social protection groups. Additionally, external shocks open windows of political opportunity to promote new protective requirements, and scientific discoveries reveal new cause–effect links associated with business practices previously believed to be appropriate and safe. Besides implementation contradictions, new government strategies and approaches by policy entrepreneurs may be developed at any stage of the policy process and thus may also trigger efforts to change even those public policies that are perceived as well executed by most influential groups.

Business responses to this feedback loop may not show levels of resistance as strong as in previous protective policy processes because of the socialization experienced by the business sector. However, the protective policy process–business response is likely to follow a similar inverted-U pattern of resistance to cooperation. For example, business responses to global climate evidence and possible regulatory demands in the US have followed this pattern despite the extensive institutionalization of policies and regulations dealing with other types of environmental challenges.

Finally, it is also important to recognize that in some exceptional "implementation" cases in the US, the institutionalized routines involve the de facto disregard of adopted public policy prescriptions and regulations due to lax enforcement and/or simple defiance arising from considering the regulations to be illegitimate or unreasonable. To better understand this dynamic, it is helpful to consider an illustrative example. Coal mining companies operating in the Appalachian Mountains have for decades shown very high incidence of accidents, despite the existence of an extensive system of federal regulations aimed at guaranteeing safe mining operation in the US (Burns, 2005; Hawkins and Thomas, 1984; Montrie, 2003; Weeks, 2003). One of the latest disasters, which resulted in the death of twenty-four miners in West Virginia, received national attention in early 2006 (Urbina, 2006). This poor compliance record is attributed by scholars and congressional investigations to strong business opposition and insufficient oversight by the Federal Mine Safety and Health Administration (Burns, 2005; Montrie, 2003; Urbina, 2006; Weeks, 2003).

Resistance to protective policies by mining companies operating in this region of the US is also evident with regard to environmental protection regulatory standards. For example, in January 2008 the US EPA levied a $20 million fine against Massey Energy Co. for more than 4,500 alleged violations of the Clean Water Act in West Virginia and Kentucky between 2000 and 2006.[24] Massey Energy, the fourth largest producer of coal in the US, agreed to pay what amounts to the largest penalty imposed by the US EPA for violations of the Clean Water Act (Copenhaver, 2008 in note XX; Fahrenthold, 2008). Yet, despite its record number of violations and consenting to pay the fine (plus $10 million in pollution control investments), Massey Energy's spokesperson continued insisting that "the company's violations were generally minor and there had been no serious damage to the environment as a result" (Hendriken, 2008, quoted in Fahrenthold, 2008). In 2007 Massey Energy was also penalized $1.5 million by the Mine Safety and Health Administration for an accident resulting in the death of two miners in West Virginia. This fine is also the largest ever levied by the federal government for coal mine-related accidents.[25]

Notes

1. This chapter is an expanded and modified version of portions of: Rivera *et al.* (2009), reproduced with kind permission of Springer Science and Business Media.
2. Policy capture: building on the seminal work of Downs (1957), Olson (1965), and Huntington (1952), in the early 1970s, economists challenged public interest perspectives of policymaking and proposed an alternative capture theory view (Stigler, 1971; Peltzman, 1976; Posner, 1974). According to capture theory, the enactment and implementation of economic policies (e.g., those directed at regulating prices, monopolies, trade, business investment, etc.) tend to primarily promote the narrow private interests of powerful businesses that dominate policymakers and regulators (Peltzman, 1976; Posner, 1974; Stigler, 1971). Capture theory's basic argument, that government policies and regulations favor the most powerful and involved business interests, assumes that businesses can better provide resources (e.g., campaign donations, expert information, lucrative post-government jobs, etc.) than other interest groups to narrow, self-interested policymakers and regulators focused on maintaining their positions, increasing their power, and/or enhancing their wealth after leaving government (Levine and Forrence, 1990). Capture theory also suggests that, compared to business interests, other interest groups involved in the policy process lack the expertise and resources to sustain the long-term advocacy required to guarantee the advancement of the public interest by government policies and regulations (Sabatier, 1975).

   Yet, political scientists have criticized these arguments, pointing out that policy capture seldom occurs in the context of the US where multiple interest groups have the expertise and resources to compete to gain the attention of policymakers, regulators, the media, and the public (Teske, 2001; 2003). This literature also points out that the ability of narrow business interests to capture the policy process in the US is significantly counterbalanced by political entrepreneurs who can generate new policy ideas and alternatives, provide information to the media, and organize new interest groups capable of occasional mobilization (Kingdon, 1995; Quirk, 1988; Wilson, 1980). Generation of new policy ideas is a factor that plays a particularly important role in US policy change. Government, business, and other interest groups are well aware of this wisdom most famously articulated by Victor Hugo: "Greater than the tread of mighty armies is an idea whose time has come" (Kingdon, 1995: 1; Lieberman, 2002). Accordingly, they invest a great amount of resources to generate new policy ideas that may sooner or – most often – later find fertile policymaking ground. This political dynamic is particularly prevalent for environmental and other social protection policies that are more likely to be on the public agenda (Levine and Forrence, 1990; Marcus, 1984). Protective regulations in the US are usually promoted and defended by multiple and well-organized actors such as environmental organizations, consumer protection groups, and unions, among others (Kraft and Kaminiecki, 2007; Marcus, 1984; Sabatier, 1975).

Neo-institutional scholars have also been very critical of capture theory by arguing that policymakers and regulators are not simply "bean counters" focused on tallying the demands and resources of different interest groups to make decisions (Carpenter, 2001; Evans *et al.*, 1985; Nordlinger, 1981). In the US, because of the legitimacy provided by the democratic process, policymakers and regulators enjoy formal authority and autonomy that allow them to develop their own professional norms, values, expertise, coercive resources, and most importantly a sympathetic constituency to confront demands from narrow special interest groups such as business and industry groups (March and Olsen, 1989; Teske, 2001; 2003).

Findings from multiple empirical studies (for reviews of this literature see Teske, 2003, and Gerber and Teske, 2000) provide little support for the argument that special interest groups are able to sustainably capture the policy process in the US. Over the last thirty years there have been numerous protective regulations enacted, many of which resulted in significant costs to business and industry (Gerber and Teske, 2000; Teske, 2003). Such findings are in contradiction with the predictions of capture theory (Culhane, 1981; Kaiser, 1980; Levine and Forrence, 1990; Meier, 1988; Sabatier, 1975; Wilson, 1980). In fact, conclusive empirical support of capture theory predictions is lacking even for economic policies (Berry, 1984; Levine and Forrence, 1990; Meier, 1988; Teske 2001; 2003; Wilson, 1980). On the other hand, it is important to keep in mind that the lack of strong evidence suggesting the low incidence of policy capture in the US since the 1970s does not imply the absence of this phenomenon in other countries with authoritarian institutions and state corporatist systems of interest representation. In these countries, opposition to business interests by well-organized environmental and social protection groups may be very weak or absent, allowing the private sector to dominate the policy process. This is one of the reasons why, in the second half of the paper, we consider countries' level of democratization and system of interest representation as two of the basic country contextual variables moderating the level of business resistance during the protective policy process.

3. The policy process stages originally proposed by Laswell (1956; 1971) were: (1) *Intelligence*, defining the major components of an emerging policy problem; (2) *Promotion*, identifying what or who determined the priority of the issue; (3) *Prescription*, proposals to alleviate the problem; (4) *Invocation*, coordinating the policy with existing norms; (5) *Application*, what later came to be called implementation; (6) *Termination*, how a policy is ended; and (7) *Appraisal*, the means of evaluating a policy's effectiveness.
4. Brewer and deLeon (1983) proposed the following stages: *Policy initiation*, how a policy need is articulated and alternatives proposed; *Estimation*, during which the proposed alternatives are assessed; *Policy selection*, how a specific policy alternative is chosen; *Policy implementation*, how a newly chosen program is executed; *Evaluation*, how policies and programs' merits/shortcomings are judged so that future iterations can be more effective in reaching their goals; and *Termination or change*, how a policy/program is ended or modified.
5. This parsimonious approach is, of course, the science-based method for studying specific relationships of interest while acknowledging that other variables may have an effect on such relationships (Kuhn, 1962; Popper, 2002; Rowley, 1997).
6. Of course, this and all of the other examples used in the book are included only for explanatory purposes and should not under any circumstances be considered as providing empirical evidence for the posited arguments.
7. Here, I follow Neil Fligstein – and the social movements literature – in using the term *incumbents* to refer to "powerful organizations or groups which have the necessary political or material resources to enforce an advantageous view of appropriate field behavior and definition of field membership on other groups" (Fligstein and McAdam, 1993: 8; Fligstein, 1996: 663). Inside an organization, incumbents "are those who have vested interests in and thus pursue the maintenance of an existing institutional model" (Kim *et al.*, 2007: 290).
8. Bazerman and Hoffman (1999) refer to this supposition as the "mythical fixed-pie assumption."
9. All websites accessed on February 11, 2008 unless otherwise noted: www.conservation.org/discover/about_us/team/bod/Pages/default.aspx; www.nature.org/aboutus/leadership/art15462.html; www.edf.org/page.cfm?tag ID=365; www.nrdc.org/about/board.asp (accessed March 3, 2008).

10. In 2008 the Boards of Environmental Defense, the Natural Resources Defense Council, and The Nature Conservancy were respectively chaired by: (1) N. J. Nicholas, Jr., a private investor with major holdings at Boston Scientific and former President of Time Inc.; (2) Dan Tishman, CEO of the Tishman Construction Corporation; and (3) John P. Morgridge, Cisco Systems' Chairman Emeritus. Additionally, Robert J. Fisher from Gap Inc. was the Chairman of the Board's Executive Committee at Conservation International (Conservation International, 2008; Environmental Defense, 2008; Natural Resources Defense Council, 2008; The Nature Conservancy, 2008).
11. An institutional order "is composed of an institutional logic and organizational forms and practices that reflect that logic. An institutional logic is made up of the cognitive maps, the belief systems carried by participants in the field to guide and give meaning to their activities." (Kim *et al.*, 2007: 289).
12. In the early 2000s the US Chemical Industry Association changed its name to the American Chemistry Council.
13. Dr. Deborah Rice, a toxicologist in the state of Maine, who chaired an EPA external review panel examining the carcinogenic effects of decabromodipheny ether (deca-bdp) was removed from the panel in 2007. Dr. Rice was dismissed in response to a complaint from the American Chemistry Council about her testimony before the Maine legislature regarding health risks of this chemical compound, banned in Europe and several US states (Dingell and Stupak 2008a; 2000b).
14. These cases included: (1) scientists employed by manufacturers of ethylene oxide (Dow Agro, ExxonMobil), acrylamide (Cytec Industries and American Cyanamid), dibutyl phthalate and trimethyl pentane (Exponent and Lyondell Chemical Co.) serving on the EPA panel examining the safety for humans of these very same compounds; and (2) EPA expert panel members being simultaneously hired/funded by the American Chemistry Council to prepare the council's public comments on the safety of the chemicals under review by these panels.
15. A study conducted between 2002 and 2004 by the US Center for Disease Control and Prevention found BPA in the urine of more than 90 percent of the population in the United States (National Institute of Health, 2008).
16. Layton, L., 2008. "Canada bans BPA from baby bottles," *The Washington Post*, April 19, A3.
17. Endocrine-disrupting substances behave like hormones and interfere with the normal regulation of metabolism, growth development, and puberty (National Institute of Health, 2008).
18. Only one of these studies paid by the chemical industry had been made available to the public and submitted for scientific peer review (Dingell and Stupak, 2008a; 2008b).

19. In October 2008, it was also discovered that the research center directed by the chairman of the FDA panel charged with judging BPA safety had received a $5 million donation – not disclosed to the FDA – from a retired medical device manufacturer and anti-regulation activist deeming BPA as "perfectly safe" (Rust and Kissinger, 2008a). The donor's medical device manufacturing company – Gelman Instrument Company – was classified in the mid-1980s as the second worst polluter in Michigan by the state's Department of Natural Resources (Rust and Kissinger, 2008b).
20. Institutional entrepreneurs "are individuals or groups who willingly invest their resources, time, effort, and power in promoting a particular institutional logic along with organizational forms and practices that reflect that logic." Challengers, according to the social movements literature, are "committed to changing the existing institutional model" (Kim *et al.*, 2007: 289–90).
21. Nullification seeks to portray that a reformer's "accusations or suggestions are invalid – the result of misunderstanding and misperceptions on his part" (O'Day, 1974: 375). It involves claims of authority, experience, and – if necessary – bureaucratic investigations to show that reformers' complaints are baseless or that their initiatives have been considered and found to be suboptimal. "The explicit message is: You don't know what you are talking about, but thank you anyway for telling us." (O'Day, 1974: 375).
22. Habitualization is understood here as "the development of patterned problem-solving behaviors and the association of such behaviors with particular stimuli" (Tolbert and Zucker, 1996: 181).
23. I use the term objectification to refer to "the development of general, shared social meanings attached to habitualized behaviors stimuli" (Tolbert and Zucker, 1996: 181).
24. (1) Copenhaver, J. 2008. "Consent decree: United States of America v. Massey Energy Company *et al.*, Civil Action No. 2:07–0299," The United States District Court for the Southern District of West Virginia.
    (2) Urbina, I. 2008. "Coal company hit with EPA's largest civil penalty," *The New York Times*, Friday, January 17, 2008. Accessed November 25, 2008: www.nytimes.com/2008/01/17/us/17cnd-mine.html?scp=2&sq=urbina%20ian%20and%20coal%20company&st=cse.
25. (1) Occupational Safety and Health Daily, 2007. "$1.5 million fine assessed for Alma Fire is largest issued for coal mine violations," *Occupational Safety and Health Daily*, March 30. Accessed January 18, 2008: subscript.bna.com/SAMPLES/ohd.nsf/c5a7ccf782cf46ca85256b57005ca5bc/7826e37e953355db852572ad007c8e49?OpenDocument.
    (2) Murray, K. *et al.*, 2007. "Report of investigation: fatal underground coal mine fire: Aracoma Alma Mine #1, Logan, West Virginia, January 19, 2006," Washington DC: US Department of Labor Mine Safety and Health Administration.

3 Country context and the protective policy process–business response relationship[1]

In the previous chapter, the discussion was limited to the US context, known for its highly institutionalized pluralistic democratic traditions, high levels of wealth, predominant reliance on stringent command-and-control regulations, and strong government capacity to enforce the law (Hillman and Keim, 1995; Vasudeva, 2005; Vig and Kraft, 2006). Yet, companies operating in other countries experience different societal fields that significantly shape the local policy process dynamic and its associated business responses (Bourdieu and Wacquant, 1992; Giddens, 1984; Jennings and Zandbergen, 1995). Hence, this chapter seeks to conceptually explore how basic political and economic country characteristics may affect business responses to protective policy process demands.

Of course, country context characteristics are not the only factors affecting business political choices and behavior when responding to the pressures and demands exerted by the protective policy process stages. Among others, global trends, in-country regional conditions, and firm- and manager-level characteristics affect not only business agency but also how firms are socialized into distinct country's cultural, political, and economic traditions (George *et al.*, 2006; Steinmo *et al.*, 1992).[2] As discussed in Chapter 2, holding these and other factors constant is, of course, the long-accepted, science-based approach to studying specific relationships of interest while acknowledging that other variables may have an effect on such relationships (Kuhn, 1962; Popper, 2002; Rowley, 1997). In Chapter 4, I discuss the effect of firm-level characteristics on the protective policy process–business response relationship.

From an institutional theory perspective, examining the effect of country characteristics on firm responses is very important because the different history and conditions experienced by countries produce disparate socially constructed realities comprising unique political and economic institutional orders with particular norms, traditions, meanings, symbols, language, and scripts (Berger and Luckmann, 1967). Indeed, one of the most deeply-rooted sociological principles posits that a country's socially constructed reality contributes to shape the behavior and preferences of individuals and organizations (Bartley and Schneiberg, 2002; Berger and Luckmann, 1967; Friedland and Alford, 1991). Thus, this suggests that strategies adopted by firms are molded in part by the country context in which they are adopted and implemented (Granovetter, 1985). In addition, empirical evidence from cross-country studies has shown that particular country contexts result in distinct cultures of production diverging from a single, ideally efficient, form (Fligstein, 1996).

Of course, a nation's public policy context is also significantly affected by global trends and pressures. However, these trends and pressures take unique forms depending on a country's distinctive contextual characteristics such as intermediate institutions that configure local politics and economic activities (Evans, 1995; Jepperson and Meyer, 1991; Meyer, 1980). Examples of these intermediate political and economic institutions include local electoral systems, policy networks, systems of interest representation, and the structure of industry associations (Steinmo *et al.*, 1992). Global trends and pressures are also more influential sources of national policies' convergence during periods of widespread prosperity and stability in the international arena, such as in the 1990s (Steinmo *et al.*, 1992).[3] The apparent "end of history" and triumphal march of globalization and free-market "Washington consensus" of the 1990s has yielded now in the early twenty-first century to significantly divergent policy approaches to deal not only with environmental and social protection but also with economic and national security challenges (Fukuyama, 1992).

To better understand the importance of country context differences, it is useful to highlight significantly distinct contextual characteristics that tend to prevail in developing countries. Evidently, it is important to stress at the outset that not all of these countries share these characteristics to the same degree. In developing nations, the government's legitimacy, and thus its stability, is more often in question (Ascher, 1999; Horowitz, 1989). Compared to western industrialized countries, democratic traditions and accepted political advocacy channels in developing nations are more likely to be limited, fragile, and incipient (Grindle and Thomas, 1991; Horowitz, 1989). Hence, influence and participation in policymaking are usually restricted to relatively few interest groups, and freedom of the press is limited resulting in a highly centralized government that faces little scrutiny and that is highly prone to corruption (Horowitz, 1989; Lim and Tang, 2002). These countries are also poor to extremely poor, making promotion of economic growth a dominant priority of the policy agenda; as such, social and environmental protection programs tend to receive scant attention by policymakers (Ames and Keck, 1997; Ascher, 1999; Rivera, 2004). Government agencies in developing countries often adopt command-and-control regulations that mimic those enacted in industrialized countries. Yet, compared to their equivalents in industrialized nations, these developing country agencies have a very limited capacity to enforce policies and regulations and tend to suffer from an endemic lack of technical, administrative, and financial resources (Ascher, 1999; Blackman and Sisto, 2005; Rivera, 2004). For instance, despite the serious and widespread environmental degradation problems confronted by China, in 2005 the State Environmental Protection Administration had just 400 employees, with 300 based in Beijing and only about 200 working on a full-time basis (Balfour, 2005: 122; Khan and Yardley, 2007). By comparison, the US Environmental Protection Agency had over 17,000 full-time employees distributed in ten regional offices and more than ten laboratories (Khan and Yardley, 2007).

The effect of these country context differences is especially prominent on national governmental regulations that, despite increasing globalization pressures, vary greatly across countries and rely on enactment and enforcement at the country level (Jepperson and Meyer, 1991; Stiglitz, 2006). I argue, accordingly, that variations in country contextual characteristics shape business political power, and its understanding and preferences for environmental and social protection policies, thus moderating – weakening or strengthening – firms' resistance to pressures and demands exerted during the different stages involved in enacting and implementing these policies. This moderating effect exerted by country context on the policy process–business response relationship arises for multiple reasons.

First, the country institutional context contributes to limit or amplify the level of influence and participation that different groups can exert on government decisions by constraining their political power, the payoffs of political involvement, and defining legitimate political action strategies (Amenta *et al.*, 1994; Bartley and Schneiberg, 2002; Friedland and Alford, 1991). Second, it also plays a role in restricting the array of policy alternatives perceived as legitimate and rational by policymakers (Lieberman, 2002). Third, besides its constraining effects, country contextual characteristics also exert a constitutive effect on individuals and organizations, contributing to giving meaning that molds the interests and identities of the actors involved in the policy process (Bartley and Schneiberg, 2002; Clemens and Cook, 1999; Hall and Taylor, 1996; Meyer *et al.*, 1997). Fourth, country context also helps to determine the availability of resources and how they are exchanged by the different actors involved or affected by the policy process (Friedland and Alford, 1991). Fifth, it also plays a role in establishing windows of opportunity or veto points that can respectively advance or derail the consideration of emerging problems, and the adoption or implementation of public policies (Steinmo *et al.*, 1992).[4]

This chapter focuses on four basic characteristics of a country's political-economic context: (1) the level of democratization; (2) the system of interest representation; (3) the regulatory approach; and (4) national economic income. Obviously, there are many other country-level socio-economic and political characteristics that have an impact on resistance to policymaking by molding how business and other actors construe their interests and configure power relations. A few examples include: political party system structure; independence of distinct government branches; specific rule of electoral competition; class structure; levels of economic inequality; and the level of state intervention in the economy (Steinmo *et al.*, 1992). However, for several reasons, I posit that it is important to begin understanding the moderating effect of these four characteristics.

First, long-standing research focused on classifying distinct country contexts has identified the levels of democratization and wealth as basic omnibus elements that provide an indication of national context development or modernity (Adelman and Morris, 1965; Baron, 2005; Jepperson and Meyer, 1991; Makino *et al.*, 2004). Institutional scholars, in particular, have stressed the importance of the degree of country "modernity" in determining the legitimacy of pursuing not only economic growth but also environmental and social protection goals (Jennings and Zandbergen, 1995; Meyer and Rowan, 1977;

Meyer and Scott, 1983). In more developed societies there is a higher prevalence of institutional rules and myths that portray environmental and social protection as appropriate social goods, facilitating the creation of formal structures and organizations focused on promoting protective regulations (Jennings and Zandbergen, 1995; Meyer and Rowan, 1977).

Second, a country's level of democratization shapes the interaction of different actors during the policy process by defining which interest groups and political strategies are legitimate, delineating appropriate advocacy procedures, and establishing rules for governmental decisionmaking (Ascher, 1999; Grindle and Thomas, 1991; Neumayer, 2001; Payne, 1995). The level of country wealth limits the resources available for political participation and government implementation of public policies and regulations (Horowitz, 1989; Jepperson and Meyer, 1991; Spencer *et al.*, 2005).

Third, besides general indicators of country development, the level of business resistance to the protective policy process can be significantly amplified or weakened depending on which interest groups dominate the policy process and by the costs and flexibility of the restrictions imposed by protective regulations. A country's system of interest representation indicates the level of government autonomy vis-à-vis business and other interest groups. Thus, it provides an indication of the ability of the business sector to capture the policy process (March and Olsen, 1989; Williamson, 1989). The regulatory approach, on the other hand, determines the costs and flexibility of protective regulations by indicating countries' preferences for the stringency of protective standards and for the combination of incentive-based and command-and-control regulatory instruments (Gunningham *et al.*, 2003; Vogel, 1986). In the next section, I start by relaxing our initial assumptions about the political context of public policymaking and then shift attention to countries' economic affluence.

Political context

Neo-institutional scholars studying businesses have highlighted the importance of a country's political context in shaping firms' responses to economic policies and regulations (Hillman and Keim, 1995; Murtha and Lenway, 1994; Spencer *et al.*, 2005). I follow other scholars in defining a nation's political context as the set of institutional

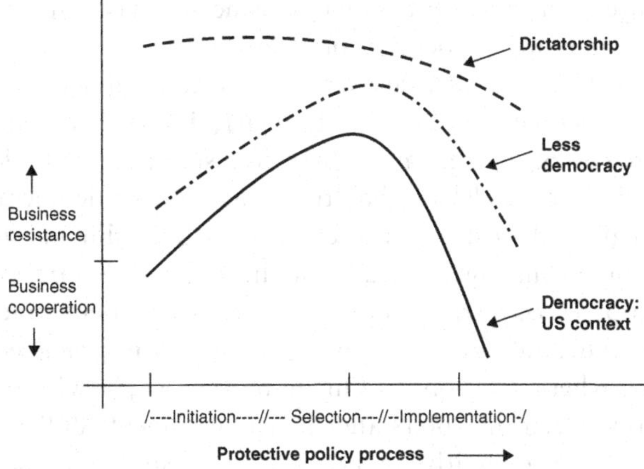

Figure 3.1 Protective policy process–business response relationship: moderating effect of different levels of democracy (rudimentary illustration)

structures, norms, roles, and their related systems of interest representation that delineate how authority, rights, and obligations are obtained and divided among state, business, and other nongovernmental actors (March and Olsen, 1989: 741; Spencer *et al.*, 2005: 322). Most studies examining business behavior and political context have focused on variations in the distinct systems of interest representation in industrialized countries and thus assume higher levels of democratic traditions as given (Hillman and Keim, 1995; Murtha and Lenway, 1994; Spencer *et al.*, 2005). However, besides differences in the types of systems of interest representation, the level of democratization and the type of protective regulations vary significantly around the world affecting the response of business during the different stages of enacting and implementing protective public policies and regulations.

Level of democratization

Regarding the level of democracy, I argue that in countries with more institutionalized democratic traditions, businesses are more likely to display more cooperation during the different stages of the public policy process than in authoritarian regimes (see Figure 3.1 for a rudimentary illustration of this moderating effect). Before I elaborate further on this proposition, I first define democracy, discuss how it is measured, and then discuss why businesses may display greater cooperation in more democratic countries.

In the most basic sense, democracy is widely defined as government by the people (Dahl, 1971; Lijphart, 1984). It is important, however, to emphasize that a vast literature spanning multiple social sciences continues to debate the "true" meaning of democracy and I cannot begin to do justice to this extensive scholarship in this book. Hence, I follow management and public policy scholars by limiting the scope of our arguments to representative democracy (also called liberal democracy), as opposed to the seldom-practiced direct democracy, where decisions are made by the people without intermediation between the voters and their government (Bollen, 1993). Here, I define representative democracy as a system of country governance in which the supreme power is vested in the people and exercised by them indirectly through representation mechanisms involving periodic free elections in which at least two parties compete, the winning party leads the government until the next election, and every citizen has a right to vote and to be elected (Bollen, 1993; deLeon, 1997; Lijphart, 1984; Przeworski *et al.*, 1996). Besides the democratic rights outlined in this definition, it is also important to emphasize that the extent of representative democracy – level of democratization – existing in a country is also determined by the degree of inherent political liberties allowing individuals the freedoms of speech and association (Bollen, 1993; Dahl, 1971; Lijphart, 1984).

There is a substantial amount of debate regarding how to measure the level of country democratization and multiple scholars have periodically published comprehensive reviews of this literature (Bollen, 1980; 1986; 1993; Elkins, 2000; Przeworski *et al.*, 1996). The controversy among scholars focuses on the indicators that should be used and most strongly on whether democracy is a dichotomous or a continuous variable. Przeworski and his co-authors (1996) argue in favor of a "minimalist" dichotomous scale that classifies countries as democracies if the chief executive position and legislative offices are filled as a consequence of periodically contested elections and authoritarian otherwise (Alvarez *et al.*, 1996: 21; Przeworkski *et al.*, 1996; Przeworkski and Limongi, 1997: 178–9). Other scholars argue that there is a substantial variation in the degree of democratization across countries over time and that this variation should not be lost in a categorical scale

Table 3.1 ***Selected illustrative examples of country classification based on their level of democratization for 2007****

Democracies	Hybrid regimes	Authoritarian regimes
(1) Sweden	(1) Singapore	(1) Pakistan
(2) Australia	(2) Turkey	(2) Egypt
(3) Germany	(3) Venezuela	(3) Cuba
(4) Canada	(4) Kenya	(4) China
(5) Costa Rica	(5) Mozambique	(5) Zimbabwe
(6) Uruguay	(6) Iraq	(6) North Korea

* For all categories, countries are listed in descending order from more democratic to less democratic.
Sources: 1. Kekik, L. 2007. *The Economist Intelligence Unit's Index of Democracy*. London: Economist Intelligence Unit.
2. Freedom House. 2008. *Freedom in the World 2008*. New York: Freedom House, Inc.

(Bollen, 1993; Elkins, 2000). I adopt the latter view and agree that the level of democracy can be measured continuously, albeit imperfectly, using a variety of indicators that evaluate two fundamental aspects of representative democracy: the existence of democratic rights and political liberties (Bollen, 1993; Dahl, 1971; Isham *et al.*, 1997). Although scholars differ on their definition and measurement of democratic rights, most scales include the right of citizens to vote, citizens' eligibility for public office, the right of political leaders to compete for support and votes, and the presence of contested free and fair elections (Dahl, 1971; Isham *et al.*, 1997). In terms of political liberties, most democracy scales use indicators of freedom to form and join organizations and freedom of expression (Bollen, 1993). Extensive time-series data for the indicators of distinct aspects of representative democracy are easily available from multiple sources and cover most countries in the world, beginning in the early 1970s (e.g., see freedomhouse.org). Finally, it is important to highlight that comparisons of different democracy scales proposed by multiple authors and organizations show very high levels of agreement (typically above 90 percent) in how countries are classified as democracies or dictatorships (Przeworkski *et al.*, 1996: 21; see Table 3.1 for a few examples of country classification based on their level of democratization).

Building upon the discussion of the meaning and measurement of representative democracy, I now examine how different levels of democratization in a country may moderate business responses to the public policy process. My focus in the following section is, however, on extreme cases (highly democratic and authoritarian countries) to illustrate how firm resistance varies with large changes in the level of democracy. Of course, as discussed above, levels of democracy and authoritarianism vary along a spectrum. The moderating effect of the level of democracy on the public policy process–business response relationship arises from traditional democratic rights and liberties. These rights and liberties establish patterns, routines, and roles of political participation, conflict, advocacy, and law enforcement, the meaning, understanding, and appropriateness of which is mutually accepted and internalized by a country's government, businesses, and other influential stakeholders (March and Olsen, 1989; Payne, 1995). Freedom of the press, speech, association, and participation, and the unhindered right to vote are core rights taken for granted in democratic systems. These rights open information and advocacy channels to multiple grassroots actors that in authoritarian regimes are traditionally, and almost exclusively, enjoyed by business, military, and political elites (Ascher, 1999; Grindle and Thomas, 1991). These freedoms are then used by supporters of social and environmental protection to expedite the process of enacting and institutionalizing protective policies and regulations.

Freedom of the press and speech

Institutionalized freedom of the press and speech allows citizens, scientists, interest groups, the media, and interested government officials to be more informed about, and to monitor the causes and effects of, social and environmental problems produced by business activities (Neumayer, 2001; Payne, 1995). In authoritarian countries freedom of the press and speech are often some of the first rights to be suppressed. For example, in Venezuela and Russia, it has been commonplace in recent years to restrain independent news media outlets by controlling the importation of paper and other printing materials, canceling TV channel licenses, threatening and violently attacking journalists, and/or shutting the media outlets down outright (Levy, 2008; Romero, 2007).

Free speech traditions make it easier to publicly and timely convey concerns and demands to the media, policymakers, and business managers about the detrimental consequences of problematic social and environmental protection routines that may be pursued by business (deLeon, 1997; Fischer and Hajer, 1999; Payne, 1995). For instance, in the fall of 2008, it was reported that more than 50,000 Chinese infants had been severely sickened by consuming baby formula adulterated with melamine, a toxic compound that produces kidney stones (Yardley and Barbosa, 2008). All affected babies appeared to have taken formula produced by Sanlu, a joint venture company partially owned by Fontera, New Zealand's leading multinational dairy company. Yet, according to international media reports, Sanlu "applied pressure to block reporting and used its political connections to prevent some other newspapers from publishing articles about the problem" (Yardley and Barbosa, 2008: A10). These tactics are easier in China where censorship and the strict control of the media are enforced by the central government. Indeed, in early summer 2008, local journalists and media outlets that were aware of an unusual number of sick babies were not allowed to report about it or to investigate the causes (Yardley and Barbosa, 2008). At this time, the Chinese government's Central Propaganda Department was focused on promoting positive news to hype the Olympic Games. In fact, new government rules enacted in 2007 demanded that Chinese media outlets secure official authorization before running any stories related to food safety. These rules were enacted in response to a large recall in the US of Chinese dog food, also adulterated with melamine (Yardley and Barbosa, 2008). In the end, news about possible problems with poisoned baby formula in China arose first in New Zealand where Fontera executives contacted local government officials (Yardley and Barbosa, 2008).

Freedom of association

Well-established freedom of association mechanisms inherent to democratic nations expedite the organization of social and environmental protection advocacy groups and coalitions that are better able to debate, promote, and sustain demands for protective policies and enforcement aimed at improving business social and environmental responsibility (Diamond, 1999; Lybecker and Horan, 2005; Payne, 1995). Indeed, the success of environmental and social protection activists depends to a large degree on their ability to establish organized groups that provide them with increased prestige, authority, management skills, international connections, and money to mobilize their supporters (Kim *et al.*, 2007).

It is hard to diminish the importance of the freedom of association to the promotion of environmental and social protection of causes. The increased resources, connections, administrative capacities, and legitimacy attained by organized groups significantly enhance their bargaining power relative to business and the government (Kim *et al.*, 2007). Because of enhanced resources and capabilities, the members and staff of organized environmental and social protection groups are also much less vulnerable than individual activists to retaliation and/or manipulation by government or other opponent organizations. Additionally, increased resources and capabilities allow more effective organization and deployment of political action. This political action may not only include traditional political action strategies including donations to political parties, issue-specific research, lobbying, public education campaigns, the creation of multi-sector alliances, drafting of laws and regulations, issue framing for agenda setting, and legal defense funds, but also more confrontational tactics such as rallies, demonstrations, sit-ins, picketing, strikes, and even violent protests (Kim *et al.*, 2007; Kingdon, 1995).

Given the enhanced freedom of the press and organization and stronger rule of law traditions, more democratic governments are also less likely to arbitrarily and/or violently restrict the advocacy efforts of social and environmental activists and their organized interest groups (deLeon, 1997; Payne, 1995). Conversely, in authoritarian states repression, threats, and other manipulation tactics are more often used to deal with the demands of these advocacy groups, particularly when they seek to promote protective regulatory restrictions on core sectors of the economy and/or businesses owned by the elite (Kim *et al.*, 2007).

For instance, in 2007 the incoming Guatemalan Minister of the Environment received pre-emptive death threats linked to his future authority to certify the environmental impact assessments of mining projects strongly opposed by local communities, the Catholic Church, and environmentalist groups all excluded from the negotiations between the government and prospective mining companies (Estrada, 2008).[5] Of course, it is important to stress that these death threats may have arisen from multiple sources – such as the military, other government officials, local firms, and/or local landowners expecting windfall profits – without any connection and/or support from the multinational mining companies involved in these conflicts. Despite their covert nature, anonymous threats of violence can be a very effective form of manipulating government officials and activists in countries like Guatemala with strong state-corporatist traditions and an unfortunate history involving extreme levels of violence, poverty, corruption, and authoritarian institutions (Petri, 2002).[6]

Freedom of political participation and the right to vote

Freedom of political participation and the right to vote also play a key role in increasing the legitimacy of protective policies, vis-à-vis economic growth policies, as citizens and groups that advocate social and environmental protection can support the election of like-minded politicians who are more likely to promote the adoption and effective enforcement of protective policies perceived as costly by the business sector (Diamond, 1999; Lim and Tang, 2002; Payne, 1995). Nondemocratic states may hold elections to give the appearance of upholding these voting and political participation rights. Yet, in these authoritarian states, multiple groups – from the government and sometimes other sectors of society – often rely on rigging practices aimed at fraudulently manipulating these "elections." Commonplace rigging practices include stuffing ballot boxes, hiring thugs to intimidate voters and opposition candidates, bribing/extorting public employees to gain their support, and using official funds to promote pro-government candidates. Even more aggressive rigging tactics may include detention or even assassination of opposition candidates. For instance, in 2007–8, intimidation and imprisonment of opposition candidates and their supporters were evident in elections held in Russia and Egypt, and in the case of Pakistan also included the assassination of the globally famous former prime minister Benazir Bhutto (Chivers, 2008; Constable and Rondeaux, 2008; Gall, 2007; Levy, 2008).[7]

Overall, the combination of greater information, demands, and organized political support for social and environmental protection institutionalized by traditional democratic rights and freedoms, constrains the level of resistance that can be offered by firms during the different stages of the policy process. Hence, I argue that businesses in more democratic countries display more cooperation as they experience greater internalization of the collectively shared meaning and importance of social and environmental protection. Firms in more democratic countries tend to take for granted the legitimacy of the activist role played by social and environmental organizations and the news media (Gunningham *et al.*, 2003; Mitchell, 1997; Schmidt, 2002). Also, because of their higher internalization of stronger social-environmental protection traditions, companies in more democratic countries more instinctively accept the enhanced use of coercive government mechanisms to enforce protective policies and regulations (Lindblom and Woodhouse, 1993; Mitchell, 1997; O'Rourke, 2004).

Of course, firms may still actively use resistance strategies to oppose protective regulations in highly democratic countries (Oliver, 1991). However, in these countries some of the most aggressive resistance tactics such as defiance – in the form of violence and disregard of government authority – are considered radical deviances of the institutionalized democratic order and thus seldom adopted or even considered by firms because of their long-standing social and legal illegitimacy (Baron, 2005; Lindblom and Woodhouse, 1993; Mitchell, 1997). Additionally, as I discussed in the policy capture section of the book (see Chapter 3), the most aggressive form of resistance – manipulation tactics aimed at capturing the policy process – is difficult to sustain by business in highly democratic countries like the US. This is mainly because in democratic regimes multiple interest groups, not just businesses, have the rights, expertise, and resources to compete and influence decisionmakers at different stages of policy process (Teske, 2003).

Conversely, in authoritarian regimes business is more likely and able to rely on manipulation tactics for multiple reasons. First, environmental and social protection groups are more likely to be excluded – violently if necessary – from policymaking advocacy and mobilization. Second, the state is less autonomous from economic interests as its legitimacy and capacity to stay in power is more dependent on economic growth than on: (1) citizen consent; and (2) its ability to democratically combine and adjudicate the myriad disparate interests held by those governed (Dahl, 1973; Lindblom and Woodhouse, 1993). Third, government decisions that are considered arbitrary can seldom be challenged successfully because of a lack of an independent judicial system and legislature (Grindle and Thomas, 1991).

To be sure, it is important to stress that manipulation strategies that enable business to capture the policy process must be maintained over time through long-term co-opt, influence, and control tactics. In authoritarian countries, because of the lack of freedom of expression and repressive tactics against opposition, these manipulation tactics are not as conspicuous as other forms of less aggressive resistance used in democratic regimes. Hence, it may seem as if businesses are not offering high levels of resistance to protective policy process demands in authoritarian countries when in fact resistance is sustained at the highest level in the form of manipulation that results in policy capture. Crises generated by big accidents offer rare opportunities to reveal aggressive manipulation tactics often used by business in authoritarian countries to resist adoption and/or implementation of environmental and social protection standards. To illustrate this point, it may be useful to consider the following example. In 2007, a coal mine explosion that killed 105 workers in Linfen, China (Shanxi Province) generated an unusual public uproar that forced the Chinese government to pursue a rare investigation (Barbosa, 2007). This inquiry revealed that the company owning the mine, Ruizhiyan Mining Co., had for a long time used illegal mining and worker safety practices that were overlooked by local public officials receiving bribes in the million dollar range from Ruizhiyan's managers (Cody, 2008). This accident, considered the second most fatal mining disaster in 2007, is just one of many contributing to a government-reported death toll of 3,786 miners in 2007, making the Chinese mining industry the deadliest in the world (Cody, 2008).[8] My argument in this section suggests the following proposition:

Proposition 2: Other things being equal, a country's level of democratization moderates the inverted U-shaped relationship between the protective policy process and firms' responses in such a way that firms operating in less democratic countries are more likely to offer higher political resistance during the different stages of the policy process than firms operating in more democratic countries.

Policy network style: pluralistic versus corporatist systems

Besides stressing the degree of democratization, political science's neo-institutional theory also highlights the importance of identifying the system of interest representation to characterize a country's political context (March and Olsen, 1989; Schmitter, 1974). A country's system of interest representation is defined as the "mechanism by which latent private desires are turned into actual public policies" (Crepaz, 1995: 401). It is usually classified into three ideal-type categories: state-corporatist, neo-corporatist (also called liberal corporatist), and pluralistic, depending on the nature of the interdependencies between the government and organized interests representing business, unions, and other advocacy groups, and on the country's emphasis on consensual policymaking (Katzenstein, 1994; Murtha and Lenway, 1994).

Corporatist systems. Since Schmitter's seminal paper in 1974, there has been a substantial amount of research that has explored the nature and characteristics of corporatist systems (Crepaz and Lijphart, 1995; Scruggs, 1999; Williamson, 1989). As originally conceptualized, Schmitter (1974) defined a corporatist structure as:

> a system of interest representation in which the constituent units are organized into a limited number of singular, compulsory, noncompetitive, hierarchically ordered and functionally differentiated categories, recognized or licensed (if not created) by the state and granted a deliberate representational monopoly within their respective categories in exchange for observing certain controls on their selection of leaders and articulation of demands and supports. (Schmitter, 1974: 93–4)

This broad definition covers two main types of corporatism that need to be distinguished: state-corporatism and neo-corporatism (Schmitter, 1974; Streeck and Kenworthy, 2005; Williamson, 1989). *State-corporatist* systems are more prevalent in authoritarian countries or those with incipient democratic practices (Schmitter, 1974; Williamson, 1989).[9] In such systems, a small number of peak associations, usually from business, are deliberately authorized by the government (via official decree and/or repression of other competing groups) to develop and implement economic and social policies. The policies developed and advocated by these peak associations generally reflect narrow industry interests and exclude the concerns of environmental and social protection groups (Schmitter, 1974; Scruggs, 1999; Streeck and Kenworthy, 2005). On the other hand, in *neo-corporatist* forms of interest intermediation, typical of some northern European democracies (e.g., Austria, Norway, and

Sweden), traditional business associations share cooperative policymaking and implementation with labor and a wider variety of other socially licensed "peak" groups such as nongovernmental organizations focused on advancing environmental and social protection causes (Scruggs, 1999; Streeck and Kenworthy, 2005). A high degree of cooperation between a relatively strong centralized state and the various peak associations in the country is strongly emphasized in neo-corporatist states (Schmitter, 1974; Williamson, 1989). Thus, in return for access to and participation in the policy process, the various peak groups enjoying influential access are expected to strive for collective benefits and social consensus in addition to advocating their own narrow interests (Jepperson, 2002; Jepperson and Meyer, 1991; Schmitter, 1974).

Pluralist systems. On the other end of the continuum from corporatist countries are pluralist ones. Schmitter (1974) defines pluralism as:

> a system of interest representation in which the constituent units are organized into an unspecified number of multiple, voluntary, competitive, nonhierarchically ordered, and self-determined (as to type of scope of interest) categories which are not specially licensed, recognized, subsidized, created or otherwise controlled in leadership selection or interest articulation by the state and which do not exercise a monopoly of representational activity within their respective categories. (Schmitter, 1974: 96)

In more pluralistic countries like the US and the UK, governments often receive input from a large number of competing interest groups and policymaking reflects these clashing interests (Scruggs, 1999; Streeck and Kenworthy, 2005; Williamson, 1989). Countries with pluralistic systems are often characterized by rivalry among multiple and fragmented interest groups that compete to provide their input in the policy process (Jepperson, 2002; Schmitter, 1974; Spencer *et al.*, 2005). Advocacy groups may be constantly changing and emerging in pluralistic societies and their roles, rights, and obligations are not reified (Jepperson, 2002; Streeck and Kenworthy, 2005). Public policies are not as consensual as in neo-corporatist countries and are more likely the outcome of domination by changing coalitions that prevail in the political battles of the moment (Jepperson, 2002; Schmitter, 1974). The state in pluralistic nations is weaker and less centralized than in neo-corporatist countries (Schmitter, 1974; Streeck and Kenworthy, 2005).

Neo-institutional scholars studying businesses have used the neo-corporatist–pluralistic variations across countries to predict firm responses to economic and industrial policies but have given scant consideration to state corporatist systems more typical of developing countries (Jepperson and Meyer, 1991; Streeck and Kenworthy, 2005). These researchers have also given less consideration to how countries' systems of interest representation affect business responses to environmental and social protection policies that could potentially generate a more confrontational business–government–society dynamic (Crepaz, 1995; Griffiths and Zammuto, 2005; Scruggs, 1999; Whitley, 1999; Windolf, 2002). Additionally, this extant literature has mostly focused on explaining business responses to the implementation of already established regulations, paying little attention to other stages of the policymaking process (Hillman *et al.*, 2004; Vasudeva, 2005). Cashore and Vertinsky's (2000) case study examining the environmental protection practices adopted by forestry companies in the US and Canada is a notable exception to the literature's lack of attention to protective policies. They theorize that forestry firms' responses to environmental protection demands are affected by the level of business domination prevalent in different types of sectoral-level policy network styles (Cashore and Vertinsky, 2000).

Building upon this seminal work, I posit that the level of resistance that firms offer during the different stages of the protective policy process is likely to be higher in pluralistic countries than in neo-corporatist ones. Conversely, compared to state-corporatist nations, firms' resistance is likely to be lower in pluralistic countries. This moderating effect on the policy process–business response relationship arises first from the variation in the levels of business participation and second from the distinct emphasis on policymaking consensus inherent to the different systems of interest representation. Compared to pluralistic countries, in a state-corporatist country businesses' likely monopolistic access to policymaking and implementation increases their capacity for using higher levels of resistance in the form of manipulation tactics, often allowing them to capture the policy process. In contrast, business resistance is likely to be lower in neo-corporatist countries compared to pluralistic countries because of shared participation with labor and other environmental/social protection peak associations capable of effectively excluding issues from the public policy agenda.

In more general terms, the previous arguments posit that business resistance is likely to follow a nonmonotonic relationship with competition for participation in policymaking. The more business has to compete for participation, as in pluralistic countries, the more likely it is to show higher resistance to the point of defiance (in cases of high levels of exclusion). Conversely, when business enjoys monopolistic access to the state, as in state-corporatist countries, it is more likely to use manipulation strategies (the highest form of resistance) to capture policymaking. It is important, however, to emphasize that business manipulation that results in policy process capture is not a one-time event. Highest business resistance in the form of manipulation needs to be sustained over a long period of time for policy capture to endure and thus make other less aggressive resistance strategies (that are usually more visible) unnecessary. In between these two extreme scenarios of business participation, business cooperation is more likely when business shares participation in the policy process with other groups as in the case in neo-corporatist countries.

The lower levels of business resistance observed in neo-corporatist countries are also the result of sedimented traditions, routines, and structures that emphasize consensus and collective rights in policymaking over pluralism's priority on political competition and individual rights, and over state-corporatism's emphasis on the exclusion of social protection groups from policymaking (Crepaz, 1995; Scruggs, 1999). In neo-corporatist countries, firms are more likely than in pluralistic and state-corporatist nations to internalize a socially shared emphasis on political harmony and community cooperation and thus consider the use of aggressive resistance strategies as illegitimate when confronting demands for social and environmental protection (Crepaz, 1995; Scruggs, 1999). Additionally, given their more frequent interaction with licensed organized social and environmental groups in the search for policy consensus, firms in neo-corporatist countries are also more likely to cooperate with licensed social activist groups during the different stages of the protective policy process (Crepaz, 1995; Hillman and Hitt, 1999; Scruggs, 1999).

Proposition 3: Other things being equal, a country's system of interest representation moderates the inverted U-shaped relationship between the protective policy process and firms' responses in such a way that firms operating in pluralistic countries are more likely to offer: (1) higher political resistance during the different stages of the policy process than firms operating in neo-corporatist countries; and (2) lower political resistance during the different stages of the policy process than firms operating in state-corporatist countries.

Regulatory approach: command-and-control versus incentive-based

Other key factors that moderate the public policy process–business response relationship are the stringency and type of regulatory instruments and mechanisms considered, enacted, and implemented to promote social and environmental protection by business. The type of regulatory instruments varies along a spectrum from command-and-control to incentive-based (Howlett and Ramesh, 1995; Salomon, 1981). Obviously, these two polar extremes of the continuum represent ideal types and countries use a combination of both command-and-control and incentive-based instruments. Yet, in most cases, a predominant preference for a particular type of policy instrument can be identified (Jennings and Zandbergen, 1995).

Because our initial focus was on the US context, I assumed in the first half of the book that a command-and-control regulation approach is the predominant type considered and prescribed by the protective policy process. Command-and-control regulations set detailed compliance standards, remediation technologies and equipment, administrative systems, reporting mechanisms, and non-compliance penalties for companies, in concert with specific government monitoring and enforcement responsibilities (Porter and van der Linde, 1995; Vig and Kraft, 2006).

Incentive-based regulations, on the other hand, seek to more efficiently and cooperatively promote social and environmental protection by avoiding prescription of specific compliance techniques and instead using economic incentives – such as taxes and/or tradable permits for undesired business practices – that give firms flexibility to continuously test and develop technology and management systems to comply with established standards (Jennings and Zandbergen, 1995; Porter and van der Linde, 1995; Vig and Kraft, 2006). Additionally, under the incentive-based regulatory approach, governments shift focus from enforcement to preventive compliance that relies on providing technical assistance to business and creating consumer or supply-chain demand for socially and environmentally responsible firms through public rating databases and awards (Gunningham *et al.*, 2003).

Compared to incentive-based regulations, command-and-control regulations designed to address social and environmental protection demands have traditionally been perceived as more inefficient and inflexible policy instruments that stifle innovation by impinging on business compliance choices (Gunningham *et al.*, 2003; Henriques and Sadorsky, 1996; Winter and May, 2001). The institutionalization of command-and-control regulations depends primarily on government coercive monitoring and enforcement whereas in the case of an incentive-based approach, business' social and environmental protective practices acquire predefined collective meaning, understanding, and acceptability, not only through government coercion but also with the help of instrumental economic pressures (Andrews, 1998; Porter and van der Linde, 1995; Scott, 2001). Thus, I posit that firms operating in countries that rely on incentive-based regulations to promote social and environmental protection are more likely to offer higher cooperation during the different stages of the policy process than firms operating in countries relying on command-and-control regulations.

Command-and-control regulations perceived as inefficient and inflexible are more likely to generate higher business resistance during the different stages of the policy process because they heighten the customary conflict between the provision of social-environmental protection by business and the already institutionalized business' profit-seeking expectations, routines, roles, and traditions (Andrews, 1998; Oliver, 1992; Zucker, 1987). Conversely, incentive-based regulations take advantage of traditional business sector strengths at finding innovative and cost-effective methods (Delmas and Marcus, 2004; Porter and van der Linde, 1995; Wheeler, 1999). Incentive-based regulations also reduce the likelihood of expensive litigation typical of a command-and-control regulatory approach, freeing firm resources to more quickly meet protective demands (Cashore and Vertinsky, 2000; Porter and van der Linde, 1995; Vig and Kraft, 2006). They may also create new markets for innovative firms that develop new technologies and management systems (Porter and van der Linde, 1995).

These innovative firms may also improve their reputations thanks to increased social and environmental legitimacy derived from their proactive practices (Porter and van der Linde, 1995; Vig and Kraft, 2006).

Besides identifying the type of regulatory instruments preferred in different countries, scholars in multiple social sciences have also long highlighted the importance of considering the stringency of the specific protective regulations proposed and adopted by a country (Gunningham *et al.*, 2003; Levison, 1996; Vig and Kraft, 2006). More stringent protective regulations involve more rigorous standards and enforcement, imposing higher costs on business, even if they rely on incentive-based regulatory instruments (Levison, 1996; Vig and Kraft, 2006). Also, the more stringent regulations are, the more restricted the technology and management choices available to businesses attempting to meet the given environmental or social regulatory performance standards. This combination of higher costs and restricted compliance choices associated with more stringent regulations again enhances the conflict between institutionalized profit-seeking business traditions and protective policy demands. Accordingly, it can be expected that firms are more likely to offer higher resistance during the different stages of the protective policy process when confronting more stringent regulatory requirements.

Proposition 4: *Other things being equal, a country's regulatory approach moderates the inverted U-shaped relationship between the protective policy process and firms' responses in such a way that firms operating in countries relying on command-and-control regulations are more likely to offer higher political resistance during the different stages of the policy process than firms operating in countries relying on incentive-based regulations.*

Proposition 5: *Other things being equal, regulatory stringency moderates the inverted U-shaped relationship between the protective policy process and firms' responses in such a way that firms operating in countries relying on stricter regulations are more likely to offer higher political resistance during the different stages of the policy process than firms operating in countries relying on less stringent regulations.*

Economic context

Finally, I also believe that it is important to highlight the intervening role played by a country's economic affluence, indicated by its gross national income (GNI) per capita, in moderating the protective policy process–business response relationship. For this I draw on arguments from neo-institutional economics and resource dependence theory (North, 1990; Pfeffer and Salancik, 1978). Gross national income is a measure of national economic activity representing the total value of all goods and services produced annually including income from abroad – called gross national product (GNP) in the old terminology of the 1968 United Nations System of National Accounts (World Bank, 2006).

The connection between national socio-political institutions and national economic income has long been recognized by multiple social science disciplines; with most scholars focusing on understanding how socio-political institutions shape the economy (March and Olsen, 1989; North, 1990; Scott, 2001). Of course, economic income reciprocally affects the process of socio-political institutional formation and change (Jepperson and Meyer, 1991; North, 1990). For example, a large body of the economics literature suggests that social and environmental protection norms and regulations may be easier to institutionalize in wealthier countries (Dasgupta *et al.*, 2002; Porter and van der Linde, 1995; Stern, 2004). These extant works have studied the relationship between country GNI per capita and social or environmental protection to test the application of the Kuznets curve hypothesis to these issues (Dasgupta *et al.*, 2002; Higgins and Williamson, 1999; Milanovic, 2005; Solimano *et al.*, 2000; Stern, 2004). The Kuznets curve hypothesis posits an inverted U association between social-environmental decline and per capita income, meaning that, in wealthier countries, economic growth is associated with social-environmental improvement (Grossman and Krueger, 1991). Social-environmental quality in poor countries, on the other hand, is expected to quickly decline with economic growth (Dasgupta *et al.*, 2002; Grossman and Krueger, 1991; Stern, 2004).

This inverted U relationship is explained by arguing that as national income per capita rises beyond lower-middle income country levels, resources and new technology available for social and environmental protection enforcement and adoption respectively become more abundant for governments and firms (Stern, 2004). Also, once citizens in upper-middle income countries and beyond have satisfied their basic needs (e.g., health, education, and safety), they shift their demands to increased social-environmental protection, prompting the adoption and effective implementation – institutionalization – of stricter protective regulations (Panayotou, 1997). Empirical studies offer mixed evidence about the precise GNI per capita levels at which turning (or "saddle") points are observed, but most point to improvements in social and environmental quality beginning in countries with upper-middle income levels – currently between $3,466–$10,725 GNI per capita (Stern, 2004; World Bank, 2006).[10]

At a micro-level of analysis, organizational theory scholars have similarly pointed out how the array of available strategies and attainable goals increases for businesses operating in more munificent environments (Castrogiovanni, 1991; Pfeffer and Salancik, 1978; Staw and Szwajkowski, 1975). Munificence is understood here as the level of "abundance of critical resources needed by firms operating within an environment" (Castrogiovanni, 1991: 542). In contexts with scarce resources, competition and conflict increases, reducing firms' profitability and survival, making it more difficult for business to pursue other goals that produce collective benefits such as social and environmental protection (Pfeffer and Salancik, 1978; Staw and Szwajkowski, 1975). Moreover, the pressure to gather limited resources in scarce environments pushes firms to engage in illegal acts such as the corruption of government officials (Husted, 1999; Staw and Szwajkowski, 1975).

Hence, I argue that firms operating in poor countries (below upper-middle GNI per capita) are more likely to offer higher resistance during the different stages of the protective policy process than those operating in wealthier countries. In these poor countries demands for social and environmental protection are more likely to be considered incompatible with legitimate subsistence practices of large numbers of barely surviving businesses (Blackman and Bannister, 1998; O'Rourke, 2004; Rivera, 2004). Moreover, it is not only that social and environmental protection demands may be perceived as trivial and illegitimate when faced with the struggle for survival; but also that these issues are usually dismissed because it is taken for granted that poor developing country governments lack the capacity and/or the will to enforce "on-paper" protective regulations (Ames and Keck, 1997; O'Rourke, 2004; Rivera, 2004; Stuligross, 1999). In addition, many business owner-managers rarely have the basic education required to understand complex social and environmental protection requirements (Rivera and deLeon, 2005).

Proposition 6: Other things being equal, a country's economic income moderates the inverted U-shaped relationship between the protective policy process and firms' responses in such a way that firms operating in poor countries with gross national income per capita below upper-middle income levels are more likely to offer higher political resistance during the different stages of the policy process than firms operating in wealthier countries.

Finally, it is important to re-emphasize a condition established at the beginning of this chapter: in developing the arguments and propositions, I assumed firm and in-country regional characteristics to be constant. The following chapter considers the effect of firm-level characteristics on the protective policy process–business response relationship. Regional variations inside countries are also important. Significant changes in the level of political freedoms, democratic rights, level of income per capita, and enforcement/monitoring of protective regulations are common inside countries and they tend to be particularly stark in developing nations even across small distances. For example, despite the pervasive weak enforcement capacity of environmental/social protection agencies in developing countries, the ability of these agencies to influence business behavior can be expected to be higher for firms located in urban areas (O'Rourke, 2004; Stern, 2004; Wheeler, 1999). In these areas, local community stakeholders can be expected to be more politically influential as they have higher economic and legal capacity, stronger leadership, and more connections with high-level government officials, the media, and environmentalists (O'Rourke, 2004; Stern, 2004; Wheeler, 1999). I do not develop an additional chapter to deal with these regional differences because the logic and propositions discussed here for country contextual variations can easily be adapted by scholars and policymakers to explore the effect of these in-country regional changes.

Notes

1. This chapter is an expanded and modified version of portions of: Rivera *et al.* (2009), reproduced with kind permission of Springer Science and Business Media.
2. Some rational choice scholars would even make the argument that political and other kinds of behavior are explained by self-interest with institutional effects being negligible (Steinmo *et al.*, 1992).

3. Similarly, during the 1950s and 1960s there was another period of international prosperity and national policy convergence in western countries that ended with an economic crisis triggered by sharp oil price increases (Steinmo *et al.* 1992).
4. Veto points are "points in the policy process where the mobilization of opposition can thwart policy innovations." (Steinmo, *et al.*, 1992: 7).
5. Personal interview with Luis Ferrate, Guatemalan Minister of the Environment, by Fernando Estrada of *Prensa Libre.* Citation: Estrada, J. 2008. Luis Ferrate: "Debo proteger la vida de dodos." *Prensa Libre*, August 3, 2008. Accessed online on August 6, 2008: www.prensalibre.com/pl/2008/agosto/03/253102.html.
6. Guatemala, one of poorest countries in the western hemisphere, suffered a twenty-five-year civil war that ended in 1996 after more than 250 thousand deaths. It has just recently adopted incipient democratic rights and liberties (Economist Intelligence Unit. 2008. *Guatemala Country Report.* London).
7. Chivers, C. J. 2008. "Gorbachev, rebuking Putin, criticizes Russian elections." *The New York Times*, January 29, 2008. Accessed online on February 18, 2008: www.nytimes.com/2008/01/29/world/europe/29russia.html.

   Constable, P. and Rondeaux, C. 2008. "Desiring a fair vote, doubting it will be: Pakistanies expect rigging by government." *The Washington Post*, February 18, 2008. Page A13.3.

   Gall, C. 2007. "Bhutto assassination ignites disarray." *The New York Times*, December 28, 2007. Accessed online on February 18, 2008: http://www.nytimes.com/2007/12/28/world/asia/28pakistan.html#.
8. Cody, E. 2008. "Safety subverted in China's mines: corruption comes to the surface after disaster that halted production." *The Washington Post*, February 18, 2008. Page A10; Barbosa, D. 2007. "105 killed in China mine explosion." *The New York Times*, December 7, 2007. Accessed online at: www.nytimes.com/2007/12/07/world/asia/07mine.html?scp=1&sq=Linfen+mine&st=nyt.
9. It is important to emphasize, however, that state corporatism and dictatorship are not synonymous.
10. The World Bank classifies countries according to their gross national income (GNI) per capita as follows: low income, $875 or less; lower middle income, $876–$3,465; upper middle income, $3,466–$10,725; and high income, $10,726 or more (World Bank, 2006).

4 *Firm-level characteristics and business responses to environmental/social protection demands*[1]

The predominant tendency among firms sharing a similar external context and policy demands is to adopt similar strategies and structures (Hoffman, 1997). However, firm-level characteristics, such as ownership, profitability, and industry, to name a few, can contribute to produce heterogeneous business responses to the political interaction observed during the different stages of the protective policy process (Issac and Griffin, 1989; Makino *et al.*, 2004; Sutton and Dobbin, 1996; Tolbert and Zucker, 1983). Indeed, there is an extensive literature on corporate political strategy that has identified how firms' characteristics are associated with differences in corporate political activity (Cavazos, 2005). In general, this research suggests that firms that are larger (Boddewyn and Brewer, 1994; Keim and Baysinger, 1988; Schuler, 1996), more diversified (Hillman and Hitt, 1999), have more slack resources (Schuler, 1996; Schuler *et al.*, 2002), and are older (Hillman, 2003) tend to show higher levels of political activity and a greater desire to exert influence on the public policy process. Similarly, a growing number of empirical studies implemented mostly in the US and Europe have identified an array of firm-level characteristics associated with higher levels of corporate environmental and social performance (Berchicci and King, 2007). However, most of these empirical studies have focused on identifying a link between different measures of profitability and indicators of corporate environmental and/or social performance (Margolis and Walsh, 2003).

The conceptual framework developed in Chapters 2 and 3 assumes firms' characteristics and in-country regional variations to be constant. This assumption allowed me to, first, focus on exploring how firm responses vary as a function of the different stages of the protective policy process in the US (Chapter 2). Second, it also made it possible to explore how variations in country context characteristics affect the protective policy process–business response relationship (Chapter 3). This chapter extends the framework of analysis to explore how variations in firms' characteristics may contribute to affect business responses to protective policy process demands.

The effect of firm-level characteristics on firms' responses to protective policy demands is particularly important during the enactment and early implementation stages of the protective policy process, when regulatory demands are not yet fully institutionalized (Tolbert and Zucker, 1983). Heterogeneous responses to protective policy demands arise for multiple reasons: first, variations in firms' resources, personnel, structures, ownership, and culture – to name a few key factors – produce different perceptions and understandings of the competitive meaning and legitimacy of institutional pressures (Delmas and Toffel, 2004; Gunningham *et al.*, 2003). Second, the intensity of coercive, normative, and mimetic institutional pressures exerted on a specific firm by policymakers, stakeholders, and other competitor companies increases based on how these external actors perceive such a firm to:

(1) be engaged in activities with high impact on the natural environment, consumers' and workers' well-being, etc;
(2) be an industry leader whose behavior may affect other competitor businesses and supply chain firms in different parts of the world;
(3) have the resources to adopt superior environmental and social protection practices without risking survival.[2]

Third, often firms operating in the same country context, and even the same organizational field, simultaneously experience conflicting institutional pressures that force managers to offer more resistance to those pressures perceived to be: less legitimate, exerted by non-influential actors, less consistent with other firm goals (e.g., profit-making), and/or exerted by actors with low capacity for coercion (Oliver, 1991).[3] Fourth, related to the last reason, multinational enterprise subsidiaries face multiple types of isomorphic pressures arising not only from host country contexts but also from home country environments and parent company culture and norms (Kostova and Roth, 2002).

Before discussing the effect of specific firm characteristics in the following sections of this chapter, it is important to stress that there is a large array of different company qualities that can contribute to shaping business responses to protective policy process demands.

Indeed, as mentioned above, there is a growing body of literature that seeks to identify the relationship between distinct firm traits and environmental/social protection practices (Berchicci and King, 2007). In this chapter, I focus only on a few of the firm characteristics that have more prominently and consistently been identified to affect these practices. They include financial performance, firm size, industry type, multinational corporation ownership, public ownership, export orientation, top managers' education and nationality, and membership in industry associations.

Resource-related firm characteristics

Financial performance

The relationship between different measures of business profitability and environmental/social performance is the subject of a large theoretical and empirical literature spanning multiple perspectives, industries, and contexts (Darnall, 2009; Margolis and Walsh, 2003). However, there is still a lack of consensus about the nature and causality of this relationship. A detailed review by Margolis and Walsh (2003) of the empirical literature published between 1972 and 2003 found 127 studies examining the business profitability and environmental/social performance relationship. Of all these studies, 42.5 percent found a positive correlation between firm performance and environmental/social performance, 5.5 percent found a negative association, and the rest suggested either non-significant or mixed findings (Margolis and Walsh, 2003).

The traditional perspective on this issue suggests that, in general, there is a trade-off between environmental/social protection and business competitiveness goals (Darnall, 2009; Palmer *et al.*, 1995). Scholars supporting this perspective argue that production expenditures are larger for firms facing more environmental and social protection regulations and that most consumers are not willing to reward enhanced protective practices adopted by businesses (Darnall, 2009; Jaffe *et al.*, 1995; Palmer *et al.*, 1995). Even when incentive-based regulations are adopted, it is argued that they impose a negative effect on business performance. In the words of Palmer *et al.*, (1995: 122): "Even incentive-based environmental regulations result in reduced profits for the regulated firms ... The addition (or tightening) of constraints on a firm's set of choices cannot be expected to result in an increased level of profits." From this perspective, it follows that more profitable firms have higher slack resources with which to develop new strategies to comply with protective regulation demands, and thus would be more likely to offer less resistance to the process of enacting and implementing these regulations (Bowen, 2002). However, it is important to note that the higher level of resources available to more profitable firms could also be used to invest in higher resistance tactics that seek to pre-empt the adoption of protective policies usually perceived as costly and inflexible (Bowen, 2002). Yet, this increased capacity to display resistance is often bounded by higher institutional expectations and monitoring exerted on more profitable firms by government agencies and other stakeholders involved in the protective policy process (Hillman *et al.*, 2004).

Beginning in the early 1990s, the view that there is an inevitable trade-off between business profitability and environmental/social performance has come under strong criticism based on theoretical arguments and empirical evidence. A growing number of scholars contend that the lose-lose view follows directly from analyzing business protective practices with a static approach that assumes away changes in environmental/social protection technologies, manufacturing processes, product characteristics, and customer preferences (Darnall, 2009; Hart, 1995; Porter and van der Linde, 1995). Consequently, it is argued that when taking into consideration the intrinsic dynamic nature of competition, technology development, and customer desires, appropriately designed protective strategies and practices can enhance firm financial performance even if they exceed regulatory requirements and/or are implemented earlier (Darnall, 2009; Hart, 1995; Porter and van der Linde, 1995b).

This alternative win-win perspective rejects the assumptions that firms facing protective regulations are operating on their production frontier, have perfect access to information, and have already discovered the best technologies to comply with environmental/social protection standards (Christmann, 1997; Porter and van der Linde, 1995). For example, in the case of environmental protection, it is assumed that, because of their reactive approach, firms have systematically failed to consider pollution as a waste of resources and as a sign of inefficient production processes. Therefore, firms often neglect opportunities to improve the efficiency of their manufacturing processes

(Darnall, 2009; Hart, 1995; Russo and Fouts, 1997). Additionally, given the growing demand for environmentally/socially responsible products and technologies, firms adopting proactive environmental/ social protection practices can improve their financial performance by obtaining price premiums and/or gaining exclusive access to new markets that favor these products and practices (Darnall, 2009; Porter and van der Linde, 1995; Rivera, 2002).

The win-win perspective on the association between firm performance and environmental/social performance suggests that more profitable firms are more likely to offer more cooperation during the different stages of the protective policy process. This increased cooperation arises from a new understanding that protective regulations may spur managerial and technological innovations that allow firms to gain cost and differentiation advantages. These protective managerial and technological innovations would have ordinarily been resisted by managers holding institutionalized biases that portray environmental and social protection practices as costly and inflexible mandates. The previous arguments suggest the following propositions:

Proposition 7: Other things being equal, higher firm financial performance is associated with higher environmental/social performance.

Proposition 8: Other things being equal, firm financial performance moderates the inverted U-shaped relationship between the protective policy process and firms' responses in such a way that firms with higher financial performance are more likely to offer lower resistance during the different stages of the policy process than firms with lower financial performance.

Firm size

Larger firms are more visible and have higher potential impact on environmental and social protection quality. Accordingly, their practices, even in developing countries, receive higher scrutiny from customers, the media, government agencies, and environmentalists (Hettige *et al.*, 1996; King and Lenox, 2000). Thus, bigger businesses are more likely to be pressured to cooperate more with national policymakers. Additionally, because of their assumed greater resources, larger facilities are held to higher standards by stakeholders and are expected to play a leadership role in social and environmental protection by showing beyond-compliance environmental/social performance. Industry associations also expect larger companies to play a leadership role and pressure them to participate in voluntary programs that promote beyond-compliance corporate environmental and social responsibility (Hoffman, 1999; Tashman and Rivera, 2008). They also are more likely to enjoy economies of scale when implementing environmental and social protection measures (Bray *et al.*, 2002; King and Lenox, 2000; Wheeler, 1999). On the other hand, it is important to recognize that, as in the case of more profitable firms, larger businesses have more resources and bargaining power that may permit them to offer higher resistance during the protective policy process (Hillman *et al.*, 2004; Oetzel, 2005). Indeed, empirical work in the US has consistently found that larger companies are more politically active and tend to obtain more access to high level policymakers (Hillman *et al.*, 2004; Oetzel, 2005).Yet, given the increased level of scrutiny and demands exerted on larger firms by the government, the media, activists, and other stakeholders, their ability to adopt aggressive levels of resistance is often more limited than in the case of smaller firms. Politically, it is also more difficult for governments and activists to exert strong protective policy pressures on small and micro-businesses that tend to have more public support and are often perceived as being more financially vulnerable and having less impact on environmental/social protection problems (see discussion below) (Blackman and Sisto, 2005). These arguments suggest the following propositions:

Proposition 9: *Other things being equal, larger firm size is associated with higher environmental/social performance.*

Proposition 10: *Other things being equal, firm size moderates the inverted U-shaped relationship between the protective policy process and firms' responses in such a way that larger firms are more likely to offer lower resistance during the different stages of the policy process than smaller firms.*

Micro-businesses and the protective policy process

Besides considering firm size in general, it is also important to highlight that a large proportion of firms in developing countries are micro-businesses that often operate outside the formal economy. Micro-businesses are generally considered as firms with between one and ten employees, although this range is somewhat arbitrary and may vary slightly from country to country (Beck *et al.*, 2005;

Blackman, 2000; De Soto, 2000).[4] These informal economy micro-firms are, in a sense, inconspicuous organizations to regulators since they tend to lack an official government license to operate, usually do not pay taxes, and have no access to credit and financial services from banks (Blackman and Sisto, 2005; De Soto, 2000). Typically, a significant number of these micro-enterprises are barely surviving financially with little resources to track or deal with emerging environmental and social protection issues (Blackman and Bannister, 1998; Garcia-Johnson, 2000; O'Rourke, 2004). Additionally, because of their micro-size and the fact that they operate extra-legally, these businesses tend to have very little influence over the actions of developing country governments that they perceive as corrupt and irrelevant to their existence (De Soto, 2000). This condition is particularly problematic since estimates are that up to 50 percent of all people in developing countries work in such micro-businesses (De Soto, 2000: 154). Environmental and social protection issues are seldom part of the institutionalized priorities of informal micro-firms as they are seen as costly and, most importantly, considered incompatible with the legitimate practices of enterprises that are barely surviving (Dasgupta, 2000; Lo and Leung, 2000; Rivera, 2002; Stuligross, 1999). Moreover, it is not only that environmental and social protection issues are perceived as trivial and illegitimate; these issues are usually dismissed because it is taken for granted that developing country governments lack the capacity and/or the will to enforce protective regulations on micro-businesses (Ames and Keck, 1997; O'Rourke, 2004; Rivera, 2004; Stuligross, 1999). In addition, owner-managers of informal micro-firms in developing countries rarely have the basic education required to understand complex environmental management requirements (Rivera and deLeon, 2005).

Industry type

The industry in which firms operate may also affect their responses to environmental and social protection policy demands (Griffin and Koerber, 2006). Compared to firms that operate in the service sectors of the economy, businesses in natural resource extraction (e.g., mining, oil and gas exploration, forestry) and heavy manufacturing industries (e.g., utilities, chemical, steel production, paper production) are more likely to generate visible environmental and social impacts.

These firms are also more often involved in intense and frequent disputes associated with their protective practices and tend to confront more regulations, oversight, and demands from governments, local communities, and other stakeholders. Accordingly, businesses operating in natural resource extraction and heavy manufacturing industries are more likely to show higher resistance to environmental and social protection policy demands that are taken-for-granted to be more costly and constraining (Rivera, 2002). These arguments suggest the following propositions:

Proposition 11: Other things being equal, firms operating in natural resource extraction or heavy manufacturing industries are associated with lower environmental/social performance than firms operating in other sectors of the economy.

Proposition 12: Other things being equal, industry type moderates the inverted U-shaped relationship between the protective policy process and firms' responses in such a way that firms operating in natural resource extraction or heavy manufacturing industries are more likely to offer higher resistance during the different stages of the policy process than firms operating in other sectors of the economy.

Firm ownership characteristics

Multinational corporation subsidiaries

Businesses owned by multinational corporations (MNCs) from the most advanced industrialized countries are also more visible to local and international stakeholders, leading to heightened expectations and monitoring of their environmental and social protection practices than those experienced by local firms and MNC subsidiaries from other countries such as China, South Korea, India, and Brazil (Christmann and Taylor, 2001; Levy and Kolk, 2002; Wheeler, 1999). Additionally, MNCs from the most advanced industrialized countries tend to have more ready access to environmental/social protection management knowledge and technologies developed to respond to more stringent protective policy standards of their home countries (Christmann and Taylor, 2001; Levy and Kolk, 2002; Wheeler, 1999). The market and cultural context in the most advanced industrialized countries is also more favorable to environmental and social protection efforts and thus may make the top managers of these countries' MNCs more receptive to protective policy concerns and regulations (Levy and

Kolk, 2002; Rivera, 2004).[5] Thus, compared to other firms, multinational subsidiaries from the most advanced industrialized countries can be expected to be more likely to offer less resistance during the different stages of protective policy process – particularly in developing countries (Garcia-Johnson, 2000; Neumayer, 2001, Christmann and Taylor, 2001; Wheeler, 1999). Drawing on the previous reasoning the following propositions can be suggested:

Proposition 12: Other things being equal, multinational corporation subsidiaries from the most advanced industrialized nations are associated with higher environmental/social performance than other types of firms.

Proposition 13: Other things being equal, ownership by a multinational corporation moderates the inverted U-shaped relationship between the protective policy process and firms' responses in such a way that MNC subsidiaries from the most advanced industrialized nations are more likely to show lower resistance during the different stages of the policy process than other types of firms.

Stock market participation

The level of resistance to the protective policy process can also vary depending on whether a company is publicly or privately owned. Compared to publicly traded companies, private companies are under less pressure to show short-term profits. This may allow privately owned firms to invest more in environmental and social protection projects that often require a long time to show positive financial returns. However, publicly traded firms are more likely to face a wider and more intense array of pressures that can constrain their ability to resist demands to invest in environmental/social protection efforts (Darnall and Edwards, 2006).

Some of these pressures arise from the small but increasing number of socially responsible investment and pension funds that favor the stocks of firms with higher environmental/social performance (Lyon and Maxwell, 2002, Dowell *et al.*, 2000). These funds provide incentives for publicly owned businesses to offer more cooperation to protective policy demands (Lyon and Maxwell, 2002, Dowell *et al.*, 2000). To be sure, publicly traded companies that consistently show higher environmental/social performance are known to have significantly higher stock market returns (Khanna *et al.*, 1998).

A reputation of poor environmental/social performance is also associated with higher exposure to greater risk of legal liabilities that can reduce a firm's stock price (Khanna, 2001). The previous arguments suggest the following propositions:

Proposition 14: Other things being equal, publicly traded firms are associated with higher environmental/social performance than privately owned ones.

Proposition 15: Other things being equal, firm ownership moderates the inverted U-shaped relationship between the protective policy process and firms' responses in such a way that publicly traded firms are more likely to show lower resistance during the different stages of the policy process than privately owned firms.

Export orientation to advanced industrialized countries

Firms exporting their products to advanced industrialized country markets with more environmental/social responsibility aware consumers can be expected to benefit from enhanced green reputations either through preferential access or, as in the case of organic products, with price premiums (Christmann and Taylor, 2001; Garcia-Johnson, 2000; O'Rourke, 2004; Rivera, 2002). The more stringent protective regulations in the US and Europe also impose enhanced requirements and monitoring on businesses seeking to export their products and services to these markets (Shah and Rivera, 2007). Moreover, export-oriented firms are increasingly facing enhanced pressures from major multinational corporations based in industrialized countries – such as Home Depot, Ikea, and Whole Foods Market, to name a few – to meet voluntary beyond-compliance environmental and social performance standards (Christmann and Taylor, 2001; Garcia-Johnson, 2000; O'Rourke, 2004; Shah and Rivera, 2007).

Additionally, environmental and social responsibility nongovernmental organizations (NGOs) and activists in advanced industrialized countries are more politically influential and have more resources that allow them to exert stronger normative pressures on businesses exporting their products to these countries. Indeed, firms with poor environmental/social performance that export to these environmentally aware markets have a higher risk of being targeted by international media and environmental organizations (O'Rourke, 2004; Garcia-Johnson, 2000). Accordingly, firms exporting their products to advanced industrialized countries can be expected to show higher willingness to cooperate with the enactment and implementation of protective policies and regulations. These arguments can be summarized as follows:

Proposition 16: Other things being equal, firms with an export orientation to advanced industrialized countries are associated with higher environmental/social performance.

Proposition 17: Other things being equal, export orientation moderates the inverted U-shaped relationship between the protective policy process and firms' responses in such a way that firms exporting their products to advanced industrialized countries are more likely to show lower resistance during the different stages of the policy process than those selling their products in less developed countries.

Industry association membership

Firms that are members of industry or trade associations often face stronger normative and mimetic pressures to show exemplary environmental and social protection performance and to show more cooperation with protective policy process demands (Delmas, 2002; Garcia-Johnson, 2000; Grasmick *et al.*, 1991; King and Lenox, 2000; Hoffman, 1999). Trade groups have a significant interest in maintaining an industry-wide reputation of superior environmental/social responsibility to avoid increased scrutiny from activists, the media, and regulators (King and Lenox, 2000). This superior reputation may also generate goodwill that can allow industry to shape the enactment of new protective regulations. However, a few facilities with poor records can significantly reduce the perceived environmental/social responsibility credibility of an entire industry (King and Lenox, 2000). Hence, industry associations tend to compel low-performing firms to improve their protective practices by relying on peer pressures and embarrassment (Grasmick *et al.*, 1991; Hoffman, 1997).

Additionally, industry associations encourage the mimetic adoption of cooperative approaches and beyond-compliance practices developed by leading firms providing technical assistance to poorly performing facilities (King and Lenox, 2000; Rivera, 2002; Tashman and Rivera, 2008). Social network theory may help explain how industry associations encourage the mimetic diffusion of capabilities associated with enhanced environmental/social protection practices

(Granovetter, 1983; Tiwana, 2008). Social network theory posits that the diffusion of knowledge occurs more readily through inter-organizational networks because they provide their members with pre-existing modes of communication, enhancing the potential for collaboration, information exchange, and mutual observation (Kraatz, 1998; Powell *et al.*, 1996). Inter-organizational networks also generate more trust and freer communication among their members.

These conditions may manifest themselves in the type of networks created by industry associations. Member firms often have the opportunity to develop and maintain an array of dyadic relationships within the industry association headquarters and other member firms. In addition, the centrality of an industry association within its network may facilitate its instrumentality in diffusing knowledge related to managing social/environmental protection issues.[6] The key point is that innovative environmental/social protection knowledge and cooperative approaches need not originate from industry associations themselves (Tashman and Rivera, 2008). They can observe better protective practices and/or more collaborative strategies from their most proactive members, incorporate this expertise into their own knowledge base, and then retransmit it to other members who do not yet possess it (Eccles *et al.*, 1992; Procassini, 1995; Tashman and Rivera, 2008). This reasoning suggests the following propositions:

Proposition 18: Other things being equal, industry association membership is associated with higher environmental/social performance.

Proposition 19: Other things being equal, industry association membership moderates the inverted U-shaped relationship between the protective policy process and firms' responses in such a way that firms that are members of an industry association are more likely to show lower resistance during the different stages of the policy process than nonmember firms.

When considering these propositions, it is important to stress a caveat. The industry associations' tendency to promote enhanced norms of environmental and social protection may be outweighed by requests from some of their members to collectively resist protective policy process demands. The greater resources and influence available to industry association members make this collective resistance more difficult to overcome. Additionally, industry associations may promote the adoption of symbolic beyond-compliance practices as an avoidance strategy aimed at pre-empting the adoption of new protective regulations.

Top manager demographic characteristics

Besides considering general firm qualities, it is also important to examine differences in the characteristics of the top managers making key decisions for their companies. Chief executive officers (CEOs), in particular, are responsible for making businesses' strategic choices, such as those that involve the selection of a firm's long-term environmental/social protection approach and tactics (Cordano and Frieze, 2000; Flannery and May, 2000; Hambrick and Mason, 1984; Hambrick and Abrahamson, 1995). CEOs also control the financial resources to implement strategic environmental/social protection choices (Hambrick and Abrahamson, 1995; Hambrick and Mason, 1984). The power of CEOs over these strategic decisions is even more important among small firms where their influence can be magnified and directly exerted over most managerial responsibilities (Chen and Hambrick, 1995; Hambrick and Mason, 1984).

Organizational psychology scholars have suggested that a person's background demographic characteristics can be important in predicting strategic choices because these traits are central to shaping the beliefs, values, attitudes, and assumptions CEOs use to assess firms' competitive alternatives and their outcomes (Hambrick and Abrahamson, 1995; Hambrick and Mason, 1984; Lasswell, 1948; Simon, 1947; Wiersema and Bantel, 1992). Next, based on evidence from previous studies, I discuss the effect of demographic characteristics suggested to be associated with higher environmental and social responsibility concerns: level of formal education, academic expertise, and nationality (Cottrell, 2003; Dunlap and Van Liere, 1978; Ewert and Baker, 2001; Kellert, 1996; Kollmuss and Agyeman, 2002).[7]

Formal education level

Among demographic variables, formal education appears to be one of the most consistently correlated with enhanced environmental and social responsibility concerns (Cottrell, 2003; Ewert and Baker, 2001; Hines *et al.*, 1987; Kollmuss and Agyeman, 2002; Smith, 1995). Individuals who are known to be more highly educated generally possess a superior ability to understand complex and uncertain problems, such as those involving environmental and social protection issues, and thus display greater awareness and concern for these issues (Ewert and Baker, 2001; Hines *et al.*, 1987; Wiersema and Bantel, 1992). Empirical evidence also suggests that higher formal education is correlated with greater willingness to donate to environmental and social protection organizations, and to engage in the practices promoted by these organizations (e.g., recycling, volunteering for social protection causes, buying from firms certified for their superior social responsibility, etc.) (Smith, 1995; Kellert, 1996; Kollmuss and Agyeman, 2002).

Based on this reasoning, it can be argued that CEOs with higher levels of formal education can be expected to be more amenable to adopting enhanced protective practices and also more willing to cooperate with protective policy process demands (Cottrell, 2003; Ewert and Baker, 2001; Hambrick and Mason, 1984; Rivera and deLeon, 2004). Higher levels of formal education are also associated with better information-processing abilities and receptivity to innovation, both key elements of beyond-compliance practices promoted by new protective policies (Cottrell, 2003; Smith, 1995; Wiersema and Bantel, 1992). This discussion suggests the following propositions:

Proposition 20: A firm's environmental/social performance is positively correlated with the level of formal education of its CEO.

Proposition 21: Other things being equal, a CEO's level of formal education moderates the inverted U-shaped relationship between the protective policy process and firms' responses in such a way that firms whose CEOs have higher levels of formal education are more likely to show lower resistance during the different stages of the policy process.

Academic major

Behavioral research has also suggested that besides the level of formal education, different academic disciplines are distinctively correlated to a person's general perspectives, outlooks, values, beliefs, and motivations (Ewert and Baker, 2001; Smith, 1995; Wiersema and Bantel, 1992). Individuals also self-select into different disciplines based on their beliefs, values, personalities, and concerns (Ewert and Baker, 2001; Smith, 1995). Likewise, several empirical studies indicate that the type of academic major is linked to different levels of an individual's environmental/social responsibility concerns and behavior (De Young, 1996; Ewert and Baker, 2001; Smith, 1995; Stern *et al.*, 1995). For example, graduates majoring in business and economics appear to be more likely to show lower pro-environmental/social responsibility concerns than those individuals majoring in other disciplines, particularly environmental studies, biology, and the humanities (Ewert and Baker, 2001; Smith, 1995). Thus, firms whose CEOs hold degrees in business and economics can be expected to offer more resistance to protective policy process demands and to show lower environmental/social performance.

Advanced industrialized country nationality

Recent scholarly work has also indicated that CEOs and managers from advanced industrialized countries can be expected to be more aware of the heightened expectations about corporate environmental/social protection exerted by international NGOs, the media, and consumers in these nations than their counterparts from developing countries (Christmann and Taylor, 2001; Rivera and deLeon, 2004; Wheeler, 1999). Empirical studies also suggest that top managers from advanced industrialized nations have easier access to information about innovative environmental and social protection management knowledge developed to respond to the more stringent protective regulations prevailing in these countries (Christmann and Taylor, 2001; Wheeler, 1999). Firms with CEOs from advanced industrialized countries may also be subjected to increased oversight by local environmental and social action groups and government agencies (King and Shaver, 2001). Hence, it can be expected that these CEOs would be more likely to adopt proactive environmental/social protection efforts and to offer less resistance to the protective policy process (Christmann and Taylor, 2001; Garcia-Johnson, 2000).

Limitations to the influence of firm characteristics

Having discussed the effect of specific firm characteristics on business responses to protective policy demands, it is important to stress a few caveats suggested by the neo-institutional literature on organizational analysis. First, isomorphic behavior in response to coercive, normative, and institutional pressures is still seen as predominant among firms sharing an organizational field (DiMaggio and Powell, 1983; Scott, 2001). The more taken-for-granted are norms and expectations, the more likely firms are to behave isomorphically. To be sure, empirical studies indicate that the firm characteristics' influence on business responses to the policy process declines, to the point of showing no significant effect, as regulations and standards become fully institutionalized (Baron *et al.*, 1986; Friedland and Alford, 1991; Tolbert and Zucker, 1983). This tendency to adopt similar strategies and structures has been observed during business participation in public policymaking. Although businesses indeed show conflicting political action while trying to shape the public policy process, empirical research by Mizruchi (1992: 250–5) and his collaborators has consistently indicated that "instances of unified behavior [by businesses] greatly dwarf those in which firms politically opposed one another" (Clawson *et al.*, 1986; Mizruchi and Bey, 2005: 321).

Notes

1. This chapter includes modified and expanded sections from the articles listed below; reproduced with kind permission of the journal publishers and co-authors: Rivera (2002; 2004), Rivera and deLeon (2004; 2005), and Rivera *et al.* (2006).
2. *Coercive pressures*, usually imposed by governments, require companies to pursue specific behaviors by relying on legal sanctions or threats (Meyer and Rowan, 1977). *Normative pressures* arise from values and norms of conduct promoted by professional networks, industry associations, and academic institutions. Normative pressures usually exert influence on organizations by relying on peer pressures and embarrassment of non-compliers (Hoffman, 1999). *Mimetic pressures* are demands that firms face to appear legitimate and competitive by imitating the institutionalized behavior of the most profitable and respected companies in their industry (DiMaggio and Powell, 1983).
3. An organization field is understood here as "those organizations that, in the aggregate, constitute a recognized area of institutional life: key suppliers, resource and product consumers, regulatory agencies, and other organizations that produce similar services or products" (Powell and DiMaggio, 1991: 64).
4. Small enterprises are generally defined as those ranging in size from eleven to fifty employees (De Soto, 2000).
5. Levy and Newell (2000) additionally suggest that American managers show lower environmental concern than European managers because of

the US' higher aversion to regulations, added emphasis on individualism, and lower political support for environmental protection than in Europe.

6. The degree of *centrality* refers to the structural position that an actor occupies within a network.
7. A person's income has also been consistently found to be correlated with higher concerns for environmental and social responsibility. Yet, given that CEOs tend to have relatively higher incomes than other members of society, this variable is not discussed here (Ewert and Baker, 2001; Cottrell, 2003; Kollmuss and Agyeman, 2002; Kellert, 1996; Dunlap and Van Liere, 1978).

5 *Is greener whiter? Resistance strategies by the US ski industry*[1]

In the late 1990s the US Forest Service (USFS) was developing revised land use plans for national forest lands, as required by the National Forest Management Act of 1976. Environmentalists' favored draft version of these land use plans proposed additional restrictions to recreational use, such as skiing and ski area development. The stringency of these restrictions was particularly high in western US national forest lands where major ski areas are located. For example, one of the proposed land use plans for Colorado's White River National Forest – home of renowned ski resorts such as Vail, Aspen, Breckenridge, Keystone, and Beaver Creek, among others – intended to forbid ski areas' expansion (Briggs, 2000).[2] Not surprisingly, the adoption of more restrictive new land use plans was resisted not only by the ski industry but also by real-estate developing companies, recreation user groups, and local politicians, among others. This chapter examines in detail one of the resistance strategies adopted by the US ski industry: the creation and implementation of a voluntary environmental initiative named the Sustainable Slopes Program.

Since the early 1990s, more than 200 voluntary environmental programs have been created in the US with the stated intent of promoting proactive corporate environmental protection (Carmin *et al.*, 2003). In the 1990s, the use of these programs as alternatives to command-and-control regulations became a core element of the federal government's environmental policy agenda (Dietz and Stern, 2002). This trend has led to an on-going debate addressing the environmental effectiveness of voluntary initiatives and the reasons why firms participate in them (Andrews, 1998; Dietz and Stern, 2002; Highley and Leveque, 2001; Khanna, 2001; O'Rourke, 2003). A few studies have assessed participation in US voluntary environmental programs but their findings are mixed and even greater uncertainty remains about the environmental effectiveness of these programs (Darnall and Sides, 2008; deLeon and Rivera, 2009). Utilizing the neo-institutional theory framework developed in the previous chapters, this chapter contributes to this debate by focusing on two main issues:

- identifing factors and facility-level characteristics related to a firm's decision to participate in a voluntary environmental program; and
- determining if participation in these programs is related to higher environmental performance.

We propose to achieve these objectives through an assessment of western ski areas' participation in the Sustainable Slopes Program (SSP), a voluntary environmental initiative established by the National Ski Areas Association (NSAA) and endorsed by the US Environmental Protection Agency (EPA), the US Forest Service, and other federal agencies. Our deliberate focus on a group of service businesses represents a clear distinction from previous work on voluntary environmental programs, which has largely studied manufacturing firms (Khanna, 2001; Rivera, 2002; Videras and Alberini, 2000; Welch *et al.*, 2000).

Supporters of voluntary programs argue that because voluntary programs provide market and regulatory benefits to participants, they can effectively promote beyond-compliance environmental protection (Arora and Cason, 1996; Khanna, 2001; Lyon and Maxwell, 2002; Rivera, 2002). It has also been suggested that these initiatives are more cost efficient, improve regulatory flexibility, and promote technology innovation (Carmin *et al.*, 2003; Delmas, 2002). However, critics remain suspicious of the claims of effectiveness of voluntary initiatives as a means to promote environmental protection. These skeptics assert that firms see participation in these programs as an avoidance-resistance strategy that allows them to pre-empt more stringent regulations and disguise poor environmental performance (Andrews, 1998; Arora and Cason 1996; Delmas, 2002; Harrison, 1999; Khanna, 2001; deLeon and Rivera, 2009). Additionally, these critics question the advocates' claims that voluntary initiatives can provide significant market incentives for firms to promote beyond-compliance (Andrews, 1998; Rivera, 2002).

The US ski industry and the Sustainable Slopes Program

Since Sun Valley in Idaho, one of the first large ski resorts in the United States, opened in the late 1930s, the American ski industry has become an important sector of the tourism and recreation economy (Hudson, 2000). Skiing and related activities experienced very rapid growth during the 1960s and 1970s, leading by 1982 to the creation of about 735 downhill ski areas (hereafter called ski areas) (Hudson, 2000; NSAA, 2003a). Beginning in the mid-1980s, however, the industry has shown a relatively stagnant demand (in terms of skier visits), leading to intense competition and significant consolidation among ski areas. During the 2002–3 season, 490 ski areas were operating in the US, a 33 percent reduction from the 1982 totals (NSAA, 2003b; Sachs, 2002). For the last twenty years, the number of annual skier/snowboarder visits has remained relatively constant, averaging about 54 million visits per year (NSAA, 2003b).[3] Snowboarding, the one segment of the market experiencing growth rates above 5 percent since 1999, constituted 29.6 percent of total demand in the 2002–3 season (NSAA, 2003b). Preliminary estimates predict a record 57.3 millions skier/snowboarder visits for the 2002–3 season (NSAA, 2003a).

The industry annual income for 2002–3 is estimated to be about $4.2 billion, 23 percent higher than five years ago (Palmeri, 2003). Nevertheless, intense competition, price discounts and large capital investments have kept profits significantly low even for the largest ski resort chains such as Vail Resorts, Intrawest, and American Skiing Company. Adult lift-ticket prices vary from an average of $59.33 for bigger ski areas to $33.82 for the smaller ones in 2002–3. The increasing reliance by ski areas on season and discount passes has reduced the yield revenue per ticket to about 54 percent in 2002–3 from yield rates of over 60 percent obtained in the mid-1990s (NSAA, 2003a). Thus, ski areas have focused on expanding their businesses to real-estate development, lodging, and retail to complement their income (Hudson, 2000; Palmeri, 2003). In recent years, over 50 percent of the industry revenue has originated from these new businesses (Hudson, 2000; Palmeri, 2003).

Western ski industry. For the present purpose of this study, western ski areas are defined as those located in the Rocky Mountain region (Colorado, Idaho, Montana, New Mexico, Utah, and Wyoming) and the Pacific West region (Alaska, Arizona, California, Nevada, Oregon, and Washington State). Currently, there are 167 ski areas in the west, 92 of which are located in the Rocky Mountains and 75 are in the Pacific West region (NSAA, 2003a). California and Colorado, with 32 and 27 ski areas respectively, are the states with the largest number of facilities (NSAA, 2003a). During the last decade, the number of annual skier/snowboarder visits has also remained relatively stable in the western United States, averaging about 18.5 million per year for the Rocky Mountains and about 10.7 million for the Pacific West (NSAA, 2003b).

Despite comprising only about one-third of all ski resorts operating in the country, during the last decade western ski resorts have consistently attracted over 50 percent of the total annual skiers. During the 2002–3 season, daily lift-ticket prices for western ski areas were on average the most expensive at $58.16 compared with an average of $45.05 for other parts of the country (NSAA, 2003a). In contrast to other regions of the US, operation in leased federal land is a distinguishing characteristic of western ski resorts, with over 90 percent of the facilities occupying some federally owned land (SACC, 2002). Foreign visitation (other than from Canada) is also higher for western ski areas. In the 2002–3 season, non-Canadian foreign visitation to western ski resorts was about 4.5 percent, three times higher than in other regions of the United States (NSAA, 2003a). Although western ski resorts show a large variation in size, the largest ski areas in the country are located in the west, particularly in the Rocky Mountains and Sierra Nevada ranges (NSAA, 2003a).

The Sustainable Slopes Program. The NSAA established the SSP in 2000. The SSP aims to promote beyond-compliance principles that cover twenty-one general areas of environmental management (see Table 5.1; NSAA, 2001; Sachs, 2002). Participant ski areas are expected to implement annual self-assessment of their environmental performance. The SSP, however, has been strongly criticized by environmentalists as a "green-washing" scheme because of its *strictly voluntary nature* (SACC, 2002; Sachs, 2002). In general, strictly voluntary programs lack critical necessary conditions to reduce "free-riding" behavior by participant businesses. These necessary conditions are: (1) specific performance-based standards of environmental protection to be adopted by participant companies; (2) periodic independent third-party audits that verify the adoption of these standards; and (3) rewards and sanctions that publicly recognize the different levels of audited performance obtained by voluntary environmental program (VEP) participants.

Table 5.1 *General aspects of environmental management covered by the SSP*

(1) Planning, design, and construction
Water resources
(2) Water use for snowmaking
(3) Water use for facilities
(4) Water use for landscaping and summer activities
(5) Water quality management
(6) Wastewater management
Energy conservation and use
(7) Energy use for facilities
(8) Energy use for snowmaking
(9) Energy use for lifts
(10) Energy use for vehicle fleets
Waste management
(11) Waste reduction
(12) Product reuse
(13) Recycling
(14) Potentially hazardous wastes
Other
(15) Fish and wildlife
(16) Forest and vegetative management
(17) Wetlands and riparian areas
(18) Air quality
(19) Visual quality
(20) Transportation
(21) Education and outreach

Source: NSAA (2001).

The imminent adoption of new – and potentially more restrictive – land use plans by the USFS in the late 1990s and the increased scrutiny of the ski industry by environmentalists were critical to push the NSAA to create the SSP. Key components of the most stringent versions of these land use plans alternatives involved considerable restrictions to recreational activities in national forest lands and limits to additional expansion of ski areas, particularly those located in Colorado (Briggs, 2000). If adopted, the implementation of these enhanced restrictions to recreational activities included in the USFS' new land use plans was scheduled to begin in 2001. Regarding the increased external scrutiny, since the mid-1990s environmental organizations have strongly criticized western ski areas' expansion plans and operation practices, highlighting landscape destruction, deforestation, water and air pollution, and damage to wildlife habitats as the most detrimental effects (Briggs, 2000; Clifford, 2002; Ski Areas Citizens' Coalition (SACC), 2002).

The NSAA developed the SSP's principles and practices by requesting comments from multiple stakeholders including ski companies, federal and state agencies, and nonprofit environmental organizations (NSAA, 2001). The resulting program enjoyed at the time the endorsement and support of an array of federal and state agencies and a few regional environmental groups, including the US Environmental Protection Agency, the Department of Energy, the Forest Service, the National Park Service, the Colorado Department of Public Health and Environment, the National Fish and Wildlife Foundation, and the Trust for Public Land (NSAA, 2003a). Moreover, the USFS and the Conservation Law Foundation provided significant funding for the development and implementation of the SSP (Clifford, 2002; NSAA, 2003a). Notably, however, none of the major environmental conservation organizations, such as the Sierra Club, the Nature Conservancy, and the Natural Resources Defense Council that were initially involved in the design of the SSP, decided to officially endorse the program (NSAA, 2000, 2001, 2003a).

Initially in 2000, 160 ski areas enrolled in the SSP (NSAA, 2000). The number of member facilities increased to 170 in 2001 and since then participation has remained constant at 173 ski areas. The self-assessment survey of environmental performance distributed by the program was completed by 79 ski areas in 2003, about 11 percent less than in 2001 and 2002 (NSAA, 2003a; 2002; 2001).

Theory and hypotheses

Neo-institutional theory and participation in voluntary environmental programs. In analyzing the voluntary environmental decisions of ski areas, we rely on the neo-institutional framework and ideas developed in Chapters 2–4 of this book. Consistent with the arguments of neo-institutional theory, recent scholarly work has pointed out the importance of considering the role of stakeholder and social pressures to understand corporate environmental voluntarism (Cashore and Vertinsky, 2000; Hoffman, 1999; Holm, 1995; Jennings and Zandbergen, 1995; King and Lenox, 2000). Drawing on this literature, the following paragraphs develop hypotheses about factors and facility-level characteristics related to higher likelihood of participation in voluntary programs.

Federal government oversight and state-level environmental pressures. Coercive institutional pressures exerted by federal and state government agencies in the form of mandatory environmental regulations, monitoring, and noncompliance penalties are well-known mechanisms to promote enhanced corporate environmental protection (Cashore and Vertinsky, 2000; Henriques and Sadorsky, 1996; Tyler, 1990; Winter and May, 2001). To be sure, even threats of new environmental regulations or explicit government support of beyond-compliance environmental practices are known to be significant incentives for managers to try to pre-empt regulatory action by improving facility environmental performance and by participating in voluntary environmental initiatives (Cashore and Vertinsky, 2000; Khanna *et al.*, 1998; Winter and May, 2001). These coercive pressures have a greater impact on facilities that operate in states with higher environmental pressures arising from more stringent regulations, stronger enforcement capacity, and higher pro-environmental opinion levels (Cashore and Vertinsky, 2000; Henriques and Sadorsky, 1996; Mazur and Welch, 1999; Winter and May, 2001). These arguments suggest the following hypotheses:

Hypothesis 1: Facilities facing higher federal government environmental oversight are more likely to participate in voluntary environmental programs.

Hypothesis 2: Facilities facing higher state-level environmental pressures are more likely to participate in voluntary environmental programs.

Facility size. As discussed in Chapter 4, due to their higher visibility and higher potential impact on the environment, larger facilities face stronger institutional pressures to display exemplary environmental management practices (Arora and Cason, 1996: 430; King and Lenox, 2000; Rivera, 2004; Winter and May, 2001). Because of their assumed greater resources, bigger facilities are held to higher standards by government agencies, environmental groups, and other stakeholders (Rivera, 2004). Industry associations also expect larger companies to play a leadership role in environmental protection (Hoffman, 1999). Accordingly, bigger facilities seeking to pre-empt and/or reduce stakeholders' institutional pressure are more likely to participate in voluntary programs that promote beyond-compliance environmental protection. This reasoning suggests the following hypothesis:

Hypothesis 3: *Larger facilities are more likely to participate in voluntary environmental programs.*

Stock market participation. The small but increasing number of "green" investors that favor the stocks of environmentally friendly firms provides incentives for corporations to adopt proactive environmental management practices (Lyon and Maxwell, 2002). Additionally, publicly traded companies that consistently show poor environmental performance are known to have significantly lower stock market returns (Khanna *et al.*, 1998). A reputation of poor environmental performance is also perceived as exposing firms to greater risk of environmental liability that can reduce their long-term profitability (Khanna, 2001). Thus, voluntary environmental programs that signal superior corporate environmental performance can be expected to be more appealing to publicly traded firms (Darnall, 2002). This reasoning suggests the following hypothesis:

Hypothesis 4: *Facilities owned by publicly traded firms are more likely to participate in voluntary environmental programs.*

Participation in industry-sponsored voluntary programs and improved environmental performance. Participation in industry-sponsored voluntary programs that seek to promote beyond-compliance environmental principles and practices has recently become a favored mechanism to signal proactive environmental behavior ("green behavior") by business facilities (Darnall, 2002). Traditionally in the US, these programs do not involve performance-based standards or sanctions for poor environmental behavior, and lack third-party monitoring (Khanna, 2001; King and Lenox, 2000; Rivera, 2004). Despite their lack of coercive mechanisms, industry-sponsored voluntary initiatives can rely on normative institutional mechanisms such as peer pressures and public attention and ridicule that could be effective to encourage participant facilities to improve their environmental performance (Hoffman, 1999; King and Lenox, 2000). Additionally, voluntary programs can offer financial incentives and technical assistance that increase the incentive to show superior environmental performance by participant facilities (Hoffman, 1999; King and Lenox, 2000; Rivera, 2002).

Trade associations enthusiastically support voluntary programs because they can help in maintaining a positive industry-wide environmental reputation that reduces scrutiny from environmentalists and the media and pre-empts the possible imposition of new regulations (King and Lenox, 2000). A few recent empirical studies suggest that in some cases voluntary initiatives can promote improved environmental performance among its participants. For example, firms that adopted the EPA's 30/50 program showed statistically significant reductions in chemical releases (Khanna and Damon, 1999). Mexican firms that have adopted ISO-14001 also appear to have significantly improved their self-reported environmental compliance (Dasgupta *et al.*, 2000). These arguments suggest the following hypothesis:

Hypothesis 5A: Facilities participating in industry-sponsored voluntary environmental programs are more likely to show higher environmental performance.

Alternatively, it can be argued that institutional pressures may motivate facilities to opportunistically participate in a voluntary program but may not be strong enough to actually induce adoption of improved environmental management practices (Khanna, 2001; King and Lenox, 2000; Rivera, 2002). Even without showing enhanced environmental performance, business facilities may improve their "green" image by enrolling in industry-sponsored voluntary programs that have been officially endorsed by federal and state government agencies (Arora and Cason, 1996; Darnall, 2002; King and Lenox, 2000). This opportunistic free-riding behavior is one of the main weaknesses of industry-sponsored voluntary programs that traditionally do not include performance-based standards and third-party monitoring, and lack sanctions for poor performing participants (Arora and Cason, 1996; Hoffman, 1999; Khanna and Damon, 1999; King and Lenox, 2000). Several empirical studies indicate that firms with lower environmental performance are more likely to join voluntary initiatives such as the Responsible Care Program, the 33/50 program, and the Climate Challenge Program (King and Lenox, 2000; Khanna and Damon, 1999; Welch *et al.*, 2000). Additionally, participants of Responsible Care and the Climate Challenge Program also appear to show lower pollutant release reductions than non-participants (King and Lenox, 2000; Welch *et al.*, 2000). These arguments suggest the following alternative hypothesis:

Hypothesis 5B: Facilities participating in industry-sponsored voluntary environmental programs are more likely to show lower environmental performance.

Methodology

Data collection. In the fall of 2001, data on ski resorts' basic characteristics were obtained from individual ski resort websites and verified by relying on public figures available at the US Forest Service and National Park Service, the National Ski Areas Association, the New York and Toronto Stock Exchanges, and Travelocity. The 2001 Sustainable Slopes Program Report (NSAA, 2001) was used to gather data on ski resort participation in this program. Additionally, we collected third-party environmental performance data for ski areas from the 2001 environmental scorecard grades produced by the SACC. Beginning in 2001, the SACC, an alliance of American environmental organizations, has been evaluating the environmental performance of ski areas in the western United States.[4]

Sample. The final sample for the study included 109 western ski resorts representing about 64 percent of all ski resorts located in the Rocky Mountains and Pacific West regions (NSAA, 2002).[5] This sample involved all 57 western ski resorts for which third-party environmental performance data were available as of 2001. The additional 52 ski resorts were randomly drawn from the remaining population of ski resorts located in the western United States.

Regression analysis technique. To test the proposed hypotheses, we used a recursive two-stage modeling process originally developed by

Heckman (1978) that controls for self-selection bias in the evaluation of voluntary choices. An array of different instrumental techniques has been developed to address the problems introduced by self-selectivity (Greene, 2000: 926–46; Maddala, 1986: 260–71). However, these techniques are considered "unnecessarily complex and cumbersome" and thus Heckman's more parsimonious two-step methodology is the preferred analytical alternative (Greene, 2000: 926–46). Moreover, Heckman's two-stage technique has been widely used to evaluate environmental and economic benefits generated by voluntary environmental programs (Arora and Cason, 1996; Hartman, 1988; Khanna, 2001; Khanna and Damon, 1999; Lee and Trost, 1978; Rivera, 2002; Welch *et al.*, 2000). Controlling for self-selection bias is necessary because firms that anticipate higher benefits from joining a voluntary initiative are expected to be more likely to participate (Hartman, 1988; Heckman, 1978; Khanna and Damon, 1999; Maddala, 1986). Thus, similar independent variables are likely to influence participation and the program environmental outcome (Khanna and Damon, 1999; Greene, 2000; Maddala, 1986).[6]

In the first stage of the analysis, a probit regression identifies independent variables, X_{1i}, significantly related to participation in the SSP, and D_i (Khanna and Damon, 1999; Maddala, 1986). This probit regression is also used to estimate the probability of participation for individual ski areas, P_i.

$$(1)\ D_i = \delta + a_i X_{1i} + \varepsilon_{1i}$$

where:

δ = regression constant term;
X_{1i} = independent variable (federal government oversight, stock exchange trading, size, state location);
a_i = regression coefficient for independent variable X_{1i};
ε_{1i} = equation (1)'s random error term.

In the second stage of the analysis, an ordinary linear regression (ordinary least-squares, OLS) models ski areas' environmental performance, Y_i. To control for self-selection bias, the OLS regression includes as one of its independent variables the probability of participation estimates, P_i, calculated using the probit model above (Khanna and Damon, 1999; Maddala, 1986).

(2) $Y_i = \alpha + b_i X_{2i} + c_i P_i + \varepsilon_{2i}$;

where:

X_{2i} = federal government oversight, stock exchange trading, size, state environmental regulatory stringency;
P_i = probability of participation in the SSP;
ε_{2i} = equation (2)'s random error term.[7]

Measures. Participation in the SSP, the dependent variable for the probit model, was measured using a dummy variable equal to one for facilities participating in the program and zero otherwise.

Environmental scorecard grades produced by the SACC were used as a measure of *environmental performance*, the dependent variable for the OLS model. The environmental scorecard grades are based on third-party performance audits that evaluate ski resorts' compliance with general criteria of environmental management, the most important being:

(1) environmental management of ski areas' expansion and related real-estate development;
(2) snowmaking practices;
(3) water management;
(4) public disclosure policies;
(5) wildlife protection practices;
(6) recycling and pollution prevention practices; and
(7) landscape management.

The environmental performance for each ski area is determined by adding the scores of all standards and dividing it by the maximum possible score to create a percentage performance rate.[8] Beginning in 2001, SACC has published the summary reports of its third-party assessments, assigning "letter grades" to the environmental performance of ski resorts in the western United States, as follows:

Environmental scorecard grade	Environmental performance letter grade publicized
77 to 100 percent	A
60 to <77 percent	B
45 to <60 percent	C
35 to <45 percent	D
<35 percent	F

Source: SACC, 2002.

These scorecard grades have received national attention in the *New York Times, USA Today*, and CNN. In the fall and winter, they are reported by local TV and newspapers, and highlighted by specialized ski magazines and web pages (Janofsky, 2000). Ski industry representatives, however, have strongly criticized the SACC's environmental scorecard grades as a biased and unrealistically stringent measure of environmental performance (Janofsky, 2000).

Land ownership of ski area facilities, classified as private, mixed, and public was respectively used as proxy for low, medium, and high *federal government environmental oversight.* Ski areas operating on leased public land experience significantly greater environmental monitoring by federal agencies such as the USFS, the US Bureau of Land Management, and/or the US National Park Service (Briggs, 2000; Clifford, 2002). To operate on public federal land, ski areas need to obtain special-use permits that require a periodic review of their master and operating plans, engineering design, and environmental impact statements for new developments (Briggs, 2000; Clifford, 2002). *Facility size* was measured as the number of skiable acres occupied by each ski area (in thousand-acre units). *Ownership by publicly traded firms* was coded as a binary variable equal to one for ski facilities owned by publicly traded firms, and zero otherwise. Estimates of *probability of participation in the SSP*, determined in the first stage of statistical analysis, were used as a proxy for program adoption in the OLS regression that models environmental performance.

Finally, we used state location and Mazur and Welch's (1999) index of state environmentalism as two alternative proxies to measure the level of *state environmental pressures* faced by ski areas. The index of state environmentalism is the average of four standardized indicators of environmentalism that include the following: (1) state population membership in the largest US environmental groups (Wikle, 1995); (2) pro-environmental opinion levels collected by the General Social Survey implemented annually by the National Opinion Research Center (Davies and Smith, 1996; Mazur and Welch, 1999); (3) League of Conservation Voters' pro-environmental ranking of states' congressional delegations; and (4) ranking of states' environmental policy implementation strength (Hall and Kerr, 1991; Mazur and Welch, 1999).

Results

Frequency distributions, means, and standard deviations for the sample of western ski resorts are displayed in Table 5.2. The majority of ski resort facilities included in the sample (74.3 percent) was participating in the SSP. It is also important to highlight that of the western ski areas that received environmental scorecard grades in 2002, the majority (70.2 percent) obtained "C" or lower grades.

Factors related to participation in the SSP.[9] Table 5.3 presents the probit regression results of two alternative specifications that yield similar findings about institutional factors related to the SSP. Model 1 includes state location as a proxy for state environmental pressures. Model 2, on the other hand, includes Mazur and Welch's index of state environmentalism as a measure of state environmental pressures (Mazur and Welch, 1999; Welch *et al.*, 2000). Compared to state location, this index of environmentalism appears to be a better proxy of state environmental pressures and it is used as an independent variable in the second stage of the regression analysis. Since lift-ticket prices and ski area size are highly correlated, we dropped the lift-ticket price variable from Model 2.

To reduce redundancy, we limit our description of the participation analysis to Model 2 findings. Results indicate that high and medium levels of federal government oversight have a positive and statistically significant association with participation in the SSP ($p<0.05$). This finding supports Hypothesis 1's argument that facilities with higher federal government environmental oversight are more likely to participate in voluntary environmental programs. The positive and significant coefficient ($P<0.1$) on the index of state environmental environmentalism suggests that higher state environmental pressures are significantly associated with higher probability of participation in the SSP. This result suggests support of Hypothesis 2. Additionally, Hypothesis 3 – that larger facilities are more likely to participate in voluntary environmental programs – appears to be supported by Model 2's positive and statistically significant coefficient on ski area size ($P<0.01$). Conversely, the evidence from Model 2 does not support Hypothesis 4. Facilities owned by a publicly traded firm do not appear to be significantly more likely to participate in the SSP. Finally, it is important to note that both Models 1 and 2 have an overall fit

Table 5.2 *Descriptive statistics*

	Full sample		SAAC ranked	
Variable	N	Percent	N	Percent
Dependent variables				
SSP participation				
Not enrolled	28	25.7	8	14.0
Enrolled	81	74.3	49	86.0
Total	109	100	57	100
Environmental performance				
77 to 100 percent (A)			8	14.0
60 to <77 percent (B)			9	15.8
45 to <60 percent (C)			16	28.1
35 to <45 percent (D)			14	24.6
<35 percent (F)			10	17.5
Total			57	100
Mean			48.9 (17.0)[a]	
Independent variables				
Federal government oversight				
Low (private land)	18	16.7	6	10.5
Medium (mixed land ownership)	17	15.7	10	17.5
High (public land)	73	67.6	41	71.9
Total	108	100	57	100
Ownership by publicly traded firms				
No	100	91.7	48	84.2
Yes	9	8.3	9	15.8
Total	109	100	57	100
Size (thousand-acre units)				
0 to 1	56	51.4	16	28.1
>1 to 2	28	25.7	20	35.1
>2 to 3	17	15.6	14	24.6
>3 to 4	6	5.5	5	8.8
>4 to 5	2	1.8	2	3.5
Total	109	100	57	100
Mean	1.3 (1.0499)		1.7 (1.0801)	

Table 5.2 *(cont.)*

	Full sample		SAAC ranked	
Variable	N	Percent	N	Percent
State location				
Alaska	2	1.8		
Arizona	2	1.8		
California	20	18.3	6	10.5
Colorado	25	22.9	18	31.6
Idaho	8	7.4	2	3.5
Montana	8	7.3	4	7.0
New Mexico	8	7.5	4	7.0
Nevada	3	2.7		
Oregon	8	7.3	4	7.0
Utah	13	11.9	10	17.5
Washington	9	8.3	7	12.3
Wyoming	3	2.7	2	3.5
Total	109	100	57	100

[a] Standard deviations are in parentheses.

significant at $P<0.01$, and are able to correctly classify more than 80 percent of the participation decisions.[10]

Factors related to ski areas' environmental performance. Findings from the OLS regression that analyzes ski areas' environmental performance are displayed in Table 5.4, Model 3. Results indicate that, other things being equal, higher probability of participation in the SSP appears to show a statistically significant relationship with lower environmental performance ($P<0.1$). This result supports Hypothesis 5B's alternative argument that ski areas adopting industry-sponsored voluntary programs are significantly associated with lower environmental performance. Facilities owned by publicly traded companies also appear to be significantly more likely to show lower environmental performance ($P<0.01$). Federal government oversight appears to have a negative but statistically insignificant relationship with environmental performance. In contrast, higher state environmental pressures show a statistically significant relationship with higher environmental performance ($P<0.01$).

Table 5.3 *Probit regression results (dependent variable: participation in the SSP)*

	Model 1	Model 2
Constant	–2.869** (1.323)[a]	–1.542*** (0.523)
Federal government environmental oversight		
High (public land)	1.006** (0.447)	1.187*** (0.383)
Medium (public-private land)	1.429* (0.796)	1.476*** (0.537)
Ownership by publicly traded firm	–1.066 (1.071)	–0.330 (0.761)
Price	0.095*** (0.037)	
Size (thousand-acre units)	0.00793 (0.337)	0.648*** (0.229)
State environmental pressures		
Index of state environmentalism		1.617* (0.838)
State location		
Alaska	–1.643 (1.325)	
Arizona	–1.165 (1.166)	
California	–0.9917 (0.700)	
Idaho	–0.545 (0.855)	
Montana	–0.0184 (0.985)	
New Mexico	–2.035** (0.792)	
Nevada	–2.742** (1.119)	
Oregon	4.436 (321.5)	
Utah	–0.658 (0.774)	
Washington	–0.208 (0.830)	
Wyoming	–1.856* (1.107)	
N	107	107
–2 Log L	68.410	90.868
χ^2 for co-variates	50.253***	27.796***
Percent correctly classified	90.6	84.6

[a] Standard errors are in parentheses.

* prob < 0.10; ** prob < 0.05; *** prob < 0.01.

Table 5.4 *OLS regression results (dependent variable: environmental performance)*

	Model 3
Constant	67.633** (7.26)[a]
Federal government oversight	
High (public land)	−6.065 (−0.78)
Medium (public-private land)	−13.117 (1.47)
Ownership by publicly traded firm	−24.391** (−3.99)
Probability of participation	−23.661* (−1.82)
Size (thousand-acre units)	−1.970 (−0.89)
State environmental pressures	39.101** (2.92)
N	55
F-value	5.69**
R2	0.415
Adj-R2	0.342

[a] t-values are in parentheses.

* prob<0.10; ** prob<0.01.

Discussion

Factors related to participation in the SSP. Consistent with previous research on environmental voluntarism by manufacturing firms, our findings highlight the importance of coercive institutional regulatory pressures as a key factor positively associated with participation in voluntary environmental programs (Henriques and Sadorsky, 1996; King and Lenox, 2000; Khanna *et al.*, 1998; deLeon and Rivera, 2009; Delmas, 2002). Ski areas facing higher federal government oversight because of their location on public land appear to be more likely to participate in the SSP. Results also indicate that facilities facing higher coercive and normative institutional forces arising from state environmental agencies, state environmental groups, and local public opinion are more likely to participate in the SSP. We posit that ski facilities that face greater federal monitoring and more state pro-environmental pressures see adoption of *strictly voluntary* programs such as the SSP as an avoidance strategy, seeking to send a signal of enhanced "green" behavior to reduce government oversight and scrutiny or demands by environmentalists and other stakeholders

(Cashore and Vertinsky, 2000; Henriques and Sadorsky, 1996; Mazur and Welch, 1999; Rivera, 2002). Strictly voluntary environmental programs are those that: (1) lack specific performance-based standards of environmental protection to be adopted by participant companies; (2) do not require periodic independent third-party audits that verify the adoption of these standards; and (3) do not include rewards and sanctions that publicly recognize the different levels of audited performance obtained by their participants (deLeon and Rivera, 2009). The explicit endorsement of the SSP – despite its strictly voluntary nature – by federal agencies such as the EPA and the USFS provides it with higher legitimacy that makes participation in the SSP a more effective avoidance-resistance strategy.

Ski area size appears to be significantly associated with higher participation in the SSP. This finding is in line with evidence suggesting that larger manufacturing facilities are more likely to participate in voluntary initiatives (Arora and Cason, 1996; Delmas, 2002; Khanna, 2001; King and Lenox, 2000; Videras and Alberini, 2000). Federal and state government agencies, the media, environmental organizations, and industry associations pay more attention to the environmental practices of larger, more visible facilities (Arora and Cason, 1996; Khanna, 2001; King and Lenox, 2000). Thus, not surprisingly, bigger more visible facilities experience stronger institutional pressures to show credible superior environmental performance, and thus are more likely to participate in voluntary initiatives (Arora and Cason, 1996; King and Lenox, 2000). For example, a large resort like Aspen in Colorado is seen as a "model" ski area by consumers and trade publications, so it would strive to demonstrate the legitimacy of that identification by actively participating and supporting the SSP.

Finally, ski areas owned by publicly traded firms do not appear to be significantly associated with higher participation in the SSP. This finding contradicts the evidence provided by a few studies that have analyzed adoption of voluntary programs by manufacturing firms (Khanna, 2001). We suggest that this result reflects the relatively low priority given by the stock market to the environmental performance of service sector corporations. Additionally, mainstream investors still pay almost exclusive attention to short-term profitability (Lyon and Maxwell, 2002). The combination of the traditional lack of attention to service firms' environmental performance and shareholders' primary focus on short-term profits can make facility managers reluctant to undertake the long-term capital investments that are necessary for adopting the principles of voluntary environmental programs (Lyon and Maxwell, 2002).

Factors related to ski areas' environmental performance. Our findings indicate that higher probability of participation in the SSP is significantly correlated with lower levels of environmental performance. In other words, our cross-sectional analysis provides initial evidence to suggest that SSP members are more likely to show lower environmental performance than non-participant ski areas. This finding suggests additional support to our view of participation in the SSP as an avoidance-resistance strategy seeking to send a symbolic "green" signal. SSP members appear to be displaying free-riding behavior expecting to improve their "green" reputation without actually implementing its beyond-compliance environmental management principles and practices. As suggested by other studies of corporate environmental voluntarism, we argue that the SSP's strictly voluntary nature may facilitate ski areas' free-riding behavior (Khanna, 2001; King and Lenox, 2000).

The data also indicate that ski areas owned by publicly traded companies are significantly more likely to show lower environmental performance. As in the case of the participation model, we argue that this finding reflects stock markets' focus on short-term profits and relatively low monitoring of service firms' environmental behavior. The increasing importance of "green" investment funds and the growing attention given by environmentalism to service sector corporations may change this trend (Lyon and Maxwell, 2002; Rivera, 2002).

Rather surprisingly, ski areas located in federal public land that face greater oversight by the USFS seem to have a negative correlation with environmental performance, although this relationship is statistically insignificant. Evidence from studies of manufacturing firms consistently indicates that higher government oversight is positively associated with higher voluntary environmental behavior (Henriques and Sadorsky, 1996; Khanna, 2001; Rivera, 2002; Videras and Alberini, 2000; Winter and May, 2001). We hypothesize that this unexpected result can be explained by the conflicting mandates received by the USFS to preserve national forest lands, follow all pertinent environmental protection regulations, and simultaneously promote ski areas development (Briggs, 2000). The National Forest Management Act of 1976 prescribes specific protection measures and plans, and the

National Forest Ski Area Permit Act approved by Congress in 1986 requires active promotion of ski areas (Briggs, 2000). The USFS also receives leasing fees that can range between 2.5 and 4 percent of the gross income of ski areas operating on federal land (Briggs, 2000; Clifford, 2002). Ski area fees are mostly retained by the local USFS offices that collect them, providing a direct economic incentive for local officials to favor ski area activities and expansion over preservation activities (Briggs, 2000; Clifford, 2002). In recent years, the USFS has even expanded its support of the ski areas through the National Winter Sports Partnership, providing funding for the marketing of ski sports (Clifford, 2002).

The only variable that appears to have a positive and statistically significant relationship with environmental performance is state environmental pressure. Ski areas facing greater state-level environmental pressures consistently appear to not only be more likely to participate in the SSP but also to show higher environmental performance. This finding stresses the positive link between corporate environmental voluntarism and states with higher support for environmental protection, stronger environmental groups, and a better capacity for implementing environmental policies and regulations. Similar results have been observed in the manufacturing sector (Khanna, 2001; Mazur and Welch, 1999; Welch *et al.*, 2000).

Conclusions

The growing popularity and government support of voluntary environmental programs as alternative environmental policy instruments has led to an intense debate about their environmental effectiveness and about the reasons why businesses participate in these initiatives (Andrews, 1998; Highley and Leveque, 2001; Khanna, 2001). Voluntary environmental programs have been posed as an innovative way in which firms can display beyond-compliance environmental behavior (i.e., appear "green"). Yet, only a few studies have evaluated manufacturing facilities' participation in US voluntary environmental programs, leading to mixed evidence (Arora and Cason, 1996; Khanna and Damon, 1999; King and Lenox, 2000; Welch *et al.*, 2000). This chapter analyzes the initial implementation of the SSP for ski areas inquiring as to whether "greener" is "better" in terms of beyond-compliance, that is, "whiter."

First of all, it is critical that we underscore the preliminary and cross-sectional nature of this study. The SSP was created in 2000 and we utilize some of the first publicly available third-party data on the environmental performance of western ski areas. The statistical correlations identified by our analysis do not imply causality. Our sample is also limited to ski areas located in the western United States and consequently the results cannot be generalized to ski areas operating in other regions of the country. The generalizability of our findings on ski areas' environmental performance is also limited by the relatively small sample used in the analysis (fifty-seven ski areas representing about 33 percent of all western facilities). The third-party evaluations of ski areas' environmental performance have been initially focused on larger ski areas; also limiting the generalizability of the environmental performance model to bigger facilities. Additionally, the objectivity of these third-party evaluations, produced by the SACC, has been sharply criticized by industry representatives that consider the coalition an "aggressive antagonist of (ski) resort developments" (Janofsky, 2000).

Consistent with previous evidence about voluntary behavior by manufacturing firms, the findings of our study indicate that participation of western ski areas in the SSP was positively related to coercive and normative institutional pressures in the form of enhanced federal oversight and higher local environmental demands exerted by state agencies, local environmental groups, and pro-environmental public opinion (Henriques and Sadorsky, 1996; Khanna *et al.*, 1998; King and Lenox, 2000; Mazur and Welch, 1999; Rivera, 2004; Delmas, 2002). Bigger facilities that are more likely to be scrutinized by stakeholders exerting these institutional pressures are, as expected, more likely to participate in the SSP (Khanna, 2001).

Regarding the environmental performance of SSP participants, our findings suggest that ski areas that are more likely to adopt the SSP are also more likely to have lower third-party environmental performance ratings. These results are in line with King and Lenox's (2000) findings for the chemical industry's Responsible Care Program. Ski areas enrolled in the SSP program appear rather to be displaying an opportunistic resistance strategy expecting to pre-empt the adoption of more restrictive USFS' land use plans by improving their "green" reputation without actually implementing the SSP's beyond-compliance environmental management principles and practices (Sachs, 2002).

This free-riding behavior by ski areas participating in the SSP is possible because of the lack of specific coercive institutional mechanisms in the current design of the SSP. That is, the SSP – like other typical industry-sponsored strictly voluntary programs – does not involve specific environmental standards, lacks third-party oversight, and does not have sanctions for poor performance (Dietz and Stern, 2002; Khanna, 2001; King and Lenox, 2000; Sachs, 2002). Additionally, endorsement of the SSP by federal agencies reinforces a weak institutional context in which opportunistic ski areas expect to pre-empt more stringent regulatory oversight as a function of their participation in strictly voluntary environmental programs even if they have poor environmental performance (Hoffman, 1999; King and Lenox, 2000; Lyon and Maxwell, 2002).

Ski areas owned by publicly traded firms do not appear to be associated with higher participation in the SSP and are also more likely to show lower environmental performance. These findings, surprisingly, challenge the evidence provided by a few studies that have analyzed the adoption of voluntary programs by manufacturing firms (Khanna, 2001). We posit that the traditional low attention given by the stock market to the environmental performance of service sector corporations and shareholders' primary focus on short-term profits can explain this unexpected finding (Lyon and Maxwell, 2002). On the other hand, ski areas experiencing higher levels of state environmental pressures appear to be significantly correlated with participation in the SSP and also with higher environmental performance ratings. Accordingly, higher state-level pressures appear to strengthen the current weak institutional forces exerted by the SPP, federal agencies, and the stock market.

Finally, based on this initial analysis of the SSP we argue that federal agencies such as the EPA and the USFS should be more selective about their endorsement of strictly voluntary programs that do not include specific institutional mechanisms for preventing free-riding behavior, such as environmental performance standards, independent monitoring of participants, and sanctions for poorly performing facilities. Official endorsement from federal government agencies significantly increases the legitimacy of strictly voluntary environmental initiatives such as the SSP. Federal backing of the SSP, despite its lack of mechanisms to prevent opportunism, may have been a tolerable compromise to trigger the initial launching of a program allegedly promoting beyond-compliance environmental protection. Alternatively, at this early stage, federal government officials and policymakers may not have been aware of the SSP as an avoidance-resistance strategy aimed at resisting new environmental requirements. To be sure, the growth and positive public profile of the SSP are currently allowing the ski industry to improve their collective "green" reputation. For environmental policymakers, however, the growing "success" of the SSP can be a desirable outcome only if it starts to effectively promote beyond-compliance environmental protection. Otherwise, federal policymakers and government officials could be providing long-term official endorsement to a symbolic self-regulatory scheme that does not appear to effectively improve industry-wide environmental protection and that allows the ski industry to effectively resist the adoption of more stringent environmental regulations. This issue is evaluated in the next chapter.

Notes

1. This chapter is a slightly modified version of Rivera and deLeon (2004), reproduced with kind permission of the journal publishers and co-author.
2. This proposal was known as the US Forest Service's Alternative D (Briggs, 2000).
3. The National Ski Areas Association defines a skier visit as "one person visiting a ski area for all or any part of a day or night for the purpose of skiing, snowboarding, or other downhill sliding" (NSAA, 2003a).
4. Environmental score grades are published on the SACC website (www.skiareacitizens.com).
5. Using power analysis and assuming a "small" effect size for the independent variables, it was determined that a minimum sample of 105 observations was necessary to have an 80 percent chance of rejecting a false null hypothesis at a 95 percent confidence level (Cohen and Cohen, 1983: 59).
6. When applying this two-stage methodology, it is sometimes argued that valid identifier variables for the probit model cannot be correlated with the dependent variable in the OLS model (Maddala, 1986). This would imply that these two models could not share the same independent variables. However, econometric studies show that the two-stage methodology does not suffer from problems of identification even when the same set of independent exogenous variables is used for both the probit and the ordinary linear regression (OLS) regressions (Khanna and Damon, 1999; Maddala, 1986: 267–71; Olsen, 1980: 1,818–19). Given that the probit model involves a nonlinear function of its independent variables,

problems of overidentification are avoided. Overidentification arises when using a linear probability model, instead of probit, for determining probability of participation (Maddala, 1986: 267–71; Olsen, 1980: 1,818–19).

7. The error terms ε_{1i} and ε_{2i} are expected to be correlated because they involve measurement error and unobserved factors associated with the adoption of the SSP and ski areas' environmental performance.
8. Detailed reports and supporting documents used to determine the environmental scorecard grades are available at www.skiareacitizens.com.
9. Condition index and variance inflation measures for the independent variables revealed weak to moderate dependencies among the independent variables. Hence, it was concluded that harmful multicollinearity did not affect the regression models (Belsley *et al.*, 1980: 105). Lack of heteroscedasticity was also determined by White's chi-square test (White, 1980). Additionally, diagnostic tests (hat matrix, dffits and dfbetas, studentized residual) and index plots did not identify influential outlier or ill-fitted observations on the probit and OLS (Belsley *et al.*, 1980; Pregibon, 1981).
10. Because Model 1 correctly classifies a greater number of participation decisions than Model 2, we used Model 1 to calculate the values of the probability of participation variable later included in the OLS regression that analyzes environmental performance.

6 *Is greener whiter yet? Resistance or beyond-compliance by the US ski industry*[1]

Is the Sustainable Slopes Program (SSP) a symbolic, self-regulatory scheme that allows its participants to improve their green reputation without actually improving their environmental protection performance? If so, the SSP may be an effective avoidance strategy that has allowed the US ski industry to resist the adoption – by the US Forest Service (USFS) – of stricter environmental regulations discussed in the previous chapter of this book. This chapter aims to help to address these issues by focusing on two general research questions: are voluntary programs effective in promoting higher environmental performance by participant firms? If so, which distinct areas of environmental performance are more likely to be improved by firms joining a voluntary environmental program? We tackle these questions by assessing the implementation of the ski industry's Sustainable Slopes Program in the western United States between 2001 and 2005.

For some time now, public policy and management scholars have been interested in identifying mechanisms that encourage environmental protection by businesses. Public policies, in terms of environmental regulations, monitoring, penalties, institutional norms, and economic incentives, have historically been identified as positively related to regulatory compliance.

Recently, these factors have also been identified with an increased likelihood of participation in voluntary environmental programs (VEPs) that seek to promote proactive corporate environmental protection in more flexible and cost-efficient ways (Carmin *et al.*, 2003; Delmas and Toffel, 2004; Khanna, 2001; King and Lenox, 2000; Rivera, 2004). Indeed, many of the George W. Bush's administration environmental policies were predicated upon VEP-type programs. Yet, empirical evidence is still scant and contradictory about whether voluntary initiatives are effective alternative environmental policy instruments or an avoidance-resistance strategy aimed at preempting the adoption of environmental regulations (Darnall, 2003a;

Khanna, 2001; King and Lenox, 2000; Potoski and Prakash, 2005; Rivera and Delmas, 2004; Welch *et al.*, 2000).

In August 2004, the *Policy Studies Journal* published Professors Rivera and deLeon's review of the SSP, which examined the first year implementation of this voluntary program as articulated by the National Ski Areas Association (NSAA; see Chapter 5). Their empirical findings indicated that institutional pressures often seemed to be motivating ski areas' participation in the SSP; however, "despite these institutional pressures, participant ski areas seem[ed] to be correlated with lower third-party environmental performance ratings" (Rivera and deLeon, 2004: 417); that is, the SSP appeared in the beginning to be attracting the "dirtier" ski areas. They suggested that this behavior was at least partially indicating, in an Olsonian (1965) way, "free rider" behavior, or using a VEP to garner, if not necessarily deliver, environmental laurels. Much to the surprise of its authors, the article generated immediate and intense media coverage, with articles being published in multiple media outlets including *The Denver Post* (two front page Business section stories and a supportive editorial based on the research), *The Rocky Mountains News,* The *Los Angeles Times, The Seattle Post,* The *Boston Globe,* The *Salt Lake City Tribune, CBS News, MSNBC News,* The *Aspen Daily News*, *Vail Trail News* and, some weeks later, The *New York Times.*

Most of the stories were supportive, a few were more "balanced," others, especially those from the ski areas' and their trade association's publications were slightly more critical, and a few were outright hostile. The crux of the criticism centered around two major points. First, that the 2001 data represented a single "snapshot" in time focused on the first year of the SSP program. Thus, even if the analysis itself were correct (a judgment to which SSP proponents do not necessarily subscribe), it reflected the initial dilemmas of any "startup program," i.e., the analysis did not accurately represent the "results" of an established program, and, besides, surely the subsequent n-year data would reflect favorably on the SSP. Second, the NSAA strongly derided the use of materials collected by the Ski Area Citizens' Coalition (SACC), claiming they were unreliable and strongly biased against ski areas' justifiable profit concern (e.g., in terms of area expansion; Dorsey, 2004; Link, 2005). In short, while the article was clearly "academic," it had, in the best traditions of the literature in public affairs, touched a much broader set of interests.

This current chapter seeks to contribute to both the immediate discussion as to the "success" of the SSP program by specifically taking the criticisms into analytic account and, just as important, by using a more longitudinal (i.e., five-year) data set. In addition, we will begin an initial discussion on the general viability of the VEP concept, using the SSP as a representative case by evaluating the link between participation in VEPs and different areas of corporate environmental performance.

Following this introduction, we first outline the theoretic underpinnings of the analysis. The next section describes the major contextual elements of the western ski industry and the SSP. Then, we provide details about our methodological approach and articulate how we have changed the analysis to address the complaints over the initial assessment of the SSP. The following sections present the analytic findings and their discussion as well as our conclusions.

Conceptual framework

Motivations for participation in VEPs

The literature on VEPs shows a growing consensus consistent with neo-institutional theory that gives external pressures a significant role in determining the adoption of these initiatives (Arora and Cason, 1996; Darnall, 2002; Delmas, 2002; Khanna and Damon, 1999; Potoski and Prakash, 2005; Welch *et al.*, 2000). Accordingly, recent empirical studies have found a statistically significant association between higher participation in VEPs and institutional pressures such as higher regulatory and monitoring requirements and greater community and environmentalist demands (Arora and Cason, 1996; Darnall, 2002; Delmas, 2002; Khanna and Damon, 1999; Potoski and Prakash, 2005; Welch *et al.*, 2000). Additionally, these studies indicate higher adoption of these initiatives by publicly traded and larger firms that are more visible and thus attract stronger institutional pressures to show superior environmental management (Arora and Cason, 1996; Darnall, 2002; Delmas, 2002; Khanna and Damon, 1999; King and Lenox, 2000; Rivera, 2004; Winter and May, 2001). In the case of the US western ski industry, the initial assessment of the SSP included in the previous chapter also found similar institutional pressures and firm characteristics significantly related to the adoption of this program.[2]

Effectiveness of VEPs

Despite the emerging consensus about the factors and firm characteristics significantly associated with participation in VEPs, research still shows contradictory perspectives and problematic evidence regarding a fundamental question for those interested in exploring the use of VEPs as alternative instruments of environmental policy (Andrews, 1998; Carmin *et al.*, 2003; Khanna, 2001; Potoski and Prakash, 2005): *Are voluntary programs effective in promoting higher environmental performance among their participants?* Let us therefore elaborate on the two basic alternative perspectives regarding the environmental effectiveness of voluntary programs.

The first theme proposes that voluntary programs serve as effective policy tools to promote enhanced environmental protection. Supporters of voluntary initiatives hypothesize that these programs provide specific incentives in the form of increased environmental management flexibility, technical assistance, and enhanced "green reputation" that directly encourage participants to adopt superior environmental protection practices (Delmas and Terlaak, 2001; Khanna, 2001). VEPs' flexibility and technical assistance protocols can allow firms to adopt an expanded variety of environmental management practices and technologies that are more cost-efficient than those required by command-and-control regulations (Delmas and Terlaak, 2001; Moon, 2005). The sharing of "best practices" and environmental management systems (EMS) approaches, typical of voluntary programs, may also facilitate environmental innovation and organizational learning at different levels of the firm, thus permitting a firm to adopt environmental protection practices found to be more cost-efficient and effective (King and Lenox, 2000). Because of their expected superior environmental practices, VEP participants may credibly improve their "green" reputation and use it to gain higher sales and/or price premiums from environmentally aware consumers (Reinhardt, 1998). For instance, hotel facilities participants in the Costa Rican Certification for Sustainable Tourism appear to gain statistically significant premium prices (Rivera, 2002). In addition, a firm's credible "green" reputation may help participants to enhance their environmental legitimacy and thus develop better relations with regulators and environmentalists that can pre-empt more stringent oversight and stringent regulations (Darnall, 2003b; Lyon and Maxwell, 2002).

Additionally, even for strictly voluntary environmental programs that lack independent monitoring, sanctions and/or rewards, neo-institutional scholars have posited that they may trigger a socialization process involving external peer and industry-wide pressures that compel members to self-regulate in order to gain or maintain a collective "green" reputation and trust from its corporate peers, regulators, stakeholders, and, ultimately, consumers (Granovetter, 1985; Hoffman, 1999; King and Lenox, 2000). VEPs' institutional socialization tactics may involve technical assistance visits and meetings, use of formal symbols – such as environmentally friendly, i.e., "green" labels – to identify participants, periodic public reports highlighting best and worst practices participants, peer pressures, and endorsement by important industry players and regulatory agencies, and environmental groups (DiMaggio and Powell, 1983; Hoffman, 1999; King and Lenox, 2000). To be sure, a few studies have suggested that voluntary initiatives that include some of these institutional socialization mechanisms, such as the US Environmental Protection Agency's (EPA) 33/50 program and ISO-14001, may have respectively been associated with lower toxic release inventory (TRI) emissions and environmental compliance by their participants (Dasgupta, 2000; Khanna and Damon, 1999; Potoski and Prakash, 2005).

Conversely, other scholars have depicted VEPs as relatively ineffective environmental policy instruments, particularly when they are strictly voluntary.[3] From this perspective, strictly voluntary environmental programs are seen as an avoidance-resistance strategy that seeks to pre-empt the adoption of more stringent environmental protection regulations by giving the appearance of proactive "green" behavior. Proponents of this perspective posit that, in general, firms seldom engage in collective action efforts beyond their narrow self-interest unless socially constrained by strong institutional pressures in the form of monitoring and sanctions for lack of cooperation (Hardin, 1968; Olson, 1965; Ostrom, 1990; Williamson, 1975). *Without these strong institutional pressures, we propose that strictly voluntary environmental programs are unlikely to promote superior environmental performance because of their lack of coercive mechanisms to prevent opportunistic participants from free-riding on program benefits* such as "green" reputation, technical assistance, etc. (King and Lenox, 2000; Rivera and deLeon, 2004; Toffel, 2005). In this case, opportunism is distinguished from usual self-interest seeking as a behavior in which voluntary program participants deliberately evade and/or misrepresent performing agreed-on environmental practices aimed at promoting higher environmental performance (Wathne and Heide, 2000; Williamson, 1975; 1985).[4,5]

The opportunistic challenges faced by strictly voluntary programs, with no monitoring and sanctions, arise from the non-excludable public good nature of some of the benefits they provide to participants (Darnall, 2002; King and Lenox, 2000; Potoski and Prakash, 2005). For instance, once created by the program, credible "green" reputations are enjoyed by all adopting firms including those opportunistically free-riding with low environmental performance because they are not differentiated from truly environmentally proactive firms (Darnall, 2003a; King and Lenox, 2000). To be sure, empirical evidence from recent evaluations of VEPs has generated doubts about the environmental effectiveness of these initiatives (Carmin *et al.*, 2003; Khanna, 2001; Moon, 2005). These studies suggest that voluntary initiatives such as the chemical industry's Responsible Care, ISO-14001, and the US Department of Energy's Global Climate Challenge, may attract firms with questionable environmental performance. Once enrolled these firms do not appear to improve significantly their environmental performance (Darnall and Sides, 2008; King and Lenox, 2000; Welch *et al.*, 2000). In the case of the ski industry's Sustainable Slopes Program, initial evidence discussed in the previous chapter of the book also suggests that its participants are more likely to have lower environmental performance (Rivera and deLeon, 2004).

Lastly, we need to appreciate that there are distinctions between different areas of environmental performance and voluntary programs effectiveness. The arguments about the role of institutional pressures in preventing opportunistic behavior can shed light on another important and related issue that has scarcely been addressed by scholarly research: *which distinct areas of environmental performance are more likely to be improved by firms joining a voluntary environmental program?* Most studies examining the environmental effectiveness of voluntary environmental initiatives have used the amount of toxic releases as a proxy for environmental performance because of the general lack of data about other areas of corporate environmental performance (Darnall and Sides, 2008; Khanna, 2001; Toffel and Marshall, 2004). Yet, of course, environmental performance is a multidimensional concept that includes not only pollution emissions but also other areas of environmental protection, such as wildlife and habitat management, resource conservation, and footprint reduction (Starik and Rands, 1995). Indeed, the SSP and other voluntary initiatives include a comprehensive list of environmental practices and standards that incorporate these and other recognized dimensions of environmental protection. Thus, it can be expected that VEP participants that do not face strong institutional pressures in the form of monitoring and sanctions for non-compliance would selectively adopt different environmental management practices depending on their cost, technical difficulty, visibility for stakeholders, and benefits.

Accordingly, *we propose that participant firms would be less likely to adopt those areas of environmental protection that are more costly and have uncertain long-term benefits with little short-term payoffs for firms.* For instance, practices such as wildlife protection and "footprint" reduction, despite their significant importance for environmental protection, offer no immediate financial benefits to ski areas (Porter and van der Linde, 1995; Walley and Whitehead, 1994). However, resource conservation practices that seek to reduce the use of energy, water, and other materials, are known to offer shorter-term payoffs, making them more likely to be adopted by participants (Walley and Whitehead, 1994).

The context of western skiing: principal actors and programs

Skiing has proven to be a very popular recreational activity in the United States and particularly in the western half of the country, constituting an important part of the area's tourism and recreation economy (see discussion in Chapter 5). Despite rapid growth in the 1960s and 1970s, during the 1980s and 1990s the ski industry experienced relatively consistent (i.e., a low-growth rate) demand in terms of the number of skier visits (Hudson, 2000; NSAA, 2004b).[6] During the early 2000s, even though the ski industry faced a number of challenges (e.g., economic uncertainty in the United States and increased travel-related security concerns), ski resorts nationwide experienced an increased number of skier visits, particularly in the Rocky Mountains and western United States (NSAA, 2004a; 2005b). The 2000 through 2004 ski seasons resulted in an average of 56 million skier visits per year, compared to an average of 52 million skier visits per year between 1982 and 1999 (NSAA, 2004a; 2004b). The three best years in terms of skier visits occurred within the 2000–4 period (NSAA, 2004a; 2004b; 2001). In addition, snowboarding continues to grow in popularity, albeit at a modest rate. The increase in skier visits has been accompanied by a consolidation and stabilization in the number of ski resorts operating within the United States. Since 2000, there have been approximately 490 ski resorts in operation each season compared to 727 resorts in operation during the 1984–5 season (NSAA, 2004b).

Given the favorable climate and terrain for skiing, resorts located in the western United States are particularly popular skiing destinations. Western ski resorts, while fewer in absolute numbers, tend to attract more skiers than resorts in other parts of the country. Skier visits to resorts in the Rocky Mountains and Pacific West region accounted for 54 percent of all skier visits during the 2003–4 season, while states in these regions contain only 34 percent of the ski resorts operating in the US in 2004 (NSAA, 2004a; 2004b). Resorts in the Rocky Mountain region also commanded higher average lift-ticket prices ($61.08 for the 2003–4 season) compared to the overall average ($53.95 for 2003–4; NSAA, 2004a). Resorts in the western United States are also more likely to operate on federal lands. Unlike resorts in the eastern United States, over 90 percent of resorts in the west are operated on property leased from the USFS under a special permitting process (SACC, 2005).

The ski industry and the USFS

A number of special interest groups have criticized the relationship between the ski industry and the USFS for the low rents charged to ski resorts for the use of public lands. Additionally, the USFS and the NSAA have created a number of partnership arrangements under which the parties work together to promote ski sports (Briggs, 2000; Clifford, 2002; Wharton, 1997b). In a 1997 speech to the ski industry, Mike Dombeck, the then head of the USFS, reflected on this relationship when he stated that outdoor recreation had surpassed timber logging as the most important activity in national forests and that there were over 31 million skier visits to national forest lands in 1996 (Wharton, 1997a).

Ski resorts operating on USFS-controlled land must obtain special operating permits, abide by various environmental regulations, and pay permit fees based on the fair market value of the use of the land using a formula that considers the revenue ski resorts generate from the use of USFS lands (e.g., revenue from lift-tickets, ski schools, and facilities on forest lands). USFS fees range from 1.5 percent to 4 percent of a ski resort's adjusted gross revenue from activities on national forest land (United States Code, 2003). Despite the requirement that fees be based on fair market value, a number of General Accountability Office (GAO) reports have found that the USFS has not been collecting appropriate fees from ski resorts (GAO, 1996; Rogers, 2002; 2003).

The USFS' increased focus on recreation has coincided with a decrease in federal appropriations for the USFS and increased pressures on the agency to generate revenue from the management of forest lands (Clifford, 2002). There are also concerns that fees generated from economic activity on USFS lands are used in part to fund special accounts and trust funds which are exempt from Congress' annual appropriation process but are used to finance local community projects and partially pay for overhead expenses such as equipment purchases and/or employee salaries (Gorte, 2000; Gorte and Corn, 1995). Some have argued that the use of this receipt-sharing process may create conflicts of interests for local USFS offices faced with reduced federal appropriations (Gorte, 2000). These potential conflicts of interests gained importance in the late 1990s and early 2000s, given that local USFS offices played a critically important role in the design and implementation of new land use plans for national forest lands (see discussion in Chapter 5).

The Sustainable Slopes Program: 2000–5 implementation

As discussed in the previous chapter, a number of governmental and non-profit organizations partnered with the NSAA in the creation of the SSP, including the EPA, USFS, Colorado Department of Public Health and Environment, US Department of Energy, Conservation Law Foundation, Leave No Trace, Inc., and The Mountain Institute (NSAA, 2000). According to the NSAA (2005a):

> The number one reason for supporting Sustainable Slopes, expressed either directly or indirectly by all Partnering Organizations, is that it leads to improved environmental performance.

A few of these partnering organizations have also provided significant funding for the SSP. For example, the USFS contributed $30,000 to finance the creation of the SSP and later funded data collection efforts used by the NSAA in the creation of SSP annual reports (Clifford, 2002; NSAA, 2005a). The SSP annual reports have also been funded by the National Fish and Wildlife Foundation (NSAA, 2001). However, a number of prominent environmental organizations (e.g., The Sierra Club, The Nature Conservancy) that were initially involved in the design of SSP chose not to become official partners of the program once it was launched in 2000 (NSAA, 2000).

The SSP charter (NSAA, 2000) involves twenty-one general categories of environmental protection for ski area planning, operations, and outreach (see Table 6.1). Since the creation of the SSP in 2000, the NSAA has issued Sustainable Slopes annual reports highlighting environmental activities of endorsing resorts and reporting on the progress of resorts in incorporating the environmental principles into their operations.

Over the years, the number of resorts endorsing the SSP has increased from 160 in 2000 (33 percent of US ski areas) to 178 in 2005 (36 percent of US ski areas; NSAA, 2000; 2005a). However, it is important to underscore that the number of resorts completing the SSP's annual self-assessment tool, a key part of the program, fell from a high of 90 (52 percent) resorts in 2002 to 54 (30 percent) resorts in 2005 (NSAA, 2002; 2005a). The 22 percent decline in submission of self-assessment reports has been experienced notwithstanding the prominent role given to responding ski areas in the SSP annual reports and despite the partial funding provided by the USFS to collect these self-assessment data.

For all its efforts, the SSP has not reduced tension between the ski industry and certain environmental groups and the media that have criticized the SSP for its lack of performance standards and independent oversight and for ignoring many important areas of environmental protection (see e.g., Hartman and Zalaznick, 2003; Langeland, 2002). As the US EPA liaison to the SSP noted in a *Vermont Law Review* article:

> The challenge for Sustainable Slopes lies in its implementation. It is a voluntary program, so ski resorts opt-in with non-binding obligations. If resorts do not employ suggested actions or do not report annually, there are no consequences. Independent of fulfilling the twenty-one principles, resorts remain able to use the program logo for marketing and advertising. (Sachs, 2002)

Table 6.1 *Basic dimensions of ski areas' environmental performance**

Basic dimension	SSP general environmental protection categories	SACC environmental protection criteria
(1) Expansion management	Planning, design, and construction	Maintaining ski terrain within the existing footprint Preserving undisturbed lands from development Preserving environmentally sensitive areas
(2) Natural resources conservation	Water use for snowmaking Water use for facilities Water use for landscaping and summer activities Energy use for facilities Energy use for snowmaking Energy use for lifts Energy use for vehicle fleets Waste reduction Product re-use Recycling	Promoting and implementing recycling, and water, land, and energy conservation strategies Conserving water and energy by avoiding new snowmaking
(3) Pollution management	Water quality management Wastewater management Potentially hazardous wastes Air quality Visual quality Transportation	Minimizing traffic, emissions, and pollution Protecting water quality
(4) Wildlife and habitat management	Fish and wildlife management Forest and vegetative management Wetlands and riparian areas Education and outreach	Protection of threatened or endangered species Wildlife habitat protection

Source: SACC, 2005 and NSAA, 2000.

* A detailed list of the underlying variables used for assessing each environmental protection criterion is available online at SACC's website: www.skiareacitizens.com/criteria.html.

Methodology

Statistical analysis

Because a ski area's environmental performance is not exogenous to its decision to adopt the SSP, we employed a recursive two-stage approach proposed by Heckman (1978; 1979) that corrects for self-selection bias in the estimation of the effects of voluntary programs. The specific application of this recursive methodology to assess benefits of voluntary environmental programs is outlined by Khanna and Damon (1999: 4–5, 13) and applied by the growing number of studies that have assessed the benefits of voluntary environmental programs (Khanna and Damon, 1999; Maddala, 1986; Potoski and Prakash, 2005; Rivera, 2002; Rivera and deLeon, 2004; Welch *et al*., 2000). Also, to avoid endogeneity, control variables that vary over time were lagged one year in both stages. To elaborate:

Stage one. In this step, we model ski resorts' participation in the SSP by using a probit regression specification with panel data. Subsequently, we use this probit model to calculate each ski resort's probability of participation in the Sustainable Slopes Program. The control variables included in these probit models seek to account for federal and stakeholder institutional pressures known to affect participation in the SSP and other voluntary environmental programs (Khanna, 2001; Rivera and deLeon, 2004).

(1) $D_{it} = \delta_i + a_1 X_{1it} + \varepsilon_{1it}$

where:

i = ith ski area;
t = observation year;
D_{it} = decision to participate in the SSP;
δ_i = regression constant term;
X_{1it} = vector of independent variables (federal government oversight, stock exchange trading, size, state location);
a_1 = regression coefficients for vector of independent variables;
ε_{1it} = equation 1's random error term.

Stage two. In this stage of the analysis, we model the different dimensions of ski resorts' environmental performance using a random effects specification estimated with a mixed generalized linear regression technique (MGLR) deemed appropriate for unbalanced panel data (Greene, 2000; Little, 1995).[7,8] The estimated probability of participation in the SSP calculated in the initial step is used here as an independent variable to assess the effect of SSP participation on environmental performance (Greene, 2000; Khanna and Damon, 1999; Maddala, 1986). The second-stage regression model also includes control variables previously found to be associated with corporate environmental performance (Darnall, 2002; Delmas, 2002; Khanna, 2001; King and Lenox, 2000; Potoski and Prakash, 2005; Rivera and deLeon, 2004). Our second-step model specification is represented by the following equation:

$$(2)\ Y_{it} = \alpha_i + b_2 X_{2it} + c_i P_{it} + \varepsilon_{2it}$$

where:

Y_{it} = *i*th ski area's environmental performance at year t;
α_i = regression constant term;
X_{2it} = vector of independent variables (federal government oversight, stock exchange trading, size, and index of state environmentalism);
P_{it} = probability of participation in the SSP;
ε_{2it} = equation 2's random error term.

The use of Heckman's two-stage recursive methodology for estimating self-selection models has been criticized by some because the first- and second-stage models usually share all or almost all identifier variables (Puhani, 2000). If a linear probability model is used in stage one for determining the inverse Mill's ratio (probability of participation variable introduced on the second stage), collinearity problems between this ratio and other independent variables arise in the second stage (Maddala, 1986, 267–71; Olsen, 1980, 1,818–19). Thus, it has been suggested that application of the Heckman methodology requires the use of identifying variables associated with the dependent variable in stage one but not associated with the dependent variable in stage two.

This methodological issue was initially addressed by Olsen (1980) in an article published in *Econometrica* and more recently by other authors (Greene, 2000: 926–46; Maddala, 1986: 267–71). They show that the Heckman techniques that use a probit model for stage one and a linear model for the second stage do not suffer problems of identification even when a similar set of independent exogenous variables is used for both stages. This is because the probit model involves a nonlinear function of its independent variables and thus the Mill's ratio calculated from it "is a nonlinear function of the exogenous variables in the model" (Olsen, 1980, 1,818).

Data and measures

Building upon the initial cross-sectional assessment of the SSP (see previous chapter), we collected panel data on SSP adoption, environmental performance, and independent control variables (e.g., ski resort location, ownership, size, etc.) for five years between 2001 and 2005. Information about SSP adoption was obtained from the program's official annual reports and website. Environmental performance dimensions data were obtained from the disaggregated SACC annual scorecard rankings. Data for the independent variables was gathered from individual ski areas' internet homepages, Travelocity.com, the NSAA, the USFS, and the stock markets in New York and Toronto.

Our final sample consisted of 110 US western ski areas, which equates to approximately 62 percent of the 178 facilities operating in the western US in 2005.[9] Included in this sample were 76 ski areas that as of the summer of 2005 had received third-party environmental performance ratings and 34 ski areas randomly drawn from the western ski resort population. The use of this sample to estimate the first- and second-step regression models is described below.

Probit regression pooled data. Because once enrolled in the SSP ski areas are not excluded from the program, their adoption decision does not have to be made every year. Thus, as suggested by Khanna and Damon (1999), once a ski area has adopted the SSP, it is dropped from the dataset. Conversely, non-adopters could choose to participate in any following year. For instance, ski areas that joined the program in 2001 are included twice in the probit regression pooled data, once as non-members in 2000, and then as SSP members in 2001 (Khanna and Damon, 1999). The resulting pooled data used for the probit analysis includes 233 observations.

Environmental performance dimensions models. In the case of the second-step regression models, all ski area observations for which environmental performance data were available between 2001 and 2005 were used, resulting in an unbalanced panel data set of 350 observations.

In the following paragraphs, we describe the measures of the variables included in our analysis beginning with the different dimensions of environmental performance, participation in the SSP, and then following with the independent variables.

Measure of environmental performance dimensions. Following the approach described in the previous chapter, publicly available data obtained from the SACC annual scorecard listing were used to estimate ski areas' environmental performance. SACC is a partnership of non-profit environmental organizations located in the western US. Since 2000, SACC has conducted assessments of the environmental performance of western ski resorts and annually publishes the results online as environmental scorecard grades. Ski areas are assigned letter grades from A (best) to F (worst) based on their percentage compliance with multiple environmental performance criteria.[10] The information used to estimate scorecard grades is obtained from government documents collected through Freedom of Information Act requests.[11] Additional information is gathered from onsite visits, an annual ski area survey, individual ski resorts' websites, corporate reports, and external sources such as media articles published by trade magazines, business press, and the general media (Dorsey, 2004; SACC, 2005).

Since their initial publication, SACC's scorecard grades have received increasing recognition as a measure of ski areas' environmental performance not only by specialized ski publications and websites but also by mainstream media in the US and abroad including: the *New York Times*, *Denver Post*, *Rocky Mountains News*, *Los Angeles Times*, *Seattle Post*, *CNN*, and *ESPN*.[12] Nevertheless, it is important to underscore that the NSAA has vehemently criticized the use of environmental scorecard grades as "an unaudited, inherently flawed, and biased measure of resort environmental performance" (Dorsey, 2004). The NSAA also strongly portrays the SACC as an alliance of radical environmental groups whose goal is to obstruct the expansion of the industry (Dorsey, 2004; Link, 2005). In particular, NSAA representatives criticize the scorecard for placing undue emphasis on penalizing ski areas involved in expansion-related activities, such as real-estate development, and those refusing to respond to SACC annual surveys (Baird, 2004; Blevins, 2004; Dorsey, 2004; Janofsky, 2000).

To be sure, the controversial perspectives surrounding the use of environmental performance data are not unique to SACC's scorecard grades. They are inherent in other widely used sources of environmental performance information such as, for example, self-reported TRI data gathered by the EPA (King and Lenox, 2000; Toffel and Marshall, 2004). It is not surprising that "hard" environmental performance data are seldom available given that in the US less than 1 percent of large regulated facilities received inspection of their air, water, and land pollution between 1996 and 1998 (Potoski and Prakash, 2005). Thus, SACC scorecard grades and other measures of environmental performance widely used in the literature are clearly imperfect measures based on judgment and interpretation of qualitative and quantitative data that inherently involve human error and biases (Waddock, 2003). In this sense, the human judgments used to develop the SACC scorecard ratings "are in many respects no different from the interpretations that underlie financial and accounting statements, which also rely on the (sometimes erroneous and sometimes felonious as witnessed in the first [decade] of the millennium) judgments of auditors, accountants, and financial analysts to determine materiality" (Waddock, 2003).

In light of the putative problems presented by the SACC scorecard, we chose to extend the approach taken in the initial evaluation of the SSP (see previous chapter). First, we tried to obtain alternative data that could verify or challenge the findings of the SACC environmental scorecard. An obvious alternative were the SSP members' annual self-reported environmental performance assessments collected by the NSAA, gathered in part through funding from the USFS (NSAA, 2005a). On different occasions, we contacted the NSAA's Director of Public Policy seeking to gain access to these data. Unfortunately, the NSAA chose to maintain the proprietary nature of these self-reported assessments and, therefore, we were denied access to these data.

The only additional publicly available indication of ski resorts' environmental performance available was the Golden Eagle Award given annually to ski resorts in recognition of their environmental excellence. This award is currently being administered by the NSAA and was previously run by Mountain Sports Media, the publisher of *Ski Magazine* (NSAA, 2005a). It is noteworthy that in the period

2000–4, Golden Eagle awardees also received SACC's highest environmental scorecard grades in four out of five cases, suggesting a high correlation between these two independent proxies of superior environmental performance.

Second, we followed an alternative approach aimed at addressing concerns related to the SACC scorecard's "overemphasis" on penalizing expansion-related activities. Instead of using the SACC's overall environmental scorecard grades, we used the disaggregated data to estimate percentage compliance ratios for four basic dimensions of ski areas' environmental performance: (1) expansion management; (2) natural resources conservation; (3) pollution management, and (4) wildlife and habitat management. Table 6.1 also lists the SACC scorecard criteria that we selected to be included under each dimension. It is important to note that we excluded SACC criteria that did not fit these categories or that were not used consistently over the period 2001 to 2005.[13] Finally, we also estimated *overall environmental performance* for each ski area as the non-weighted average of the four basic environmental performance dimensions' percentage compliance ratios.

Measure of other variables. Adoption of the SSP is measured using a discrete variable that takes a value of one for enrolled facilities and zero for non-participants. Low, medium, and high levels of *federal government environmental oversight* are measured respectively by identifying the type of private, mixed, and public land ownership occupied by ski area facilities. As suggested by previous authors (Briggs, 2000; Clifford, 2002; Rivera and deLeon, 2004), facilities located on public land owned by the federal government faced significantly higher levels of environmental oversight. *Ski area size* is calculated as the total amount of skiable acres possessed by each ski area. *Ownership by a publicly traded firm* is measured by a dummy variable equal to one for ski areas belonging to corporations traded on a stock exchange and zero otherwise. *Probability of participation in the SSP* is measured on a zero to one continuous scale and its values were estimated using the probit model calculated in the first stage of the statistical analysis (Hartman, 1988; Khanna and Damon, 1999). Lastly, the level of *state environmental pressures* is measured with two alternative proxies: state location or Mazur and Welch's (1999) index of state environmentalism used by other researchers (Potoski and Prakash, 2005; Toffel, 2005). This index is estimated using four standardized indicators: (1) state membership in the largest

US environmental organizations; (2) level of pro-environmental public opinion as measured by the National Opinion Research Center; (3) the congressional delegation's League of Conservation Voters pro-environmental ranking; and (4) the state's environmental policy implementation strength ranking (Mazur and Welch, 1999).

Results and discussion

Table 6.2 shows descriptive statistics for SSP participation and performance rates for different areas of environmental protection. Descriptive statistics for the independent variables for 2005 are presented in Table 6.3. These descriptive figures suggest that, as has been the case for the overall population of US ski resorts, the level of SSP participation for our sample of western ski resorts has increased less than 3 percent over the 2001 to 2005 period (see Table 6.2). Regarding overall environmental performance, the descriptive results indicate that the proportion of ski areas (SSP members and non-members) receiving the lowest rates (F grades) has decreased from about 28 percent in 2001 to 12 percent in 2005, with the mid-rate environmental performance ranking (C grades) increasing the most from approximately 21 percent in 2001 to about 51 percent in 2005 (see Table 6.2). It is also interesting to note that in terms of individual dimensions of environmental protection, expansion management is the dimension where the largest proportion of sampled ski resorts (45.45 percent) received the highest grade (A grade). Indeed, no ski resorts received an A grade for pollution management and wildlife protection and only 3.95 percent scored an "A" for natural resource conservation (see Table 6.3).

Adoption of the SSP

Findings for two probit regression specifications that model ski areas' participation decisions are presented in Table 6.4. Each model uses a different proxy for state environmental pressures: Model 1 relies on state location whereas Model 2 uses Mazur and Welch's index of state environmentalism (1999). Given that the two models are statistically significant ($P<0.01$) and offer similar results, we only discuss the results of Model 2.[14,15] In accordance with previous research on voluntary environmental programs, the probit findings indicate that ski

Table 6.2 *Descriptive statistics for program participation and overall environmental performance*

	2001		2002		2003		2004		2005		Full period (2001–5)	
Variable/year	N	Percent	N	Percent	N	Percent	N	Percent	N	Percent	N	Percent
Sustainable Slopes Program adoption												
Yes	79	71.82	81	73.64	82	74.55	81	73.64	82	74.55	405	73.64
No	31	28.18	29	26.36	28	25.45	29	26.36	28	25.45	145	26.36
Total	110		110		110		110		110		550	
Overall environmental performance (percentage score for SSP members and non-members)												
77 to 100 (A)	4	7.02	4	5.71	4	5.71	4	5.26	3	3.90	19	5.43
60 to <77 (B)	7	12.28	7	10.00	7	10.00	13	17.11	5	6.49	39	11.14
45 to <60 (C)	12	21.05	21	30.00	28	40.00	33	43.42	39	50.65	133	38.00
35 to <45 (D)	18	31.58	24	34.29	15	21.43	16	21.05	21	27.27	94	26.86
<35 (F)	16	28.07	14	20.00	16	22.86	10	13.16	9	11.69	65	18.57
Total	57		70		70		76		76		350	
Average performance	44.86 (16.23)[a]		45.66 (14.52)		47.65 (15.44)		50.66 (15.44)		48.00 (12.48)		47.53 (14.82)	

[a] Standard deviations are in parentheses.

Table 6.3 *Descriptive statistics for the year 2005*

Variable	N	Percent	Variable	N	Percent
Expansion management (percentage score)			Federal government oversight		
77 to 100 (A)	35	45.45	Lower	19	17.27
60 to <77 (B)	12	15.58	Medium	15	13.64
45 to <60 (C)	11	14.29	Higher	76	69.09
35 to <45 (D)	7	9.09	Total	110	
<35 (F)	12	15.58			
Total	77				
Mean score		67.30 (26.31)[a]			
Natural resource conservation			Ownership by a publicly traded firm		
77 to 100 (A)	3	3.95	Yes	10	9.09
60 to <77 (B)	3	3.95	No	100	90.91
45 to <60 (C)	6	7.89	Total	110	
35 to <45 (D)	11	14.47			
<35 (F)	53	69.74			
Total	76				
Mean score		31.37 (18.04)			

Table 6.3 (*cont.*)

Variable	N	Percent	Variable	N	Percent
Pollution management			Size (thousand acres)		
77 to 100 (A)	0	0.00	0 to 1	57	51.82
60 to <77 (B)	12	15.58	>1 to 2	28	25.45
45 to <60 (C)	54	70.13	>2 to 3	17	15.45
35 to <45 (D)	0	0.00	>3 to 4	6	5.45
<35 (F)	11	14.29	>4 to 5	2	1.82
Total	77		Total	110	
Mean score		50.54 (11.19)	Mean score		1.3 (1.04)
Wildlife and habitat management			State location		
77 to 100 (A)	0	0.00	Alaska	2	1.82
60 to <77 (B)	0	0.00	Arizona	2	1.82
45 to <60 (C)	36	46.75	California	20	18.18
35 to <45 (D)	6	7.79	Colorado	25	22.73
<35 (F)	35	45.45	Idaho	8	7.27
Total	77		Montana	8	7.27
Mean score		32.17 (19.97)	New Mexico	8	7.27
			Nevada	4	3.64
			Oregon	8	7.27
			Utah	13	11.82
			Washington	9	8.18
			Wyoming	3	2.73
			Total	110	

[a] Standard deviations are in parentheses.

Table 6.4 *Results from probit regression models (dependent variable: participation in the SSP)*[21]

	Model 1	Model 2
Constant	-1.68 (0.42)[a] ***	-2.50 (0.36)***
Federal government environmental oversight		
High (public land)	1.29 (0.32)***	1.17 (0.28)***
Medium (public-private land)	1.81 (0.42)***	1.69 (0.34)***
Ownership by publicly traded firm	0.99 (0.84)	1.45 (0.78)*
Size (thousand-acre units)	0.73 (0.17)***	0.66 (0.14)***
State environmental pressures		
Index of state environmentalism		1.21 (0.51)**
State location		
Alaska	-1.13 (0.70)	
Arizona	-0.12 (0.72)	
California	0.51 (0.34)	
Idaho	-1.34 (0.46)***	
Montana	-0.59 (0.47)	
New Mexico	-1.03 (0.43)**	
Nevada	-0.81 (0.44)*	
Oregon	0.72 (0.55)	
Utah	-0.24 (0.41)	
Washington	-0.32 (0.42)	
Wyoming	-1.19 (0.61)**	
N	233	233
-2 Log L	216.45	236.57
χ^2 for covariates	91.46***	71.34***
Percent correctly classified	83.8	80.2

[a] Standard errors are in parentheses.

* prob<0.10; ** prob<0.05; *** prob<0.01.

areas are significantly more likely to participate in the SSP when facing higher levels of federal government oversight, $p<0.05$ (Darnall, 2003a; Henriques and Sadorsky, 1996; Khanna and Damon, 1999; Rivera, 2004). Also, consistent with previous studies of VEP participation, the results suggest that larger ski area size ($P<0.01$), and greater levels of state environmental pressures ($p<0.05$) are significantly correlated with adoption of the SSP (Darnall, 2002; Khanna, 2001; King and Lenox, 2000; Toffel, 2005).[16] The effect of ownership by a publicly traded firm is less conclusive as only Model 2 suggests a positive relationship with SSP participation at 90 percent confidence. Given that participation in the SSP has changed little over the 2001–5 period, it is not surprising that our findings are congruent with Rivera and deLeon's (2004) assessment of the first year participation in the SSP (see previous chapter).

Overall, this evidence is consistent with neo-institutional theory concepts suggesting that coercive pressures in the form of regulatory demands, arising at either the federal or state level, are a key incentive for promoting corporate "green" signaling in the form of adoption of self-regulatory initiatives, such as the SSP (Darnall, 2003a; Delmas and Terlaak, 2001). Similarly, larger ski areas and those traded in the stock market are more visible to a wider array of stakeholders (i.e., the media, environmentalists, consumers, the industry association) that exert stronger normative institutional pressures on these facilities to show greater proactive environmental behavior (Darnall, 2003a; King and Lenox, 2000). Thus, we suggest that independent of their actual environmental practices, these resorts use SSP adoption as a relatively low-cost and conspicuous "green legitimacy" building strategy that may have helped to delay the adoption and reduce the stringency of additional environmental regulatory demands under consideration by the USFS' land use plan revisions (Darnall, 2003b; Lyon and Maxwell, 2002). Larger or publicly traded facilities may also find the adoption of SSP practices easier because they tend to have more resources and greater access to innovative environmental management technologies as compared to smaller or privately owned ski areas (Hoffman, 1999; King and Lenox, 2000).

Environmental effectiveness of the SSP

More important than identifying factors associated with participation is determining whether adoption of voluntary programs, such as the SSP, actually promotes higher environmental performance by participants (Andrews, 1998; Potoski and Prakash, 2005). Seeking to address this question, we estimated five different regression models that analyze the outcome of the SSP in different areas of environmental protection: overall environmental performance, expansion management, natural resources conservation, pollution management, and wildlife and habitat management (see Table 6.5). For all models, the chi-square statistic indicates a significant fit for the independent variables included in the models ($P < 0.01$) (alternative model specifications are displayed in Table 6.6).[17]

Model 3 on Table 6.5 presents the results for overall environmental performance. We find that the coefficient on probability of participation is not statistically significant, even at 90 percent confidence. This finding indicates that ski areas' adoption of the SSP is not significantly correlated with higher overall environmental performance for the 2001–5 period. Similarly, the results suggest that during this period, enrollment in the SSP does not have a statistically significant correlation with higher performance in the following individual dimensions of environmental protection: expansion management (see Model 4), pollution management (Model 6), and wildlife and habitat management (Model 7). In these three cases, the coefficients on the probability of a participation variable are statistically insignificant ($P < 0.1$). Compared to non-adopting ski resorts, SSP participants only appear to show a statistically significant correlation with higher natural resource conservation performance rates ($P < 0.05$; see Model 5).

These results indicate lack of statistical evidence to conclude that between 2001 and 2005, ski areas adopting the SSP displayed superior performance levels than non-participants for most areas of environmental protection. SSP adoption only seems to be associated with higher performance in natural resources conservation practices. These non-significant findings are consistent with the neo-institutional theory arguments positing that purely voluntary initiatives are bound to suffer free-riding behavior because of their lack of robust coercive and normative mechanisms that can differentiate between proactive and opportunistic participants (Hardin, 1968; King and Lenox, 2000; Olson, 1965; Ostrom, 1990; Williamson, 1975).

As highlighted by the initial selection assessment of the SSP, discussed in the previous chapter of the book, a significant number of poor environmental performing facilities appear to self-select into the program because of the strictly voluntary nature of the program's charter. Between 2000–5, the SSP did not establish performance-based standards, did not require independent third-party monitoring of its members' environmental practices, and lacked sanctions or rewards for respectively poor or superior environmental performance (Dorsey, 2004; Rivera and deLeon, 2004; Sachs, 2002). Our five-year

Table 6.5 *MGL regression results (dependent variable: environmental performance)*

	Overall environmental performance (Model 3)	Expansion management (Model 4)	Natural resources conservation (Model 5)	Pollution management (Model 6)	Wildlife and habitat management (Model 7)
Constant	55.96 (5.29)[a] ***	85.12 (8.81)***	31.87 (7.94)***	57.53 (5.38)***	62.16 (7.56)***
Federal government oversight					
High (public land)	−7.00 (3.86)*	−4.68 (5.94)	−13.32 (6.21)**	−0.52 (4.23)	−10.38 (6.38)
Medium (public-private land)	−10.81 (4.61)**	−8.54 (7.01)	−18.97 (7.53)**	1.20 (5.13)	−17.45 (7.92)**
Ownership by publicly traded firm	−2.06 (4.18)	−15.97 (6.65)**	−2.28 (6.51)	−2.15 (4.42)	−3.81 (6.40)
Probability of participation	8.75 (8.32)	−11.90 (14.00)	32.70 (12.43)**	12.59 (8.41)	−4.27 (11.85)
Size (thousand-acre units)	−4.47 (2.1)**	−7.0 (3.5)**	−7.0 (3.1)**	2.0 (2.1)	−0.45 (2.9)
State environmental pressures	−0.19 (7.57)	9.60 (12.61)	16.66 (11.31)	−14.71 (7.65)*	−7.76 (10.65)
N	348	348	348	348	348
−2 Log L	−590.6	−321.1	−223.7	−481.9	−117.9
χ^2 for covariates	272.27***	330.34***	191.37***	175.92***	88.79***

[a] Standard errors are in parentheses.

* prob < 0.10; ** prob < 0.05; *** prob < 0.01.

Table 6.6 *New MGL regression results: excluding size and ownership by publicly traded firm as control variables (dependent variable: environmental performance dimensions)*[a]

	Overall environmental performance (Model 3)	Expansion management (Model 4)	Natural resources conservation (Model 5)	Pollution management (Model 6)	Wildlife and habitat management (Model 7)
Constant	0.53 (0.051)[b]	0.89 (0.074)	0.091 (0.10)	0.56 (0.05)	0.62 (0.069)
Probability of participation	−0.053 (0.056)	−0.039 (0.083)**	0.29 (0.10)*	0.050 (0.053)	−0.082 (0.073)
N	348	348	348	348	348
−2 Log L	−609.8	−459.4	−74.8	−504.7	−140.2
χ^2	282.89**	362**	182.62**	174.31**	87.86**

[a] Additional independent variables included in the models (Federal government oversight and state environmental pressures) not shown.

[b] Standard errors are in parentheses.

* prob < 0.05; ** prob < 0.01.

evaluation contributes to the initial SSP assessment by showing a lack of statistical evidence suggesting that once enrolled and over time, enough participants improve their practices in agreed-upon SSP dimensions of environmental protection such as expansion management, pollution management, and wildlife and habitat management. Facing the SSP's weak institutional mechanisms for preventing opportunistic behavior, it appears that once enrolled, program participants may predominantly adopt those environmental management practices that are highly visible, such as recycling, or those that offer immediate short-term benefits with relatively small investments such as energy and water conservation (Porter and van der Linde, 1995; Walley and Whitehead, 1994).

To be sure, our findings suggest that compared to non-adopting ski areas, the only dimension of environmental protection for which SSP members seem to show a statistically significant improvement is natural resources conservation. This dimension includes recycling, energy, and water conservation practices (see Table 6.1) that profit-driven firms are more likely to adopt without a socialization process spurred by strong coercive and normative institutional pressures (Delmas, 2002; Hoffman, 1999; King and Lenox, 2000; Scott, 2001). On the other hand, the other three major dimensions of environmental protection involve practices that may not have evident short-term financial benefits, or as in the case of relatively more profitable pollution prevention measures, require larger financial investments that run against ski areas' capital budget constraints (Walley and Whitehead, 1994).

Regarding the control variables included in the environmental performance specifications, we found that ski areas' location on federal land or mixed land appears to have a statistically significant correlation with lower overall environmental performance (Model 3) and natural resource conservation performance (Model 5). In addition, location in mixed land also shows a significant correlation with lower wildlife and habitat management performance (Model 6). The coefficient on ownership by a publicly traded firm (Model 4) also indicates a statistically significant association with lower performance for expansion management. Finally, larger ski areas appear to have a statistically significant correlation with lower overall environmental performance ($P < 0.05$). Similarly, larger ski areas are significantly related to lower performance rates for expansion management (Model 4) and natural resource conservation (Model 5).

These findings for ski areas located on federal or mixed land were unexpected (Henriques and Sadorsky, 1996; Khanna, 2001). After all, ski areas occupying federal land administered by the USFS are periodically subjected to greater coercive institutional pressures in the form of enhanced government oversight through a Special Use Permit process. These Special Use Permits call for ski areas' operations and development plans to be consistent with USFS resource management plans and fee structures (Briggs, 2000; Clifford, 2002; Rivera and deLeon, 2004). Holding Special Use Permits also involves obtaining approval of Environmental Impact Statements for any new development.

Yet, the lower performance of ski areas occupying national forest lands may reflect weak institutional pressures that result from at least three contradictory mandates and conflict of interest conditions experienced by the USFS. For instance, as suggested in the previous chapter, the USFS has opposing mandates that require it to regulate ski areas' environmental impacts and concurrently promote ski industry growth. Second, promoting increasing economic activities on national forest land directly increases the hundreds of millions of dollars annually allocated to the off-budget trust funds sometimes used by the USFS to partially finance overhead expenses such as employee salaries (Dombeck, 2000; Gorte and Corn, 1995).[18] Third, the USFS is required by law to share 25 percent of its gross commercial revenue from national forests with local counties for roads and school financing (Rey, 2005; Gorte, 2000).[19] Accordingly, local western congressional representatives and county officials with national forest lands in their districts tend to actively advocate for increasing economic activities in national forests against the demands from environmentalists for reduced economic activity (Dombeck, 2000; Gorte, 2000; Rey, 2005). In addition, it can also be argued that the lack of exclusive private property rights intrinsic to ski areas located on federal land pre-empts any incentives that ski firms may have to engage in environmental protection practices that involve uncertain long-term benefits (Hardin, 1968; Olson, 1965; Ostrom, 1990).[20]

Despite the higher visibility of ski areas owned by publicly traded corporations, the lack of evidence linking them to higher scores for overall environmental performance, natural resources conservation, pollution management, and wildlife habitat management was not surprising. The same can be said of their significant association with lower expansion management performance. Wall Street does not exert normative environmental pressures on firms and instead focuses on demanding consistent double-digit increases in financial performance which, in the case of ski resorts, is accomplished by focusing on aggressive real-estate development and expansion activities that inherently have a negative impact on the environmental footprint of ski resorts (Hudson, 2000; Palmeri, 2003). The emphasis on quarterly profits also reduces the appeal of investments in other areas of environmental protection that involve uncertain long-term payoffs (Walley and Whitehead, 1994). We suggest that a similar underlying logic applies to the overall lower environmental performance shown by larger ski areas that are known for their aggressive focus on real-estate development around skiable terrain (Palmeri, 2003).

Conclusions

This study contributes to answering a basic issue regarding the use of VEPs as alternative environmental protection policy tools: *are voluntary programs effective in promoting higher environmental performance by participant firm facilities?* We also contribute to the literature by highlighting the importance of analyzing an additional issue related to the environmental policy effectiveness of voluntary environmental initiatives: *which distinct areas of environmental performance are more likely to be improved by firms joining a voluntary environmental program?* We addressed these two questions by assessing the implementation of the SSP in the western United States.

Consistent with neo-institutional theory, our findings indicate that participation in the SSP is related to coerceive and normative pressures in the form of enhanced federal oversight and higher state environmental demands exerted by state agencies, local environmental groups, and public opinion (Darnall, 2003a; Khanna, 2001; King and Lenox, 2000; Rivera, 2004). Additionally, our five-year study found no statistical evidence to conclude that compared to non-participants SSP ski areas have higher overall environmental performance or higher scores in the following individual dimensions of environmental protection: expansion management, pollution management, and wildlife and habitat management. SSP participants only appear to show a statistically significant correlation with higher natural resource conservation performance rates.

These findings are also consistent with the neo-institutional perspective argument that strictly voluntary initiatives that lack specific performance-based standards, third-party oversight, rewards for exceptional behavior, and/or sanctions for poor performance, are bound to suffer free-riding behavior because of their lack of robust institutional mechanisms that can differentiate between proactive and opportunistic participants (Hardin, 1968; King and Lenox, 2000; Olson, 1965; Ostrom, 1990; Rivera and deLeon, 2004; Scott, 2001; Williamson, 1975).

Facing SSP's weak institutional mechanisms for preventing opportunistic behavior, it appears that once enrolled, ski areas may predominantly adopt natural resources conservation practices that are known to be easier and more visible for their customers (such as recycling) or those that offer immediate short-term benefits with relatively small investment such as energy and water conservation (Porter and van der Linde, 1995; Walley and Whitehead, 1994). Unfortunately, without an effective institutional socialization process spurred by strong coercive and normative pressures, we found no evidence of similar adoption of practices affecting other major dimensions of environmental protection such as expansion management and wildlife habitat management. These other dimensions may not have evident short-term financial benefits or customer visibility, or as in the case of relatively more profitable pollution prevention measures require larger financial investments that run against firms' capital budget constraints (Delmas, 2002; Hoffman, 1999; King and Lenox, 2000; Scott, 2001; Walley and Whitehead, 1994).

For policymakers, the findings of this study suggest reservations about a priori assuming that strictly voluntary programs can be effective in promoting comprehensive superior environmental protection. Of course, given the limited nature of this particular inquiry, we cannot judge VEPs in general. However, we do present the distinct possibility that strictly voluntary environmental initiatives are much more problematic than their proponents would generalize. This research suggests caution for federal agencies about officially endorsing strictly voluntary environmental initiatives – such as the ski industry's SSP – that lack independent monitoring, performance standards, and any type of sanctions/rewards for poor/superior environmental performance.

Overall, the findings of this study suggest that by helping to improve the green image of the ski industry, the SSP creation and implementation contributed to delay for a couple of years the required adoption of new land use plans by the USFS (see previous chapter). Most importantly, for most national forests in the western US, the land use plans finally adopted reversed the planned restrictions to ski area expansion included in the USFS' preferred alternatives specified in the late 1990s. For example, in the case of Colorado's White River National Forest, the USFS' initial official preference was for the so-called Alternative D. This alternative intended to restrict ski area expansions to their current size and limit ski area use of water for snowmaking (Briggs, 2000; USFS, 2002). Yet, the land use plan finally adopted in mid-2002 (known as Alternative K), specifically allows expansion of ski areas consistent with population growth in Colorado and optimistic industry projections of future skier visits (USFS, 2002). Additionally, the Alternative K adopted also reverses the emphasis from ecosystem protection to promotion of recreation and other economic activities (USFS, 2002).

Finally, it is important to stress an important limitation of our study. Although the SACC environmental scorecard is the best available measure of ski areas' environmental performance, its validity has been strongly challenged by the NSAA. We repeatedly requested access to alternative environmental performance data collected by the SSP but NSAA officials denied us access to the data. In future studies in this area we hope researchers may be able to access these proprietary environmental performance data collected by the SSP or are able to use other alternative environmental performance measures.

Notes

1. This chapter is a slightly modified version of Rivera *et al.* (2006), reproduced with kind permission of the journal publishers and co-authors.
2. The previous chapter provides a detailed outline of a neo-institutional theory model of participation in voluntary programs that interested readers should examine. Khanna and Damon (1999) also develop an alternative model of voluntary participation in the initiatives.
3. As specified in the previous chapter of the book, strictly voluntary programs lack critically necessary conditions to reduce "free-riding" behavior by participant businesses. These necessary conditions are:
   (1) specific performance-based standards of environmental protection to be adopted by participant companies;

(2) periodic independent third-party audits that verify the adoption of these standards; and
(3) rewards and sanctions that publicly recognize the different levels of audited performance obtained by VEP participants.

4. Williamson (1975: 6) originally defined opportunism as "self-interest seeking with guile." He later characterized guile as "lying, stealing, cheating, and calculated efforts to mislead, distort, disguise, obfuscate, or otherwise confuse" (Williamson, 1985: 47).
5. Free-riding is understood as avoiding cooperating in the provision of a collectively produced good while expecting to derive individual benefit from it (Delmas and Keller, 2005; Olson, 1965).
6. The term skier visit refers to one skier or snowboarder visiting a resort for any portion of one day (NSAA, 2005b).
7. A fixed-effects model is inappropriate due to the time-invariant nature of some of the independent variables (Hsiao, 1986). A Housman test is normally used to select between fixed and random effects models for specification without time-invariant independent variables (Greene, 2000).
8. The MGLR technique is better suited to handle unbalanced panel data than the traditional generalized least squares techniques (Little, 1995; Rubin, 1976). This mixed linear regression methodology employs a maximum likelihood estimation approach and allows the unknown random error vector to exhibit both correlation and heterogeneous variances (Little, 1995).
9. We classified western ski areas as those located in the Rocky Mountains and Pacific West regions of the US.
10. The environmental criteria's underlying variables and the grading methodology are available online at www.skiareacitizens.com/criteria.html.
11. These government documents – available online at SACC's website – include, among others: USFS environmental impact statements, master development plans, expansion proposals, and forest management plan revisions; and also formal biological opinions prepared by the US Fish and Wildlife Service (SACC, 2005).
12. A quick Google search of the term "ski area environmental scorecard grades" generates links to over 200 stories and articles on the scorecard rankings and more than 500 hits.
13. Criteria left out involve for instance: opposing/supporting environmentally sound policy positions and those that in the early 2000s penalized ski areas for not responding to the SACC's annual survey.
14. Model 1 yields a slightly higher percentage of correctly classified participation decisions and it is used to estimate the values of ski areas' probability of participation in the SSP – one of the independent variables included in the second stage of the regression analysis. Calculating the probability

of participation with Model 1 also reduces the chance of overidentification since this model does not include all the same independent variables used in the second stage of the analysis (see note 6).

15. To assess heteroskedasticity problems in the probit models, we used the David and Mackinnon test: it did not indicate problems ($P<0.05$).
16. State location, the alternative measure of state environmental pressures used in Model 1, similarly suggests that domicile in states with lower environmental pressures, such as Idaho ($P<0.01$), New Mexico ($P<0.05$), Nevada ($P<0.01$), and Wyoming ($P<0.05$), is significantly related to lower participation in the SSP.
17. We thank one of the anonymous reviewers for requesting that we explore alternative model specifications that may have revealed the presence of identification problems in the second stage of analysis (see description of these possible problems in the methodology section of this article). To do so, we re-calculated all the second stage MGL regression models excluding the following independent variables: (1) ski area size; and (2) ownership by publicly traded firm. These two variables showed the highest collinearity with the probability of participation variable (inverse Mill's ratio) calculated in stage one and thus could have led to identification problems. See Table 6.6 for findings of alternative model specifications.

    With the exception of the expansion management regression (Model 4), all other models produced similar results for the probability of participation variable (our key independent variable of interest in the analysis). In the case of the expansion management regression, the new coefficient for the probability of participation variable shows a negative and significant association with the dependent variable (expansion management percentage score). This specific new finding actually suggests that in expansion-related practices, SSP participants have lower performance than non-participants.
18. Forest Service trust fund allocations are independent of the US Congress' annual appropriation process (Dombeck, 2000; Gorte and Corn, 1995).
19. Since 1908, the 25 Percent Fund Act (16 USC. sec. 500) has required these payments in lieu of property taxes (Rey, 2005).
20. We thank Nicole Darnall for pointing out this alternative explanation.
21. Model 1 is used to predict ski areas' probability of participation given that it has a higher percentage of correctly classified adoption decisions.

7 *Institutional pressures and proactive environmental protection: evidence from the Costa Rican hotel industry*[1]

A quick reading of Chapters 2–4 may lead to a broad conclusion: more business resistance can be expected in developing countries. However, the specific point highlighted by Chapters 3 and 4 is that differences in countries' context and firm characteristics affect the level of resistance/cooperation offered by the business to environmental and social protection demands. Indeed, relatively high levels of business cooperation can be observed in some developing countries. This chapter and the following seek to illustrate this point by focusing on the study of a voluntary environmental certification program for hotels – the Certification for Sustainable Tourism (CST) – launched in Costa Rica in 1997. This program was established to improve the environmental performance of the Costa Rican hotel industry and was developed and implemented by the Costa Rican government with direct cooperation of the business sector, environmentalists, and academics. Remarkably, this was done in the mid- to late-1990s when voluntary environmental certification programs were still an innovation in the US.

Costa Rica is a country whose leadership in environmental – and social – protection is hard to explain based solely on its gross national income per capita ($5,560 in 2007, ranking sixty-fourth in the world, according to the World Bank). This middle-income level is significantly lower than the level of other countries (such as, for example, Mexico, Botswana, Russia, and Libya) with considerably poorer records of environmental protection. I argue that the higher levels of business cooperation that have gone hand in hand with Costa Rica's environmental protection accomplishments and innovations can be explained in part by the country's long tradition of democracy, its neo-corporatist system of interest representation, and its willingness to experiment with some incentive-based regulations.

Despite the recent growth of the literature on voluntary environmental programs, very few articles have evaluated their implementation in developing countries (Andonova, 2003; Christmann and

Taylor, 2001; Rivera, 2002; Utting, 2002; Wehrmeyer and Mulugetta, 1999). In addition, empirical evidence is still contradictory about businesses' motivations for participating in voluntary programs and about the environmental effectiveness of these initiatives (Carmin *et al.*, 2003; Delmas, 2002; Khanna, 2001; Rivera, 2002). This chapter helps to address these gaps by evaluating how institutional factors are correlated with participation and environmental performance in the CST for 2000.

In particular, this chapter focuses on three research questions: (1) Are institutional pressures correlated with participation and higher environmental performance in voluntary environmental programs? (2) Is participation in voluntary programs related to superior beyond-compliance environmental performance? (3) Do foreign-owned facilities operating in developing countries show different environmental performance than local ones?

Results indicate that voluntary environmental programs, such as the CST, that include performance-based standards and third-party certification, may be effective in promoting beyond-compliance environmental behavior when they are complemented by institutional pressures exerted by government environmental monitoring and trade association membership. Surprisingly, findings also suggest that foreign-owned and multinational subsidiary hotels do not seem to be significantly correlated with higher CST participation and superior beyond-compliance environmental performance.

The Certification for Sustainable Tourism

In 1997, the Costa Rican Ministry of Tourism began organizing a voluntary environmental program for hotels, the Certification for Sustainable Tourism (CST). This voluntary initiative was conceived as an incentive-based alternative to address the increased environmental problems generated by the boom of tourism and hotel facilities in Costa Rica (Lizano, 2001). The rapid growth of visitors and hotel investment in Costa Rica has led to significant environmental problems around the most popular parks and beaches. Hotel construction and operations, in particular, are associated with the pollution of rivers and beaches, deforestation, and destruction of wetlands (Rivera, 2002, Stem *et al.*, 2003; Wildes, 1998; Weinberg *et al.*, 2002).

The CST program aims to ameliorate these ecological problems by certifying the adoption of beyond-compliance environmental practices. It is assumed that third-party certification of beyond-compliance environmental performance can allow participant hotels to gain higher sales and/or price premiums from environmentally aware consumers who visit Costa Rica. These financial benefits are expected to promote superior environmental performance by participant hotels. In 2002, I published a journal article that examines this issue for CST firms participating in 2000. Findings from this evaluation suggest that hotel room price premiums – but not higher sales – are correlated with higher certified environmental performance in CST (Rivera, 2002). Nonetheless, the causal nature of this correlation is not clear yet. More expensive hotels may simply have more resources to adopt the CST standards (Khanna, 2001; Rivera, 2002).

The CST certification process is carried out by third-party audit teams that assess hotel performance in four general areas of environmental management (see Table 7.1). A National Accreditation Board that includes representatives of the Ministry of Tourism, environmental organizations, the local hotel trade association, and academic institutions, is responsible for establishing the CST standards and overseeing the auditing process (Jones *et al.*, 2001; Rivera, 2002).

Like the general quality ratings that classify hotels from zero to five stars, the CST program rates hotel environmental performance by granting zero to five "green leaves" of beyond-compliance. At the beginning of 2002, nearly 200 hotels were participating in the CST and 54 had received certification on a first come first served basis.[2] Since its launching, the CST program has been used by the World Tourism Organization as a model for promoting the development of other programs aimed at certifying the environmental performance of hotels in other countries.

Tourism and the evolution of the Costa Rican hotel industry

Costa Rica is one of the best examples of a country that has become a popular tourist destination thanks to its political stability and an extensive system of national parks and reserves that cover about 25 percent of the country's territory (INCAE, 2002; Gentry, 1998). Opinion surveys consistently show that visiting the rainforest and observing biodiversity is regarded as one of the most important reasons to visit Costa Rica by more than 85 percent of tourists (INCAE,

Table 7.1 *CST general areas of beyond-compliance environmental protection**

(A) Management of hotel surrounding habitat
Policies and programs
Emissions and wastes
Gardens
Natural areas
Protection of flora and fauna
(B) Environmental management of hotel facilities
Formulation of policies
Water consumption
Energy consumption
General supplies consumption
Waste management
Employee training
(C) Guest environmental education
Communication of environmental programs
Room information and management
Incentives for environmental awareness
Measurement of environmental satisfaction
(D) Cooperation with local communities
Direct benefits to local communities
Indirect benefits to local communities
Contribution to local culture
Contribution to public health
Contribution to local infrastructure and safety

* *Source*: Rivera (2002).

2002; Rivera, 2002). Hotels located on the buffer zones of national parks own more than 70,000 acres of private reserves (Bien, 2000; Wildes, 1998).

In 2001, more than 1.1 million tourists visited Costa Rica, a fourfold increase since 1987. (In 2008, the number of visitors was about 2 million.) (ICT, 2002; 2009). This extraordinary rate of growth has made tourism one of the most important sectors of the Costa Rican economy. In 2001, hotels and other tourism-related businesses generated about 45 percent of total foreign revenue produced by Costa Rica (ICT, 2002). During the 1990s more than one-third of the foreign direct investment to the country, about $1.2 billion, was devoted to establishing hotels and related businesses (Rivera, 1998). About 2,000 hotels were operating in the country in 2001. (The number of hotels in 2008 was about 2,600.) (ICT, 2002; 2009). Remarkably, more than 75 percent of these hotels did not exist in the mid-1980s (ICT, 2002; INCAE, 2002). Most hotels are small, offer basic services, compete based on price, and are located close to national parks and beaches (Rivera, 2002). Specifically, in 2001, the average hotel size in Costa Rica was sixteen rooms and five-star hotels represented less than 2 percent of all facilities (ICT, 2002; INCAE, 2002). The impressive dynamic of the hotel industry in Costa Rica is both cause and effect of the existence and growth of a national park system that is possibly the best-managed in Latin America. This symbiotic relationship is remarkable for Costa Rica, a country that despite its outstanding environmental reputation has simultaneously experienced one of the highest deforestation rates in Latin America (Gentry, 1998).

Theory and hypotheses

As discussed in Chapter 5, a firm's enrollment in a voluntary environmental initiative is not only driven by financial considerations but also by the need to attain socially constructed environmental legitimacy. In this social process, different stakeholders exert coercive, normative, and mimetic institutional pressures that promote participation and isomorphic adoption of beyond-compliance environmental management practices. Consumers, government agencies, the media, industry associations, and environmental groups are usually the most influential stakeholders. Using institutional mechanisms such as public embarrassment, even voluntary initiatives that lack sanctions and third-party oversight may be able to motivate isomorphic adherence to beyond-compliance standards among participants (Delmas, 2002; Hoffman, 1999; King and Lenox, 2000). Additionally, most voluntary programs offer to provide technical assistance to facilitate the adoption of proactive environmental management practices by participant facilities. The following paragraphs use the ideas and propositions developed in Chapter 4 to generate hypotheses about specific factors and facility-level characteristics related to a higher likelihood of participation in voluntary programs and to higher beyond-compliance environmental performance. To avoid repetition, these hypotheses are limited to factors and facility-level characteristics not already addressed in Chapter 5. Specifically, although I include government monitoring and facility size in the regression analysis, no hypotheses are developed for them (see Chapter 5 pages 92–3).

Affiliation to industry trade associations. Previous research has found that firms that are members of trade associations face stronger normative and mimetic pressures to show exemplary environmental performance and to get involved in voluntary environmental initiatives that aim to promote proactive environmental management (Delmas, 2002; Garcia-Johnson, 2000; Grasmick *et al.*, 1991; Hoffman, 1999; King and Lenox, 2000). A few environmentally irresponsible facilities can significantly reduce the perceived environmental credibility of an entire industry. Hence, industry associations are increasingly promoting beyond-compliance standards and providing technical assistance to poorly performing facilities (King and Lenox, 2000; Tashman and Rivera, 2008). Trade groups have a significant interest in maintaining a positive industrywide environmental reputation to avoid increased scrutiny from environmentalists, the media, and regulators that may lead to the imposition of new regulations (King and Lenox, 2000). For instance, the main industry association of the hotel sector in Costa Rica has been an active supporter of the CST program. This reasoning suggests the following hypotheses:

Hypothesis 1: Industry association member facilities are more likely to participate in voluntary environmental programs.

Hypothesis 2: Trade association membership is positively related to beyond-compliance environmental performance.

Foreign-owned and multinational subsidiary facilities. Foreign-owned facilities and multinational subsidiaries are also more visible to local and international stakeholders, leading to heightened expectations and monitoring of their environmental practices (Christmann and Taylor, 2001; Wheeler, 1999). These facilities are also more likely to have easier access to cost-efficient pollution prevention technologies developed to respond to industrialized countries' stringent environmental standards (Christmann and Taylor, 2001; Wheeler, 1999). Hence, foreign-owned facilities and multinational subsidiaries can be expected to be more likely to participate in voluntary programs that promote the adoption of beyond-compliance standards

(Garcia-Johnson, 2000; Neumayer, 2001; Christmann and Taylor, 2001; Wheeler, 1999). On the other hand, foreign investors may participate in voluntary programs motivated to pre-empt mandatory command-and-control regulations (Christmann and Taylor, 2001; Garcia-Johnson, 2000). Drawing on the previous reasoning the following hypotheses can be proposed:

Hypothesis 3: *Foreign-owned facilities are more likely to participate in voluntary environmental programs.*

Hypothesis 4: *Foreign ownership is positively related to beyond-compliance environmental performance.*

Hypothesis 5: *Multinational subsidiary facilities are more likely to participate in voluntary environmental programs.*

Hypothesis 6: *Multinational subsidiary facilities show a positive relationship with beyond-compliance environmental performance.*

Research methodology

Data collection and sample

Following Dillman's Total Design Method (Dillman, 1978), I developed and pre-tested a survey questionnaire to gather information on hotels' basic characteristics. The top managers of 164 hotels operating in different regions of Costa Rica agreed to provide information and completed the survey during face-to-face interviews. This final sample of 164 included all 52 hotels that as of December 2000 had been audited and certified by the CST program. The other 112 hotels were obtained from a survey of a sample of 250 hotels (yielding a 44.8 percent response rate).[3] The 250 hotels surveyed were selected using stratified random sampling based on hotel geographic location.[4] Data collected about hotel basic characteristics (e.g., size, location, quality rating, and ownership) were verified using archival information available at the Costa Rican Chamber of Tourism, the Ministry of Tourism, and the Costa Rican Association of Small Hotels.

Data analysis

To test the hypotheses proposed, I used a recursive two-stage technique that combines probit and ordinary linear regression models to control for self-selection bias in the evaluation of voluntary social behavior (Greene, 2000; Maddala, 1986). This technique, originally developed by Heckman (1978), is the standard statistical methodology used to assess benefits of participation in voluntary environmental programs (Hartman, 1988; Khanna and Damon, 1999; Rivera, 2002; Welch *et al.*, 2000). Controlling for self-selection bias is necessary because firms that anticipate higher benefits from joining a voluntary initiative are also expected to be more likely to participate (Hartman, 1988; Heckman, 1978; 1979; Khanna and Damon, 1999; Maddala, 1986). In other words, the decision to participate and its outcome are endogenous variables jointly determined by similar factors (Greene, 2000). Evaluations that do not consider the impact of self-selectivity bias are likely to overestimate the benefits of participation in voluntary programs (Greene, 2000; Hartman, 1988; Khanna and Damon, 1999; Maddala, 1986).

In the first stage of the regression analysis a probit model identifies variables significantly related to participation (Khanna and Damon, 1999; Maddala, 1986). This probit model is also used to estimate the probability of participation for each hotel. In the second stage, an ordinary linear regression (OLS) models the environmental performance of hotels certified by the CST program. To control for self-selection bias the OLS regression includes as one of its independent variables the probability of participation estimates calculated during the first stage of the analysis (Khanna and Damon, 1999; Maddala, 1986).

Variable measures

Variable metrics are described in the order in which they appear in the theory section, beginning with dependent variables and following with independent ones.

Participation in the CST program. This variable was coded using a dummy variable, with a value of one for hotels enrolled in the CST program by December 2000 and zero otherwise.

Beyond-compliance environmental performance. Lack of available data on firms' environmental performance is a pervasive problem in developing countries (Utting, 2002). There is little agreement about appropriate measures and existing publicly available data is generally self-reported (Rivera, 2002; Wheeler, 1999). The CST program has probably generated the first third-party database on beyond-compliance environmental performance for service sector firms operating in a developing country.

For the purpose of this research, I used CST percentage scores as a measure of hotel beyond-compliance environmental performance. The CST program certifies hotels based on 153 beyond-compliance standards divided into four general areas of environmental protection that include: (1) management of surrounding habitat; (2) management of hotel facilities; (3) guest environmental education programs; and (4) cooperation with local communities (see Table 7.1).

Each CST standard assesses adoption of a specific environmental practice and contributes one to three points to the final CST certification score depending on its level of importance assigned by the CST National Accreditation Commission. The final CST percentage score received by each hotel is calculated by computing the coefficient between its total adoption score for all CST standards and its maximum possible score to yield percentage performance rates (Jones *et al.*, 2001; Rivera, 2002).

Trade association membership was identified using a dummy variable equal to one for members of the main hotel industry association, the Costa Rican Chamber of Tourism, and zero otherwise.

Foreign ownership (foreign investors) was measured by a dummy variable equal to one for hotels with majority ownership by foreign investors and zero otherwise.

Multinational subsidiaries were coded using a dummy variable equal to one for those facilities that were either owned or managed by an international chain of hotels (e.g., Marriott, Best Western, Spanish Barceló) and zero otherwise.

Government monitoring. Hotel location, classified as park, beach, and city, was used as a proxy for the different levels of government monitoring faced by hotel facilities. Park and beach categories included those hotels situated within ten miles of a national park or the beach respectively. City hotels were those operating in the greater metropolitan area of the Costa Rican capital (San Jose). Previous research in Costa Rica suggests that the level of environmental monitoring for hotels is higher for hotels located close to national parks, medium for hotels located in the greater metropolitan area of San Jose, and lower for hotels situated close to the beach (Ascher, 1999; Boo, 1990; Farrell and Marion, 2001; Honey, 1999; Jones *et al.*, 2001; Rivera, 2002; Steinberg, 2001; Stem *et al.*, 2003; Weinberg *et al.*, 2002; Wildes, 1998).

Nevertheless, it is important to highlight that hotel location can also be an indicator of the main segment of consumers demanding the services of a hotel.[5] Park hotels accommodate mainly eco-tourists, whereas beach and city hotels also serve leisure and business travelers (INCAE, 2002). Ideally, a better measure of government monitoring should have been used. However, the lack of consistent and reliable data prevented the use of a better indicator.

Hotel size (size) was measured as the logarithm of the number of hotel rooms.

Hotel quality (quality) was measured using the number of "stars" assigned to each hotel by the Costa Rican Ministry of Tourism based on international quality standards developed by Triple A, Mobil, and Michelin. Controlling for hotel quality is important because of previous evidence in the literature suggesting a link between a firm's general quality standards and its environmental performance standards (Arora and Cason, 1996; Khanna, 2001; Lyon and Maxwell, 2002).

Results and discussion

Descriptive statistics

Frequency distributions, cross-tabulations and comparison of means by CST participation are displayed in Table 7.2. This table provides initial evidence that CST participation is associated with: affiliation with a multinational subsidiary, higher hotel quality, larger hotel size, and trade association membership. Of course, these results are preliminary because they identify linear relationships and do not control for other independent variables included in the model (Greene, 2000). The probit regression analysis described in the following section corrects for this limitation (Aldrich and Nelson, 1984).

Participation in the CST program

Model 1 in Table 7.3 presents the findings of the probit analysis of hotel participation in the CST program. This model shows a statistically significant overall fit ($p < 0.05$) and correctly classifies 87.8 percent of the decision to participate in the CST program. As expected, more expensive, higher-quality hotels are positively correlated with participation in the CST program.

Table 7.2 *Frequency distributions and comparison of means by CST status*

Variable		Total sample		Not participating in the CST		Participating in the CST	
		N	Percent	N	Percent	N	Percent
CST participation (percent)				97	59.15	67	40.85
Environmental performance	0 to 20					0	0
	>20 to 40					10	19.23
	>40 to 60					21	40.38
	>60 to 80					16	30.77
	>80 to 100					5	9.62
	Total					52	100
	Mean						56.48 (15.60)[a]
	Non-CST certified					15	
Foreign investors	No	83	50.61	52	53.61	31	46.27
	Yes	78	47.57	44	45.36	34	50.75
	Missing data	3	1.83	1	1.03	2	2.99
	Total	164	100	97	100	67	100
							χ^2: 1.491
Multinational subsidiary	No	154	93.90	96	99.0	58	86.6
	Yes	10	6.10	1	1	9	13.4
	Total	164	100	97	100	67	100
						χ^2:10.645**	

Location:	Beach	44	26.8	31	32	13	19.4
	City	32	19.5	16	16.5	16	23.9
	Park	88	53.7	50	51.5	38	56.7
	Total	164	100	97	100	67	100
						χ^2: 2.438	
Quality (# of stars):	0	76	46.3	66	68	10	14.9
	1	3	1.8	2	2.1	1	1.5
	2	7	4.3	3	3.1	4	6
	3	53	32.3	20	20.6	33	49.2
	4	23	14	6	6.2	17	25.4
	5	2	1.2	0	0	2	3
	Total	164	100	97	100	67	100
						χ^2: 48.318***	
	Mean	1.69 (1.67)		0.95 (1.45)		2.78 (1.34)	
						t-test: –8.16***	
Size (# of rooms):	0 to 10	42	25.8	37	38.1	5	7.5
	>10 to 20	44	27	29	29.9	15	22.4
	>20 to 30	37	22.7	18	18.6	19	28.4
	>30 to 40	15	9.2	8	8.2	7	10.4

Table 7.2 *(cont.)*

Variable		Total sample		Not participating in the CST		Participating in the CST	
		N	Percent	N	Percent	N	Percent
Size (# of rooms)(*cont.*):	>40 to 50	7	4.3	2	2.1	5	7.5
	>50 to 100	9	5.5	1	1	8	11.9
	>100	9	5.5	2	2.1	7	10.4
	Missing data	1	0.6	0		1	1.5
	Total	164	100	97	100	67	100
						χ^2: 33.665***	
	Mean	31.08 (41.68)		19.82 (25.77)		47.62 (53.67)	
						t-test: −4.41***	
Trade association	No	133	81.1	91	93.8	42	62.7
Membership	Yes	31	18.9	6	6.2	25	37.3
	Total	164	100	97	100	67	100
						χ^2: 25.048***	

* prob < 0.10; ** prob < 0.05; *** prob < 0.01.

[a] Standard deviations are in parentheses.

Table 7.3 *Regression results*

Model 1: probit regression (dependent variable: participation in the CST)[11]		Model 2: OLS regression (dependent variable: CST environmental performance)[12]	
Constant	-2.613*** (0.646)[a]	Constant	38.176** (2.65)[b]
Foreign investors	0.043 (0.256)	Foreign investors	5.404 (1.26)
Location:		Location:	
City	0.036 (0.382)	City	19.776*** (3.60)
Park	0.873*** (0.325)	Park	26.565*** (2.99)
Multinational subsidiary	0.343 (0.664)	Multinational subsidiary	-0.514 (-0.08)
		Probability of participation	-55.988* (-1.85)
Quality	0.400*** (0.099)	Quality	5.582 (1.41)
Size	0.325* (0.193)	Size	2.567 (0.56)
Trade association membership	1.00*** (0.379)	Trade association membership	22.888** (2.38)
N	159	N	49
-2 Log L	139.954	F-Value	2.78**
χ^2 for covariates	77.987***	R2	0.36
Percent correctly classified	87.8	Adj-R2	0.23

[a] Probit Model 1: standard errors are in parentheses.
[b] OLS Model 2: t-values are in parentheses.
* prob<0.10; ** prob<0.05; *** prob<0.01.

The results suggest that compared to beach hotels, park hotels facing higher government monitoring appear to be significantly correlated with higher probability of participation in the CST program ($p<0.05$). These findings suggest that institutional pressures directly wielded by the government may play an important role in promoting adoption of voluntary environmental programs. The interpretation of this finding is limited, however, by the fact that hotel location can also be an indicator of tourist preferences. Thus, the statistical significance of this finding may also reflect higher demands for environmental protection by "green" tourists visiting national parks.[5]

Also, as expected, trade association membership (Hypothesis 1) seems to show a positive and statistically significant relationship with the CST program adoption ($p < 0.05$). This outcome implies that normative institutional pressures exerted by the Costa Rican Chamber of Tourism may be linked to higher probability of participation in voluntary environmental initiatives, such as the CST program (Cashore and Vertinsky, 2000; Delmas, 2002; Hoffman, 1999; King and Lenox, 2000; Rivera, 2002).

Larger hotels as well appear to show a significant association with a higher probability to participate in this program, although this relationship is statistically significant only at the 90 percent confidence level ($p < 0.1$). This result suggests that increased facility visibility generated by larger size may not attract institutional pressures as strong as those generated by park location and trade association membership.

Surprisingly, foreign-owned facilities (Hypothesis 3) and those affiliated with multinational hotel chains (Hypothesis 5) do not seem to have a significantly higher probability of participation in the CST program than locally owned hotels ($p < 0.05$). These findings suggest that in the future, as more foreign-owned and multinational chain hotels are established in Costa Rica, significantly stronger institutional pressures from government, environmentalists, the industry association, and other stakeholders, may be necessary to promote participation in the CST program. Otherwise, adoption of the CST program may decrease.

The lack of support for Hypotheses 3 and 5 also challenges the conventional wisdom about the behavior of foreign-owned and multinational subsidiary facilities operating in developing countries (Delmas, 2002; Garcia-Johnson, 2000; Neumayer, 2001; Christmann and Taylor, 2001; Wheeler, 1999). Supporters of this conventional wisdom posit that easier access to innovative pollution prevention technology and enhanced scrutiny by international and local stakeholders leads foreign-owned and multinational subsidiary facilities to be more likely to participate in voluntary environmental programs (Garcia-Johnson, 2000; Neumayer, 2001; Christmann and Taylor, 2001; Wheeler, 1999).

Different explanations can be offered to elucidate these surprising results. First, given their greater access to information, managers of foreign-owned and multinational subsidiary facilities may be more aware of the CST program's implementation costs than managers of local hotels (Rivera, 2002). Second, because of their longer experience in adopting global environmental standards, such as ISO-14001, some multinational and foreign-owned hotels may prefer to adopt these better-known and more lax international standards than the CST standards (Delmas, 2002). Additionally, multinational and foreign-owned hotels may have greater resources than local hotels to fend off institutional pressures from international and local stakeholders to signal their "greenness" by adopting the CST program (Christmann and Taylor, 2001; Darnall, 2001; King and Shaver, 2001).[6]

To explain these surprising results, in-depth personal interviews were conducted with the general managers of large international chain hotels. These hotels are predominantly located in the metropolitan area of San Jose, the Costa Rican capital. They include hotels such as Marriott, Intercontinental, and Spanish-owned Melia and Barceló. Managers of these hotels agreed that the CST program could probably help to improve the environmental reputation of their hotels. However, they argued that it was too expensive to adopt CST standards. Most importantly, these managers were not convinced of the appeal of "green" reputations to business travelers, their main customer base.

Beyond-compliance environmental performance

Results of the environmental performance OLS regression are displayed in Table 7.3, Model 2.[7] The overall model fit tests indicate that the independent variables significantly account for 23 percent of the variance in environmental performance (adjusted R-square = 0.23; $p<0.05$).

Model 2's findings suggest that, after controlling for other factors, park hotels and trade association membership (Hypothesis 2) are significantly associated with higher CST environmental scores ($p<0.05$). These results highlight, as predicted by institutional theory, that higher government monitoring pressures and normative industry association influences tend to not only be associated with higher CST participation but are also related to superior beyond-compliance environmental performance.

City hotels also appear to be significantly correlated with higher CST scores than beach hotels ($p<0.05$). A preliminary analysis of the CST program has suggested that city hotels exhibit higher environmental performance because they have easier access to environmental management expertise and resources (Jones *et al.*, 2001). City hotels may also exhibit higher CST scores because their location in the metropolitan area of San Jose imposes enhanced demands for isomorphic environmental management behavior from government agencies, environmentalists, the media, and other stakeholders headquartered in San Jose. Model 2 also indicates that hotel quality is positively, but not significantly, correlated with CST environmental performance scores ($p<0.1$). This finding suggests that higher quality hotels may only be adopting the CST program symbolically with little intention of actually improving their beyond-compliance environmental performance.

Surprisingly, hotel size does not appear to be significantly correlated with higher CST environmental performance scores ($p<0.05$). These results provide additional support to suggest that in Costa Rica the increased visibility of larger hotel facilities may not yet attract enough institutional pressures from government agencies and other stakeholders to promote significant adoption of beyond-compliance environmental practices. This result is also surprising given that larger facilities are known to enjoy economies of scale in the adoption of superior environmental management practices (Delmas, 2002; Hettige *et al.*, 1996; King and Lenox, 2000; Khanna and Damon, 1999).

Foreign-owned (Hypothesis 4) and multinational subsidiary hotels (Hypothesis 6) do not exhibit a statistically significant relationship to higher beyond-compliance environmental performance ($p<0.05$). Moreover, the regression coefficient for multinational chain hotels seems to indicate a negative relationship to CST environmental scores. These unexpected findings may be attributed to the wide variance in beyond-compliance behavior exhibited by facilities included in these two hotel categories. To be sure, some of the hotels with the highest CST environmental scores are either foreign-owned or multinational subsidiaries. Yet, some foreign-owned and multinational subsidiary hotels in the sample also receive very low CST environmental scores.

These results are surprising given that foreign-owned facilities, and particularly multinational subsidiaries, are thought to face higher institutional environmental demands from stakeholders (Christmann and Taylor, 2001; Garcia-Johnson, 2000; King and Shaver, 2001; Wheeler, 1999). They are also known for having more resources and easier access to environmental expertise available in the international markets (Christmann and Taylor, 2001; Garcia-Johnson, 2000; King and Shaver, 2001; Wheeler, 1999).

Multinational and foreign-owned hotels displaying lower environmental performance than locally owned hotels may be opportunistically participating in the CST program trying to improve their "green" reputation without significantly improving their environmental practices. Follow-up interviews with the general managers of these low-performing hotels tend to indicate that they decided to participate in the CST to avoid increased monitoring and more stringent regulations. These managers appear to perceive the CST program as a preferred yet expensive alternative to more rigorous environmental regulations and monitoring.

Recent facility-level empirical studies implemented in other developing countries suggest that this mixed environmental performance behavior is not unique to the Costa Rican hotel industry. Evidence from manufacturing facilities in South and Southeast Asia (Hettige *et al.*, 1996; Pargal and Wheeler, 1996), Korea (Aden *et al.*, 1999), and Mexico (Dasgupta *et al.*, 2000) indicate lack of statistically significant association between foreign ownership and superior environmental performance.[8]

Finally, the probability of participation variable derived from the probit model (Model 1) and included in the OLS regression (Model 2) to control for self-selection bias suggests a negative association with CST environmental performance scores. This association is, nevertheless, statistically significant only at the 90 percent confidence level ($p<0.1$). This finding implies that of the CST-certified hotels, those with higher predicted probability of participation appear to be significantly correlated with lower levels of CST environmental performance scores. For some hotels that enrolled in the program and expected to receive high CST scores, these results could indicate a lack of environmental management expertise and resources to keep up with the paperwork and management changes required by the CST. In fact, absence of technical assistance was a common complaint expressed by the hotel managers interviewed for this study. On the other hand, this result also suggests opportunistic behavior by some hotel facilities that expect to improve their "green" reputation without actually adopting the environmental management practices required by the CST program.

Conclusions

The literature on voluntary environmental programs suggests that short-term financial incentives are correlated with proactive environmental behavior by businesses (Andrews, 1998; Khanna, 2001; Rivera, 2002). Following a similar logic, previous research based in Costa Rica suggests that this country's exceptional national park system and growing ecotourism industry generates economic incentives that can promote beyond-compliance environmental protection (Boo, 1990; Gentry, 1998; Honey, 1999; Rivera, 2002; Weinberg *et al*, 2002). My initial assessment of the CST program suggests that hotel room price premiums are both cause and effect of higher certified environmental performance in this program (Rivera, 2002).

Using the neo-institutional theory framework developed in the initial chapters of the book, this study contributes to this literature by suggesting that the CST program may not work effectively despite being correlated with market incentives and involving third-party oversight and performance-based standards. To effectively promote voluntary environmental behavior, the CST program appears to require the complement of coercive institutional pressures in the form of government environmental monitoring and normative pressures arising from industry association membership. Findings of this study suggest that these coercive and normative institutional pressures are significantly correlated with a higher likelihood of participation and higher environmental performance in the CST. In sum, besides market incentives, this study suggests that institutional pressures may also be necessary conditions for making the CST program an effective policy instrument for promoting beyond-compliance environmental behavior by hotels.

In addition, this chapter contributes to the research examining the environmental performance of multinational and foreign-owned businesses in developing countries. Despite some exceptional cases, findings suggest that multinational subsidiary and foreign-owned hotels do not exhibit significantly higher participation and superior environmental performance in the CST program than locally owned facilities.[9] For multinational hotel chain facilities these results are startling given their greater resources, easier access to technology, and longer experience responding to stronger institutional pressures wielded by international environmental organizations, the media, and more stringent home-country environmental regulations (Christmann and Taylor, 2001; Weinberg *et al.*, 2002; Wheeler, 1999; 2001). These findings indicate that stronger institutional pressures by the government and other stakeholders may be necessary to assure that foreign-owned and multinational subsidiary hotels operating in Costa Rica bring with them advanced environmental management technologies and show superior environmental performance than domestic firms.

Although the evidence from this single case study cannot be extended to other nations, policymakers trying to promote the use of voluntary programs in other developing countries need to be aware that even in the case of Costa Rica, where the hotel industry is mainly driven by ecotourism, the superior environmental performance of foreign-owned and/or multinational facilities cannot be taken for granted. To be sure, some multinationals and foreign investors have played a remarkable leadership role in supporting the creation of the CST program and have displayed some of the highest beyond-compliance environmental performances. However, other multinational subsidiaries and foreign-owned facilities have also shown more reactive environmental behavior displaying little interest in adopting the CST program or participating in it for opportunistic reasons.

Limitations and future research

The discussion of results and the conclusions from this chapter need to be considered in the context of five important limitations. First, social desirability and common variance problems could have been generated by the use of a survey instrument to collect data on hotel basic characteristics (Pedhazur and Schmelkin, 1991). To minimize this problem, the survey information collected was triangulated with archival data available at the Ministry of Tourism and the Costa Rican Chamber of Tourism. Second, despite the statistical significance of the regression models, it is important to highlight that the relatively small sample size involved in the analysis limits the precision of the findings.[10] In the future, as the CST program expands, additional assessments need to take advantage of the availability of new data to use a larger sample of hotels. Third, the use of cross-sectional data precludes identification of any causal relationships between institutional pressures exerted over hotels and their participation and environmental performance in the CST program. Future research needs to collect longitudinal data to determine the causality of the relationships identified here. Fourth, some of the measures of institutional pressures analyzed in this study are evidently rudimentary as in the case of using hotel location as an indicator of government monitoring. Future studies may be able to overcome this problem as new databases are generated in Costa Rica and other developing countries. Finally, the generalizability of the findings to other nations and other voluntary programs is prevented by the exclusive focus of this study on the implementation of the CST program in Costa Rica. Additional assessment of voluntary programs implemented in other countries and other industries is clearly necessary. Despite these limitations, I hope that this study can provide initial guidance to the policymakers in charge of expanding the CST program to other developing countries.

Notes

1. This chapter includes a slightly modified version of Rivera (2004), reproduced with kind permission of the journal publishers.
2. Certification results and CST ratings can be accessed online at: www.turismo-sostenible.co.cr/.
3. Using power analysis and assuming "small" effect size for the independent variables, it was determined that a minimum sample of 138 observations was necessary to have an 80 percent chance of rejecting a false null hypothesis at 95 percent confidence (Cohen and Cohen, 1983: 59).
4. No comprehensive list of all the hotels operating in Costa Rica was found. Thus, a sample frame list including 649 hotels was prepared. Sources of information consulted for building the sample frame included: archival data available at the Ministry of Tourism; the Costa Rican Chamber of Tourism; the Association of Small Hotels; the 2000 Costa Rican Phone Directory; and the most popular travel guides to Costa Rica. The travel guides consulted were: *A New Key to Costa Rica* (Blake and Becker, 1998); *The Berkeley Guide to Central America* (Nystrom and Smith, 1996); *Lonely Planet* (Rachowiecki, 1997); and *Fodor's Costa Rica 99* (Rockwood, 1998). Subsequently, I categorized the sample frame list into six geographic groups and randomly drew observations from each group to build a survey sample of 250 hotels.
5. The author thanks one of the anonymous reviewers for highlighting the limitations of using hotel location as a measure for government monitoring.
6. I am grateful to an anonymous reviewer for pointing out this alternative explanation.
7. *OLS regression model.* Condition index and variance inflation measures for the independent variables revealed weak to moderate dependencies among the independent variables. Hence, it was concluded that harmful multicollinearity did not affect the regression (Belsley, *et al.*, 1980: 105). Lack of heteroscedasticity was also determined by White's chi-square test (White, 1980).

8. Two studies assessing participation in ISO-14001 and the chemical industry's Responsible Care Program have found that multinational subsidiaries operating in China, Mexico, and Brazil are more likely to participate in voluntary environmental programs (Christmann and Taylor, 2001; Garcia-Johnson, 2000). It is important to note, however, that ISO-14001 and Responsible Care lack performance-based standards and do not required third-party overseeing of the environmental behavior of participants.
9. These exceptional cases include five foreign-owned or multinational subsidiary hotels that have received some of the highest CST environmental scores.
10. An increase in sample size (assuming no change in population standard deviation) results in a decrease of the standard error, thereby affording more precise estimates (Pedhazur and Schmelkin, 1991).
11. Diagnostic tests (hat matrix, dffits and dfbetas, studentized residual) and index plots identified two influential outlier observations that were dropped from the sample (Belsley *et al.*, 1980; Pregibon, 1981). Also, three observations had missing data and were excluded from analysis.
12. OLS regression model (see Model 2, Table 7.3). Three observations had missing data and were excluded from analysis. Ownership was missing for two hotels and size was also missing for another hotel.

8 Chief executive officers and proactive environmental protection: evidence from the Costa Rican hotel industry[1]

In developing countries, policymakers and officials from donor agencies have repeatedly stressed the importance of formal education and technical assistance to promote enhanced environmental protection by the private sector (Ascher, 1999; Wheeler, 1999). It has been argued that businesses would significantly improve their environmental performance if their managers were more educated and knew about innovative pollution prevention technologies that make their firms more competitive by being "green," that is, manifesting an environmental conscience (Porter and van der Linde, 1996). By much the same argument, businesses run by managers born in industrialized countries are also expected to display higher environmental performance as one way to highlight their competitive advantage (Christmann and Taylor, 2001; Wheeler, 1999). Foreign chief executive officers (CEOs) may be more likely to adopt proactive environmental efforts because of their increased awareness of international environmental requirements and easier access to environmental management information (Christmann and Taylor, 2001; Garcia-Johnson, 2000; Wheeler, 1999). Yet, there is scant empirical evidence that higher education, greater environmental management expertise, and CEO nationality are correlated with superior environmental performance by businesses operating in the developing world (Andonova, 2003; Ascher, 1999; Christmann and Taylor, 2001; Utting, 2002).

This chapter seeks to contribute to filling this gap by evaluating whether CEOs' education, environmental expertise, and nationality are associated with enhanced participation and environmental performance in voluntary programs. Data were collected from the Certification for Sustainable Tourism (CST) program in 2000 (see a detailed description of the CST and the hotel industry in Costa Rica in Chapter 7). This additional assessment of CST relies directly upon the conceptual arguments developed in Chapter 4 about the association between environmental performance and the following CEOs' demographic characteristics: (1) formal education level; (2) academic major in college; and (3) advanced industrialized country nationality. (To see the specific arguments, please see pages 81–3 in Chapter 4; to avoid repetition, these arguments are not included here.) The behavioral focus on top hotel managers complements Chapter 7's assessment of the institutional pressures associated with hotel participation and environmental performance in the CST program. We first present the methodology and results, before discussing the results and offering a set of conclusions.

Methods

Data collection

Following Dillman's Total Design Method (Dillman, 1978), we developed and pre-tested a survey questionnaire to gather information on CEO demographics and hotels' basic characteristics. Results of a power analysis indicated that a sample of at least 138 observations was necessary to have an 80 percent chance of rejecting a false null hypothesis at 95 percent confidence (Cohen and Cohen, 1983).[2] Seeking to reach this minimum sample size, we identified two groups of hotels. First, we contacted and collected information from all 52 hotels that as of December 2000 had been audited and certified by the CST program. Second, we contacted a control group of 250 hotels. This control group was selected using stratified random sampling based on hotel geographic location.[3] Of the 250 control group hotels, 112 provided information.[4] Thus, from 302 hotels contacted, a total of 164 provided information during face-to-face interviews, yielding an overall 54.3 percent response rate. Data collected about hotel basic characteristics (e.g., size, location, quality rating, and ownership) were verified using archival information available at the Costa Rican Chamber of Tourism, the Ministry of Tourism, and the Costa Rican Association of Small Hotels.

Data analysis

To test the proposed hypotheses, a recursive two-stage technique was used that combines probit and ordinary linear regression models to control for self-selection bias in the evaluation of voluntary social behavior (Greene, 2000; Maddala, 1986). This technique, originally developed by Heckman (1978), is the standard statistical methodology used to assess benefits of participation in voluntary environmental programs (Hartman, 1988; Khanna and Damon, 1999; Rivera, 2002; Welch *et al.*, 2000). Controlling for self-selection bias is necessary because firms that anticipate higher benefits from joining a voluntary initiative are also expected to be more likely to participate (Hartman, 1988; Heckman, 1978; 1979; Khanna and Damon, 1999; Maddala, 1986). In other words, the decision to participate and its outcome are endogenous variables jointly determined by similar factors (Greene, 2000). Evaluations that do not consider the impact of self-selection bias are likely to overestimate the benefits of participation in voluntary programs (Greene, 2000; Hartman, 1988; Khanna and Damon, 1999; Maddala, 1986).

In the first stage of the regression analysis, a probit model identifies variables significantly related to participation in the CST program (Khanna and Damon, 1999; Maddala, 1986). This probit model is also used to estimate the probability of participation for each hotel. In the second stage, an ordinary linear regression (OLS) models the environmental performance of hotels certified by the CST program. To control for self-selection bias, the OLS regression includes the probability of participation estimates calculated during the first stage of the analysis as one of its independent variables (Khanna and Damon, 1999; Maddala, 1986).

Variable measurements

Variable metrics are described in the order in which they appear in the preceding theory section of this paper, beginning with dependent variables and following with independent ones. *Participation in the CST program*, the dependent variable for the probit model, was coded using a dummy variable equal to one for hotels enrolled in the CST program by December 2000 and zero otherwise. *Beyond-compliance environmental performance*, the OLS model dependent variable, was measured using percentage scores assigned by the CST program. The CST program has probably generated the first third-party database on beyond-compliance environmental performance for service sector firms operating in a developing country. It certifies hotels based on

153 beyond-compliance standards divided into four general areas of environmental protection that include: (1) management of surrounding habitat; (2) management of hotel facilities; (3) guest environmental education programs; and (4) cooperation with local communities (Jones *et al.*, 2001).

Each CST standard assesses adoption of a specific environmental practice and contributes one to three points to the final CST certification score, depending on its level of importance assigned by the CST National Accreditation Commission. The final CST percentage score received by each hotel is calculated by computing the coefficient between its total adoption score for all CST standards and its maximum possible score, to yield percentage performance rates (Jones *et al.*, 2001; Rivera, 2002).[5]

Key independent variables were measured as follows: *Hotel CEO education* was measured using dummy variables to identify different ascending levels of formal education received: high school degree, some college education, college degree, and graduate degree. *Hotel CEO major in college and graduate school* was also identified by creating discrete dummy variables for the following areas of specialization: business administration; hotel-tourism management; humanities; environmental management; and social sciences. *Manager nationality* was coded as one for CEOs from industrialized countries and zero for CEOs from Costa Rica and other developing countries.

Other CEO demographic characteristics used as control variables were measured in the following ways: *age* was quantified in years, *gender* was coded as a dummy (1 = female, 0 = male), and *income* was measured in annual earnings in US dollars. We also controlled for a variety of hotel basic characteristics used in previous assessments of the CST program (Rivera, 2002; 2004). *Foreign ownership (foreign investors)* was measured by a dummy variable equal to one for hotels with majority ownership by foreign investors and zero otherwise. *Hotel location* was classified using dummy variables for park, beach, and city hotels. Park and beach categories included those hotels situated within ten miles of a national park or the beach, respectively. City hotels were those operating in the greater metropolitan area of the Costa Rican capital (San Jose). *Multinational subsidiaries* were coded using a dummy variable equal to one for those facilities that were either owned or managed by an international chain of hotels and zero otherwise. *Hotel general quality (quality)* was measured using the number of Michelin-type "stars" (*not* CST "green leaves") assigned to each hotel by the Costa Rican Ministry of Tourism based on international quality standards developed by Triple A, Mobil, and Michelin.[6] *Hotel size (size)* was measured as the logarithm of the number of hotel rooms. *Trade association membership* was identified using a dummy variable equal to one for members of the main hotel industry association, the Costa Rican Chamber of Tourism, and zero otherwise.

Findings[7]

Frequency distribution and other descriptive statistics for CST participation, environmental performance, and CEO demographics are displayed in Table 8.1. About 41 percent of the hotels included in the sample participated in the CST program. The average environmental performance for hotels that have received third-party certification was 56.48 percent adoption of CST standards, with about 40 percent of the certified hotels showing higher environmental performance than this average. For the overall sample, about 53 percent of the hotel CEOs had a college degree and about an additional 5 percent held a graduate degree. These proportions increased for CST certified hotels to 80 percent of CEOs with a college degree and an additional 14 percent of CEOs with a graduate degree.

Table 8.2 provides the frequency distributions for the academic major pursued by CEOs and also their specific nationalities. Business administration (15 percent) and hotel-tourism management (11.88 percent) appear to be the most popular academic majors pursued by hotel CEOs with a college degree. Only about 6 percent of the CEOs with a college degree majored in environmental management. In graduate school, humanities becomes the area of study pursued by the largest percentage (2.44 percent) of hotel top managers, business administration is second highest (1.83 percent). None of the top managers pursued a graduate degree in environmental management studies. Approximately 70 percent of the hotel CEOs were from Costa Rica, about 25 percent from industrialized countries, and the remaining 5 percent originated from other countries in Latin America.

Table 8.1 *Frequency distributions*

	Full sample		CST certified*	
Variable	N	Percent	N	Percent
Dependent variables				
CST participation				
Not enrolled	97	59.15		
Enrolled	67	40.85		
Total	164	100		
Environmental performance[a] (percent of compliance with CST standards)				
0 to 20%			0	0
>20 to 40			10	19.23
>40 to 60			21	40.38
>60 to 80			16	30.77
>80 to 100			5	9.62
Total			52	100
Mean			56.48 (15.60)[b]	
Hotel CEOs' demographics				
Age				
20 to 29	26	16.05	7	14
30 to 39	58	35.80	19	38
40 to 49	38	23.46	13	26
50 to 59	26	16.05	10	20
60 or older	14	8.64	1	2
Total	162	100	50	100
Mean	41.36 (11.82)		41.06 (9.63)	
Education				
High school	35	22.15	1	2
Some college	31	19.62	2	4
College	84	53.16	40	80
Graduate school	8	5.06	7	14
Total	158	100	50	100
Gender				
Female	49	30.43	16	32
Male	112	69.57	34	68
Total	161	100	50	100

Table 8.1 *(cont.)*

	Full sample		CST certified*	
Variable	N	Percent	N	Percent
Income (thousands US$ per year)				
≤9	47	30.32	4	8.16
>9 to 15	35	22.58	10	20.41
>15 to 27	35	33.58	14	28.57
>27 to 39	12	7.75	5	10.2
>39 to 51	7	4.52	3	6.12
>51 to 56	18	11.61	13	26.53
Total	155	100	49	100
Mean	21.10 (15.28)		29.63 (17.63)	

* Certified hotels have been audited and received beyond-compliance environmental ratings by the CST. Hotels that enroll in the CST are certified on a first come, first serve basis.

[a] Higher percentage indicates better hotel environmental performance (see text for details).

[b] Standard deviations are in parentheses.

CST participation and CEO education and expertise

The probit regression models used to analyze the decision to participate in the CST are displayed in Table 8.3. Model 1 assesses the relationship between hotel CEO level of education and participation in the CST while controlling for hotel basic characteristics and other CEO demographics. This model correctly classifies 87.7 percent of the participation decisions. The positive and significant coefficient ($P<0.1$) on CEO college and graduate levels of education supports Chapter 4's arguments suggesting that a firm's participation in voluntary environmental programs is positively related to the level of education of its CEO. Model 1's results do not suggest significant relationships between participation and other CEO demographic characteristics such as age, gender, income, and industrialized country nationality.

Table 8.2 ***Frequency distributions, CEOs' academic major and nationality***

	Full sample		CST certified*	
Variable	N	Percent	N	Percent
Major in college				
Business administration	24	15.00	11	22
Environmental management	10	6.25	6	12
Hotel-tourism management	19	11.88	14	28
Humanities	11	6.88	7	14
Social sciences	17	10.63	4	8
Other	10	6.25	5	12
No college degree	69	43.12	3	4
Total	160	100	50	100
Major in graduate school				
Business administration	3	1.83	2	4
Humanities	4	2.44	4	8
Other	1	0.61	1	2
No graduate degree	156	95.12	43	87
Total	164	100	50	100
Nationality				
From developing countries	122	74.85	38	74.51
From industrialized countries	41	25.15	13	25.49
Total	163	100	51	100
Nationality: specific countries				
Developing countries				
Brazil	1	0.61		
Costa Rica	114	69.94	36	70.59
Colombia	1	0.61		
Mexico	3	1.84	1	1.96
Nicaragua	1	0.61		
Peru	1	0.61	1	1.96
Venezuela	1	0.61		
Industrialized countries				
Belgium	1	0.61	1	1.96
Canada	4	2.45	2	3.92
Denmark	2	1.23		

Table 8.2 *(cont.)*

	Full sample		CST certified*	
Variable	N	Percent	N	Percent
France	2	1.23		
Germany	3	1.84		
Holland	4	2.45	2	3.92
Italy	10	6.13	1	1.96
Spain	5	3.07	2	3.92
Switzerland	2	1.23	1	1.96
USA	8	4.91	4	7.84
Total	163	100	51	100

* Certified hotels have been audited and received beyond-compliance environmental ratings by the CST. Hotels that enroll in the CST are certified on a first come, first serve basis.

Model 2 assesses the link between CEOs' college major and participation in voluntary environmental programs. This model (also shown in Table 8.3) correctly classifies 89.9 percent of the hotel participation decisions. The coefficient on college major in environmental management suggests an insignificant relationship with participation in the CST program. This finding does not support Chapter 4's arguments suggesting that a firm's participation in voluntary environmental programs is positively correlated with the environmental management expertise of its CEO. Additionally, Model 2 results indicate that hotel CEOs with a major in the humanities are more likely to participate in the CST program ($P<0.05$). We originally intended to also test this relationship for graduate level expertise but the small number of managers with a graduate degree prevented the use of regression analysis for this purpose.

CST participation and CEO nationality

Model 1 also examines whether CEOs from industrialized countries are more likely to participate in voluntary environmental programs.

Table 8.3 ***Probit regression models (dependent variable: participation in the CST)***

	Model 1 (demographics)	Model 2 (major in college)
Constant	-3.424*** (0.912)[a]	-3.949*** (1.177)
Foreign investors	-0.330 (0.321)	-0.389 (0.340)
Location		
City	-0.258 (0.394)	0.045 (0.425)
Park	0.607* (0.332)	0.980** (0.382)
Multinational subsidiary	0.449 (0.660)	0.412 (0.679)
Quality	0.330*** (0.107)	0.320*** (0.115)
Size	0.434** (0.216)	0.589** (0.252)
Trade association membership	0.430 (0.377)	0.640 (0.418)
Managers' demographics		
Age	0.007 (0.012)	0.004 (0.013)
Gender	0.274 (0.301)	0.277 (0.324)
Income	0.008 (0.010)	0.007 (0.010)
Nationality	0.228 (0.369)	0.435 (0.411)
Education		
High school		-0.163 (0.617)
Some college	-0.327 (0.386)	0.444 (0.488)
College	0.616* (0.328)	
Graduate	1.254* (0.703)	0.223 (0.731)
Academic major in college		
Business administration		0.302 (0.561)
Humanities		1.433** (0.710)
Hotel-tourism management		0.782 (0.611)
Environmental management		1.032 (0.742)
Social sciences		0.146 (0.629)
N	152	151
-2 Log L	131.099	118.357
χ^2 for covariates	75.148***	86.815***
Percent correctly classified	87.7	89.9

[a] Standard errors are in parentheses.

* prob < 0.10; ** prob < 0.05; *** prob < 0.01.

The statistically insignificant coefficient on CEO nationality does not support this hypothesis. This somewhat surprising finding challenges previous claims, and suggests that further research is necessary to elucidate on the relationship between CEOs' nationality and participation in voluntary environmental programs in developing countries.[8]

Beyond-compliance environmental performance and CEO education and expertise

Table 8.4 reports the findings of the OLS models used to test hypotheses about the association of hotel environmental performance and CEO education and nationality. Model 3's results indicate that a CEO's graduate education level (graduate degree) is positively and significantly related to his or her hotel's environmental performance ($P<0.05$). This finding supports Chapter 4 Proposition 20, suggesting that a firm's environmental performance is positively correlated with the education level of its CEO. The small number of CEOs with formal education below college graduate ($n=3$) prevented us from testing for differences between other education levels. Additionally, Model 3's results do not indicate significant associations between environmental performance and other CEO demographic characteristics such as age, gender, and income.

Model 4 incorporates different college majors pursued by CEOs to examine the correlation with hotel environmental performance. The positive and statistically significant ($P<0.05$) coefficient on environmental management major supports the argument suggesting that a firm's environmental performance is positively correlated with the environmental management expertise of its CEO.

Beyond-compliance environmental performance and CEO nationality

Model 3 also examines the association between CEOs from industrialized countries and beyond-compliance environmental performance. The nationality coefficient does not appear to show a statistically significant association with beyond-compliance environmental performance.

Table 8.4 *OLS regression models (dependent variable: CST environmental performance)*

	Model 3 (level of education)	Model 4 (major in college)
Constant	26.870 (1.56)[a]	21.640 (1.10)
Foreign investors	1.146 (0.23)	-3.864 (-0.74)
Location		
City	16.391** (3.08)	14.862** (2.98)
Park	6.588 (0.99)	11.657 (1.64)
Multinational subsidiary	-1.633 (-0.25)	-0.942 (-0.14)
Probability of participation	11.724 (0.53)	-10.719 (-0.42)
Quality	1.355 (0.45)	3.116 (0.90)
Size	-0.963 (-0.24)	6.004 (1.35)
Trade association membership	-1.724 (-0.26)	0.626 (0.10)
Managers' demographics		
Age	0.178 (0.65)	-0.093 (-0.33)
Gender	-1.292 (-0.29)	-3.908 (-0.87)
Income	0.097 (0.68)	0.132 (0.97)
Nationality	3.461 (0.60)	2.890 (0.54)
Education		
Graduate school	17.160* (2.30)	14.637* (2.06)
Academic major		
Business administration		-2.543 (-0.40)
Humanities		10.943 (1.49)
Hotel-tourism management		-5.600 (-0.95)
Environmental management		20.343* (2.09)
N	48	48
F-Value	2.78**	3.02**
R2	0.52	0.63
Adj-R2	0.33	0.42

[a] t-values are in parentheses.

* prob < 0.05; ** prob < 0.01.

Discussion

In general, the results from the regression models provide support for the argument that more highly educated CEOs are more likely to participate in voluntary environmental programs. Even more important, participant hotels run by CEOs with a graduate degree appear to be associated with higher beyond-compliance environmental performance than hotels managed by CEOs with lower levels of formal education.

As expected, the findings also suggest that hotels' environmental performance is positively correlated with the environmental management expertise of their CEOs. Yet, participation in voluntary programs does not appear to be significantly correlated with a college major in environmental management. Additionally, other CEO demographic characteristics such as gender and income were not significantly associated with either levels of participation or environmental performance.

A necessary question, then, is what is it about a CEO's higher formal education and expertise in environmental management that facilitates a positive association with beyond-compliance environmental performance? Previous conceptual work suggests that higher levels of formal education and environmental expertise *may* allow CEOs to better understand environmental management problems that are inherently complex and whose benefits are ambiguous (Ewert and Baker, 2001; Hart, 1995; Russo and Fouts, 1997; Wiersema and Bantel, 1992). This greater understanding is reflected in an enhanced awareness of and concern for environmental issues that motivates managers to adopt more proactive environmental management practices, such as those involved in showing superior beyond-compliance environmental performance. More highly educated managers are also more receptive to organizational innovation, a key element of successful adoption of beyond-compliance practices promoted by voluntary certification programs (Hambrick and Mason, 1984; Hart, 1995; Russo and Fouts, 1997; Wiersema and Bantel, 1992).

However, to better understand the regression findings, in-depth follow-up interviews were conducted with two non-overlapping groups of hotel top managers. The first group included all the CEOs (n = 8) that had earned a graduate degree; the second group consisted of all the CEOs (n = 10) that had a college major in environmental management. They were questioned about the main motivations and rationales for their decisions to enroll (or not to enroll) their companies in the CST.

Seven out of the eight CEOs with a graduate degree said that they had adopted the CST because they believed that proactively protecting the environment was a critical societal responsibility of their hotels, but also because they believed that proactive environmental management could contribute to improved financial performance. Regarding contributions to the hotel's finances, these managers specified that higher environmental performance certified by the CST could improve the "green" reputation of their hotels and thus attract a greater number of environmentally aware customers that visit Costa Rica. They also argued that some of the energy, water, and recycling management practices promoted by the CST helped their hotels to reduce costs. The one manager with a graduate degree whose hotel was not participating in the CST explained that it was his policy to comply with government regulations but that he believed that the CST was too costly with unrealistically stringent and complex standards for Costa Rica.

CEOs with a college major in environmental management also expressed a sense of environmental altruism. Six out of the ten CEOs who were educated in environmental management argued that the main reason to participate in the CST program was because proactive environmental protection was the "right thing to do." These six managers also mentioned that they believed that beyond-compliance environmental protection was a critical element for the competitiveness of their hotels. Another manager, aside from the six above, said that being what he considered "the best ecologically managed" hotel in Costa Rica was the basis of the superior financial performance for his hotel. In his words:

> At more than $200 per night our hotel is one of the most expensive in Costa Rica and we are more than 95 percent booked for the whole year ... our reputation as the best eco-hotel in the country attracts so many guests that we have to turn down the majority of potential customers.[9]

Three CEOs with environmental management majors had decided not to participate in the CST program. One of these CEOs believed that proactive environmental management was an important element of corporate social responsibility, yet, surprisingly, he said that his hotel was not participating in the CST because he did not know about the program. The other two managers argued that despite their pro-environmental protection inclinations, they considered that the CST program was too costly, biased in favor of big hotels, and too stringent given what they perceived to be the economic reality of Costa Rica.

Our findings also indicate that CEOs from industrialized countries do not appear to be significantly more likely to participate in voluntary programs than their counterparts from developing countries, and, when enrolled in these initiatives, are not more likely to show higher beyond-compliance environmental performance. These findings challenge the "conventional wisdom" that these CEOs are more environmentally aware and ready to transfer to host developing countries the more proactive environmental management practices that are the norm in industrialized nations (Christmann and Taylor, 2001; Garcia-Johnson, 2000; Wheeler, 1999). Yet, our results are consistent with the emerging empirical literature that indicates a lack of association between enhanced environmental performance and firms whose investors and/or parent companies are from industrialized countries (Aden *et al.*, 1999; Christmann and Taylor, 2001; Dasgupta *et al.*, 2000; Hettige *et al.*, 1996; Pargal and Wheeler, 1996). We argue that the wide variety of approaches taken by the CEOs from industrialized countries operating hotels in Costa Rica explains this surprising result. To be sure, some of the hotels with the highest beyond-compliance environmental performance rankings are managed by CEOs from Europe, the USA, or Canada. Yet, CEOs from these nations also operate some of the hotels that show the lowest predicted probability of participation and some of the lowest certified environmental performance. CEOs' education and environmental expertise, rather than an origin from a developed country, appear to be the critical factors related to beyond-compliance environmental behavior.

Conclusions

This analysis contributes to the public policy and environmental management literatures by increasing the understanding of how CEOs' personal backgrounds or characteristics are associated with pursuing corporate beyond-compliance environmental performance in a developing country. Previous research on environmental behavior and individual demographic characteristics has been mostly limited to samples of households, students, travelers, and members of environmental organizations, and has not considered corporate top managers (Cordano and Frieze, 2000; Cottrell, 2003; Egri and Herman, 2000; Ewert and Baker, 2001; Kellert, 1996; Kollmuss and Agyeman, 2002; Smith, 1995).

Illustrating how differences in top corporate decisionmakers' characteristics are linked to beyond-compliance environmental performance is essential to improving the effectiveness of alternative incentive-based environmental policy instruments currently promoted in the developing world. Self-interested calculations aimed at pre-empting new mandatory regulations and reducing environmental monitoring by government agencies and environmental groups can explain the decision to participate in voluntary programs and the adoption of proactive environmental practices by a significant percentage of CEOs (Cashore and Vertinsky, 2000; Henriques and Sadorsky, 1996; Rivera and deLeon, 2004; Tyler, 1990; Winter and May, 2001). Yet, other motivations also seem to be important, particularly in developing countries characterized by a context of problematic regulations, poor government monitoring and enforcement capabilities, and a weak environmental community (Utting, 2002; Wheeler, 1999).

This study indicates that CEOs' level of formal education appears to be significantly associated with higher corporate participation in voluntary programs and also with greater beyond-compliance environmental performance ratings, more so than the more apparent income indicators or country of national origin. CEOs with expertise in environmental management also show a significant link with higher levels of beyond-compliance environmental performance. Contrary to the conventional wisdom (Christmann and Taylor, 2001; Garcia-Johnson, 2000; Wheeler, 1999), CEOs from industrialized countries do not appear to be more likely to participate in voluntary programs and also do not seem to be more likely to show higher beyond-compliance environmental performance.

In-depth follow-up interviews with CEOs who have had formal graduate education and those with majors in environmental management indicate that beyond-compliance environmental choices are motivated by ecological altruism and a belief that "it can pay to be green." Previous studies highlight a significant link between regulatory pressures and participation and higher environmental performance (Cashore and Vertinsky, 2000; Henriques and Sadorsky, 1996; Rivera, 2004; Tyler, 1990; Winter and May, 2001). Nevertheless, regulatory incentives – typically governmental regulations and monitoring – were not among the main motivations for beyond-compliance environmentalism mentioned by highly educated managers or those with expertise in environmental management.

Higher education and environmental expertise may increase a CEO's recognition in Costa Rica of the intrinsic value of nature and his/her perceived sense of an ethical duty to protect it (Cottrell, 2003; Ewert and Baker, 2001; Hambrick and Mason, 1984; Wiersema and Bantel, 1992). Moreover, CEOs with higher education and environmental expertise can also be expected to be more aware of innovative technologies that lead to cost savings in the form of reduced waste, energy savings, and recycled materials, again as a function of their educational experiences. Lastly, as part of their business acumen, these CEOs may also have a better understanding of how an enhanced "green" reputation, generated by superior certified beyond-compliance environmental performance, could generate differentiation advantage benefits in the form of price premiums and higher profit margins for their hotels.

Admittedly this study has presented a very small cross-sectional sample of CEOs, and was limited to one developing nation in a short time frame. Moreover, the study was exclusively focused on experience in the "green" hotel business. For this reason, our ability to generalize our findings to other policy arenas or nations is limited at best. Future research should include longitudinal data to examine, in other industries and other countries, how CEO socio-demographic characteristics are related to beyond-compliance environmental performance.

Still, for policymakers this research indicates an environmental rationale for higher education, often graduate education, with environmental management training being especially salient. With the future of "command-and-control" environmental regulations increasingly giving way to "beyond-compliance" regimens, it would seem that formal higher education and environmental technical assistance would lay an important foundation.

Notes

1. This chapter is a slightly modified version of Rivera and deLeon (2005), reproduced with kind permission of the journal publishers and co-authors.
2. We assumed in the power analysis that environmental performance, the independent variable of interest, had a "small" effect size on the regression model (about 5 percent unique variance of the dependent variable explained).
3. No comprehensive list of all the hotels operating in Costa Rica was found. Thus, a sample frame list including 649 hotels was prepared. Sources of information consulted for building the sample frame included: archival data available at the Ministry of Tourism; the Costa Rican Chamber of Tourism; the Association of Small Hotels; the 2000 Costa Rican Phone Directory; and the most popular travel guides to Costa Rica. The travel guides consulted were: *The New Key to Costa Rica* (Blake and Becker, 1998); *The Berkeley Guide to Central America* (Nystrom and Smith, 1996); *The Lonely Planet Guide: Costa Rica* (Rachowiecki, 1997); and *Fodor's 99: Costa Rica Travel Guide* (Rockwood, 1999). Subsequently, we categorized the sample frame list into six geographic groups and randomly drew observations from each group to build a survey sample of 250 hotels.
4. A Pearson chi-square statistic was used to test whether there was a difference in the geographic frequency distribution for respondents and non-respondents of the control group (Goodmann and Kruskal, 1972; Pedhazur and Schmelkin, 1991). This test indicated that respondent and non-respondent hotels did not differ significantly in terms of location ($p<0.05$).
5. Certification results and CST ratings can be accessed online at: www.turismo-sostenible.co.cr/.
6. Controlling for hotel quality is important because of previous evidence in the literature suggesting a link between a firm's general quality standards and its environmental performance standards (Arora and Cason, 1996; Khanna, 2001; Lyon and Maxwell, 2002).
7. Following the practice used by empirical studies that rely on small sample sizes we used a $p<0.1$ criteria to determine the statistical significance of our findings. This practice has been widely accepted for studies implemented in developing countries, given that the power of the statistical

tests is positively affected by the number of observations (Pedhazur and Schmelkin, 1991: 198–203, 388).

8. We thank one of the anonymous reviewers for highlighting the need for additional research to elucidate the nature of the relationship between CEO nationality and participation in voluntary programs.
9. Personal interview with the CEO of one of the hotels with the highest certified environmental performance in Costa Rica, Costa Rica, December 2000. Authors explicitly agreed to keep hotel and manager names confidential.

9 *Certified beyond-compliance and competitive advantage in developing countries*[1]

Besides evaluating how institutional factors and top manager characteristics are associated with business environmental protection practices, it is also critical to assess how these practices are associated with economic benefits (Khanna, 2001; Porter and van der Linde, 1995). This is particularly important for voluntary environmental programs such as those discussed in Chapters 5–8. Given their non-mandatory nature, voluntary initiatives that generate short-term economic gains increase the likelihood that participant firms may show more cooperation with environmental protection demands during the different stages of the policy process (Andrews, 1998). This chapter aims to evaluate whether higher performance in voluntary environmental programs is related to differentiation advantages that yield higher prices or higher sales for participants. It also seeks to identify key conditions that have to be met by voluntary programs in order to generate these differentiation advantages. As in Chapters 7 and 8, data were gathered from a sample of hotels participating in the Costa Rican Certification for Sustainable Tourism (CST). (See description of the CST and Costa Rica's tourism industry in Chapter 7.)

Results indicate that participation in the CST program alone is not significantly related to higher prices and higher sales. Only hotels with higher environmental performance show a significant relationship with price premiums. The findings also suggest key conditions that are met by the CST program to selectively generate differentiation advantages that yielded price premiums. First, the CST program targets a market with a significant segment of environmentally aware consumers. Second, it provides clear and credible indications of firms' superior environmental performance. This allows environmentally aware consumers to differentiate the most environmentally proactive firms from the least proactive.

Voluntary environmental programs and economic benefits to firms

Scant attention has been paid to assessing the financial benefits derived by firms from their participation in voluntary environmental programs. This is surprising given the significant growth of the literature focusing on corporate environmental management issues. According to Margolis and Walsh (2001), more than fifty-five empirical studies have analyzed the relationship between environmental performance and firm profitability since 1972. Yet, hardly any has specifically looked at firms' economic benefits derived from participation in voluntary environmental programs. This issue has been overlooked to even greater degree in the public and environmental policy literature (Andrews, 1998; Khanna, 2001; Berchicci and King, 2007).

The lack of attention in the public policy literature may arise because assessing firms' economic benefits is seen as a business management topic. Nevertheless, given their non-mandatory nature, to effectively promote beyond-compliance, voluntary environmental programs have to generate short-term financial gains for participant firms (Andrews, 1998; Highley and Leveque, 2001). As stressed in this book, firms show cooperation with environmental protection demands in response to institutional pressures (Andrews, 1998; Bansal and Roth, 2000). Economists have for a long time emphasized that firms are also profit-driven and would exhibit higher environmental protection if they can obtain net economic benefits from it (Andrews, 1998). Consequently, evaluating economic benefits generated by voluntary programs is critical for their effective use as environmental policy tools. Effective voluntary environmental programs also have to discourage "free-riding" behavior by opportunistic firms (King and Lenox, 2000). So, it is also necessary to understand what conditions allow these programs to prevent "free-riding" behavior.

Findings of an assessment of the Environmental Protection Agency (EPA) 33/50 program indicate that participation had a negative impact on short-term profitability. Yet, investors perceived a positive effect for profitability in the long term (Khanna and Damon, 1999). Studies of consumers' willingness to pay for environmental quality also suggest that participation in voluntary environmental programs may allow companies to gain differentiation advantages that yield higher prices and/or higher sales (Khanna, 2001; Sen and Bhattacharya, 2001;

van Ravensway and Blend, 1999). Nevertheless, there is limited empirical evidence that directly links enrollment in voluntary environmental programs with price premiums or enhanced sales (Andrews, 1998; Khanna 2001; Lyon and Maxwell, 2002). The following section uses the resource-based theory to develop a better understanding of the conditions under which voluntary environmental programs can lead to differentiation advantages that generate higher prices or higher sales.

Resource-based theory of the firm

The resource-based theory provides valuable insights into the competitive implications of firms' responses to environmental policy demands. This theory is concerned with the relationship between a firm's internal resources and its competitiveness relative to other firms (Barney, 1991; Conner, 1991; Wernerfelt, 1984). According to the resource-based view, firms gain competitive advantage by possessing and deploying heterogeneous and immobile resources that result in more efficient manufacturing processes and/or products/services with a higher value for customers (Barney, 1991). Firm resource heterogeneity refers to how physical, human, and intangible organizational resources differ among competitors. Conversely, in the traditional industrial organization (IO) business strategy model, firm resources are viewed as homogeneous across all the competitors of a specific industry (Barney and Hesterley, 1996). Firm resource immobility refers to the inability of competing firms to mimic or purchase resources from other firms. IO strategic theories, on the other hand, consider that firm resources are mobile and can be purchased or copied.

At the core of the resource-based view is the issue of what makes a competitive advantage sustainable. Sustainable competitive advantages are those that cannot easily be imitated and substituted by competitors (Barney, 1991). A firm resource that provides sustained competitive advantages must fulfill four necessary conditions (Barney, 1991). First, it must add positive value to the firm. Second, it must be unique or rare among current and potential competitors (Reed and DeFillippi, 1990). Third, it cannot be easily substituted with another resource by competing firms (Dierickx and Cool, 1989). Finally, the resource must be imperfectly imitable because it possesses either path-dependent, causally ambiguous or socially complex characteristics (Reed and DeFillippi, 1990). These criteria highlight the point that firms cannot expect to imitate or purchase resources to obtain sustainable competitive advantages. These advantages need to be generated based on the development of rare, imperfectly imitable, and non-substitutable resources and capabilities.

Resource-based theory and voluntary environmental programs

The resource-based theory has traditionally been used to understand how internal environmental management resources can increase process efficiency and lead to cost advantages (Russo and Fouts, 1997; Sharma and Vredenburg, 1998). Nevertheless, this theory also highlights the importance of consumers' environmental perceptions and preferences (Hart, 1995). Consumer perceptions of a firm's environmental performance are critical for determining differentiation advantages that yield price premiums, and/or enhanced sales. Beyond-compliance environmental performance does not guarantee that a firm can create superior value for consumers that results in differentiation advantages. Two necessary conditions need to be satisfied for a firm's superior environmental performance to produce differentiation advantages: (1) consumers' buying decisions and willingness to pay have to be positively affected by superior environmental performance (Christmann, 1997; Reinhardt, 1998); and (2) compared to its competitors, a firm has to be perceived by consumers as having a credible reputation of superior environmental performance (Christmann, 1997; Reinhardt, 1998).

Businesses have found that it is very difficult to obtain and maintain the fidelity of "true blue" environmentally aware consumers whose buying decisions and willingness to pay is positively affected by a firm's superior environmental performance. Only a handful of companies enjoy clearly recognized reputations of superior environmental performance (green reputations). Credible green reputations are rare and difficult to create or imitate because self-proclaimed promotion of superior environmental performance is typically met with strong suspicion by the public and increased scrutiny by the media and environmental community (Hart, 1995; Klassen and McLaughlin, 1996). Hence, even when targeting environmentally aware consumers, superior environmental performance does not necessarily allow firms to gain price premiums or enhanced sales (Hart, 1995; Russo and Fouts, 1997).

Voluntary environmental programs can help to overcome the problem of lack of credibility intrinsic to self-reported environmental efforts. By granting eco-labels or environmental certifications, voluntary initiatives can distinguish firms with superior environmental performance. It is critical, however, that the programs themselves are perceived as somehow autonomous from participants in order to grant credible green reputations. Thus, they have to fulfill two basic requirements. First, they have to be controlled by an independent third party. Second, based on performance-based standards, they have to provide a clear indication of a firm's superior environmental performance. Accordingly, green consumers can differentiate the most environmentally proactive firms from the least proactive. The previous arguments suggest the following hypotheses:

Hypothesis 1: *Higher environmental rating in a third-party performance-based voluntary environmental program is positively associated with higher product prices.*

Hypothesis 2: *Higher environmental rating in a third-party performance-based voluntary environmental program is positively associated with higher product sales.*

Research methods

Sample selection

Survey and archival data were collected from the same cross-sectional sample of 164 Costa Rican hotels used for the studies discussed in Chapters 7 and 8.[2] The sample consisted of two groups. The first group included all 52 hotels enrolled and evaluated by the CST program as of December 2000. The second group of 112 hotels was drawn from a stratified random survey of 250 hotels (see details in Chapter 7, page 150).

Statistical analysis techniques

Firms that are more likely to receive economic benefits from voluntary programs are also more likely to self-select into them. Unless corrected, this self-selectivity leads to biased estimates of program benefits when simply comparing gains for participants and non-participants (Hartman, 1988; Heckman, 1978; 1979; Maddala, 1986). Thus, to test the hypotheses proposed, in this chapter I also used a recursive two-stage estimation method that corrects for self-selection bias and provides consistent estimates of participation benefits (Hartman, 1988; Heckman, 1978; 1979; Lee and Trost, 1978; Maddala, 1986).

Application of the two-stage methodology to assess price/sales benefits of the CST program

First, it is assumed that Y_i, the expected participation benefits for the *ith* hotel in the form of price premiums or higher sales, are determined by a vector of hotel characteristics X_i (e.g., location, size, quality), by its decision to participate in the voluntary environmental program, D_i, and by its environmental performance, Env_i.

$$(1)\ Y_i = \alpha + a_i X_i + b_i D_i + c_i Env_i + u_i$$

where:

X_i = equal to location, quality, size, trade association affiliation, and transnational affiliation;
D_i = the decision to participate in the voluntary environmental program;
Env_i = hotel environmental performance;
u_i = the random error term.

In this model D_i is treated as an endogenous variable because the decision to participate in the program is based on self-selection (Maddala, 1986). This also implies that D_i is likely to be determined by some of the same X_i characteristics that affect Y_i. To correct for self-selection bias the decision to participate in the program, D_i is concurrently determined with Y_i (Khanna and Damon, 1999). Thus, in the first stage, a probit regression models the decision to enlist in the CST Program, D_i. It is assumed that D_i is determined by the unobserved net benefit of participation for each individual hotel, E_i as follows:

$$(2)\ D_i = \begin{cases} 1 \text{ if } E_i > 0 \\ 0 \text{ if } E_i \leq 0 \end{cases}$$

Using the estimated probit model (2), the probability of participation in the CST program, P_i is calculated. Next, equation (1) is re-specified replacing D_i by P_i as a control variable:

$$(3)\ Y_i = \delta + a_i X_i + b_i P_i + c_i Env_i + u_i;$$

Finally, in the second stage, equation (3) is estimated using ordinary least-squares (OLS) regression.

When applying this two-stage methodology, it is sometimes argued that valid identifier variables for the probit model cannot be correlated with the dependent variable in the OLS model (Maddala, 1986). This would imply that these two models could not share the same independent variables. However, econometric studies show that the two-stage methodology does not suffer from problems of identification even when the same set of independent exogenous variables is used for both the probit and the OLS regressions (Khanna and Damon, 1999; Maddala, 1986: 267–71; Olsen, 1980: 1,818–19). Given that the probit model involves a nonlinear function of its independent variables, problems of overidentification are avoided. Overidentification arises when using a linear probability model, instead of probit, for determining probability of participation (Maddala, 1986: 267–71; Olsen, 1980: 1,818–19).

Dependent variable measures

Enrollment in the CST program (first stage, probit model dependent variable). This is coded as a binary variable equal to one for hotels participating in the program as of December 1999 and zero otherwise.

Hotel price and sales (second stage, OLS model's dependent variables). Average room price per night and occupancy rates are used as measures for hotel price and sales respectively.

Independent variable measures

Environmental performance. Dummy variables are created for identifying the environmental performance obtained by each hotel participating in the CST program, using hotels not participating in the program as a reference group.

The environmental rating assigned to each CST hotel is determined by independent audits performed by the CST program. These audits measure overall environmental performance based on a scale that grants hotels zero to five "green leaves" of environmental excellence. The ratings are intended to be similar to traditional quality ratings of hotels in which higher general quality is indicated progressively from zero to five stars. The number of "green leaves" obtained by a hotel is based on its score in four general areas of environmental management: (1) management of the physical and biological environment; (2) environmental management of hotel facilities; (3) guest environmental education; and (4) cooperation with local communities. These general areas are divided into twenty subcategories of environmental management (see Table 7.1, Chapter 7) that contain 153 yes/no questions. Each question evaluates compliance with a specific environmental practice (yes = compliance, no = non-compliance, N/A = not applicable) and was assigned a relative level of importance on a scale from one to three, three being the score for the most important yes/no questions.

The environmental rating for each general area is determined by adding the scores to all questions within that area, and dividing the total by the maximum possible score to create a percentage performance rate. Then, the final number of green leaves of environmental excellence obtained by a hotel is determined by the lowest percentage performance rate among the four general areas as follows:

Green leaves obtained	Minimum percentage performance among the four general areas
0	<20
1	20 to <40
2	40 to <60
3	60 to <80
4	80 to 94
5	>94

Competitive focus. Location is used as a proxy to measure hotel competitive focus. It is classified in three different categories: park, beach, and city hotels. Park and beach hotels are those located within ten miles of a national park or the beach respectively. City hotels, on the other hand, are those located in the metropolitan area that includes Alajuela, San Jose, and Cartago, the three major Costa Rican cities.

Previous studies of the Costa Rican tourism industry have shown that hotel location provides a good indication of the main purpose of guests staying at different hotels (ICT, 1999; 1995; INCAE, 2002). For example, park hotels focus mainly on tourists who travel to Costa Rica to enjoy nature and visit the rainforest. On the other hand, city and beach hotels cater to more diverse types of guests, including business and leisure travelers respectively.

Government monitoring. The level of general government monitoring is coded as a binary variable equal to one for those hotels that had an official "Declaration" from the Ministry of Tourism, and zero otherwise. "Declared" hotels receive tax exemptions and free promotion at international tourism fairs from the Ministry of Tourism. Declared hotels are also more closely supervised by the government and have to submit periodic information on their operations to the Ministry of Tourism and to the Treasury.

Hotel size. Hotel size is measured as the natural logarithm of the number of hotel rooms.

Hotel name recognition. Hotels affiliated or owned by an international chain are generally better known by tourists, travel agencies, and government officials. Hence, hotel name recognition is coded as a binary variable equal to one for those facilities that were either owned or managed by an international chain of hotels (e.g., Marriott, Best Western, Intercontinental), and zero otherwise.

Quality. Quality is measured by the number of stars assigned to each hotel by the quality classification system administered by the Ministry of Tourism. This quality rating system was reviewed in 1998 to reflect the standards used in the US by AAA, Mobil, Michelin, and major hotel chains (Mesa and Inman, 1999).

Probability of participation in the CST program (CST probability). Both the price and occupancy models were corrected for self-selection bias by introducing probability of participation in the CST program as a control variable. This variable was calculated using the probit model of participation determined in the first stage of the regression analysis.

Trade-association membership. Membership in the National Chamber of Tourism, the main trade association of the industry, is coded as a categorical variable equal to one for hotels affiliated with the Chamber of Tourism, and zero otherwise.

Results

Correlation values and other descriptive statistics such as means and standard deviations are reported in Table 9.1. Frequency distributions of CST-audited hotels according to their level of environmental performance are presented in Table 9.2. The majority of CST hotels

Table 9.1 *Correlation matrix and descriptive statistics*

	Variable	1	2	3	4	5	6
1	Affiliation to trade association	1.00					
2	Government monitoring	.38***	1.00				
3	Beach hotels	–.02	.02	1.00			
4	City hotels	.23**	.26***	–.31***	1.00		
5	Park hotels	–.16*	–.23**	–.66***	–.52***	1.00	
6	Occupancy	.05	.08	–.01	.11	–.08	1.00
7	Quality	.44***	.92***	.02	.28***	–.24**	.13
8	Price	.42***	.60***	.05	.11	–.12	.21**
9	Size (log)	.57***	.45***	.12	.20*	–.27***	.11
10	CST participation	.39***	.53***	–.10	.09	.02	–.11
11	CST probability	.62***	.86***	–.16*	.15†	.02	.09
12	Name recognition	.27***	.23**	.01	.13†	–.11	.13
Environmental performance variables							
13	Non-audited[a]	.01	–.01	–.10	–.16*	.22**	–.19*
14	0 Green leaves	.07	.18*	.02	–.01	–.01	–.04
15	1 Green leaf	.18*	.32***	.11	–.10	–.02	–.13†
16	2 Green leaves	.30***	.28***	–.09	.35***	–.19*	.11
17	3 to 4 Green leaves	.14†	.18*	–.16*	.13†	.04	.01
	N	164	164	164	164	164	162
	Mean	N/A	N/A		N/A	N/A	58.44
	Std. dev.	N/A	N/A		N/A	N/A	17.18

† prob<0.10; * prob<0.05; ** prob<0.01; *** prob<0.001.
[a] Non-audited are CST hotels whose environmental performance had not yet been evaluated as at December 1999.

7	8	9	10	11	12	13	14	15	16	17
1.00										
.72***	1.00									
.65***	.53***	1.00								
.54***	.41***	.33***	1.00							
.88***	.65***	.73***	.62***	1.00						
.32***	.29***	.41***	.25**	.41***	1.00					
–.06	.04	.06	.38***	.07	–.8	1.00				
.19*	.08	.13†	.23**	.19*	.09	–.06	1.00			
.32***	.18*	.22***	.47***	.33***	.12	–.12	–.08	1.00		
.30***	.09	.26***	.37***	.32***	.29***	–.10	–.06	–.12	1.00	
.21**	.38***	.12	.31***	.21**	.04	–.08	–.05	–.10	–.08	1.00
164	162	163	164	159	164	164	164	164	164	164
1.70	56.17	31.08	N/A	0.40	N/A	N/A	N/A	N/A	N/A	N/A
1.67	33.69	41.68	N/A	0.31	N/A	N/A	N/A	N/A	N/A	N/A

Table 9.2 *Environmental performance of CST-audited hotels*

	Number of hotels	Percentage
Environmental performance		
(# of Green leaves)		
0	6	11.5
1	22	42.3
2	14	26.9
3	9	17.3
4	1	1.9
5	0	0
Total	52	100
Non-audited hotels†	15	

† Non-audited are CST hotels whose environmental performance had not yet been evaluated as at December 1999.

Table 9.3 *Decision to participate in the CST program*

Constant	-2.870*** (0.652)[a]
City	0.048 (0.374)
Government monitoring	1.336* (0.608)
Name recognition	0.402 (0.656)
Park	0.947** (0.326)
Quality	0.038 (0.192)
Size	0.344† (0.197)
Trade association membership	1.077** (0.396)
N	159
-2 Log L	135.06
χ^2 for covariates	82.879***
Per cent correctly classified	88.2

[a] Standard errors are in parentheses.
† prob<0.10; * prob<0.05; ** prob<0.01; *** prob<0.001.

showed low levels of beyond-compliance environmental performance. Almost 81 percent obtained between zero and two "green leaves," about 19 percent obtained between three and four "green leaves," and none obtained five "green leaves." Results of the probit regression analysis are displayed in Table 9.3 (see discussion of participation in the CST in Chapters 7 and 8).[3]

Table 9.4 *Comparing means of price and occupancy for CST and non-CST hotels*

Environmental performance	N	Price (year average)	Occupancy (year average)
Not enrolled in CST (reference group)	96	44.71 (28.47)	59.97 (16.06)
Non-audited	15	60.50† (32.54)	48.46† (23.40)[a]
0 green leaves	6	70.17* (16.93)	54.94 (15.44)
1 green leaf	20	71.22*** (34.12)	53.31† (15.01)
2 green leaves	13	66.04*** (15.05)[a]	64.92 (15.33)
3 green leaves	9	108.39** (46.03)[a]	60.90 (14.41)
3 to 4 green leaves[b]	10	105.30** (44.48)[a]	64.81 (18.37)
5 green leaves	0	None had obtained 5 green leaves as of December 1999.	

t-test: † prob < 0.10; * prob < 0.05; ** prob < 0.01; *** prob < 0.001.
Test Ho: no significantly different means. Values in parentheses are standard deviations.
[a] Test of equality of variances showed that variances are unequal for these data. Therefore the Satterthwaite's nonparametric approximation was used to compare the means.
[b] Only one hotel obtained four green leaves. This category was created for comparison purposes.

CST environmental performance and differentiation advantage benefits

Price premium benefits

Findings from the correlation matrix (see Table 9.1) suggest that hotel room price is positively correlated with higher environmental performance. Table 9.4 compares means for price at different levels of environmental performance. The t-tests indicate that at all levels of environmental performance, hotels participating in the CST program have average room prices that are significantly higher than the average price for non-participant hotels ($p < 0.05$). The average price premium varies between \$25.46 to \$60.59 for hotels with zero, to three to four "green leaves" respectively.

It is interesting, however, to note that average price premiums for hotels with two green leaves are significantly smaller than the average price premiums for hotels with zero and one green leaf. The lack of a monotonic effect for two green leaves hotels can be explained by their predominant focus on business travelers. Most two green leaves hotels (71 percent) are located in the capital of Costa Rica and cater to a more significant proportion of business travelers (INCAE, 2002; ICT, 1999). Studies of willingness to pay for environmental quality, by visitors to Costa Rica, consistently show that business travelers are not as willing to pay higher prices for environmental quality as tourists visiting national parks (DeSharzo and Vega, 1999; INCAE, 2002).

These results provide preliminary evidence that CST hotels with higher environmental performance tend to have higher room prices. However, for these results to be more conclusive, it is necessary to determine whether price premiums remain after controlling for basic hotel characteristics and self-selection bias. The price regression model described in the following section controls for these factors.

Price linear regression model.[4] Model 1 in Table 9.5 displays the linear regression analysis for hotel room price. Findings indicate that CST-affiliated hotels with higher levels of environmental performance (hotels receiving three to four green leaves) show a significant relationship with higher room prices. Yet, participation in the CST program alone, without showing a superior level of environmental performance, is not significantly related to price premiums. These results provide support for the Hypothesis 1 argument that higher environmental rating in a third-party performance-based voluntary environmental program is positively associated with higher product prices. According to their regression coefficient, three to four green leaves hotels show room prices that are about $30 per night higher than the room prices of hotels not enrolled in the CST program. This finding, despite its significance ($p < 0.001$), should be tempered by the fact that to date only ten hotels have attained three to four green leaves of environmental excellence.

Overall, these results are consistent with resource-based theory arguments that firms showing credible superior environmental performance and targeting "green" consumers can gain differentiation advantages that yield price premiums (Christmann, 1997; Hart, 1995; Porter and van der Linde, 1995a). These conditions are satisfied in Costa Rica where: (1) the CST program provides a credible and clear indication of superior environmental performance for hotels; and (2) more than 85 percent of the tourists consider national parks and the rainforest the most important places to visit in Costa Rica (INCAE, 2000).

Sales benefits

Correlation values (see Table 9.1) provide preliminary evidence indicating that higher environmental performance is not significantly correlated to higher hotel occupancy. Similarly, means comparisons suggest that hotels with more green leaves fail to show higher average occupancy (see Table 9.4).

Occupancy linear regression model.[5] According to Hypothesis 2, a higher environmental rating in a third-party, performance-based voluntary environmental program is positively associated with higher product sales. Nevertheless, results suggest that, independently of the level of environmental performance achieved, participation in the CST program is not significantly related to enhanced sales as measured by hotel occupancy (see Model 2 on Table 9.5). Moreover, although only the coefficient for one green leaf hotels is significant ($p<0.05$), all levels of environmental performance show a negative relationship with occupancy level.

These findings, however, should be considered with caution because the overall model fit of the occupancy model is very poor. The adjusted multiple correlation indicates that independent variables in the model explain only 7.3 percent of the variance in occupancy. This is particularly striking when compared to the price model for which 58.5 percent of the variance in price is explained by the independent variables.

The low explained variance for the occupancy model and the lack of significance for the environmental performance variables may be attributed to the problems encountered in obtaining reliable hotel occupancy data. Other hotel characteristics such as price, location, size, quality, and trade association membership were verified using archival information available at the Ministry of Tourism and other public sources. Yet, hotel occupancy figures could only be verified for a handful of hotels. Additionally, face-to-face interviews with managers showed a great deal of variation in the quality and sophistication of occupancy data provided by hotels. The bigger and

Table 9.5 *CST performance and differentiation advantage benefits*

Linear regression models (stage two)

	Model 1: room price[a]	Model 2: hotel occupancy[b]
Constant	11.027 (1.123)[c]	46.058** (7.163)
City	-9.930† (-1.800)	2.151 (0.507)
CST probability	5.990 (0.411)	-11.464 (-1.037)
Occupancy	0.238* (2.193)	
Park	-3.027 (-0.584)	3.172 (0.806)
Quality	12.304** (5.005)	1.328 (0.656)
Price		0.138* (2.193)
Size (log)	3.681 (1.266)	2.539 (1.147)
Non-audited	11.639 (1.647)	-12.771* (-2.402)
0 green leaves	-9.393 (-0.939)	-7.726 (-1.016)
1 green leaf	-2.933 (-0.459)	-10.663* (-2.229)
2 green leaves	-13.915† (-1.788)	2.281 (0.381)
3 to 4 green leaves	29.897** (3.697)	-3.353 (-0.521)
N	154	154
F-Value	20.603**	2.104*
R2	0.615	0.140
Adj-R2	0.585	0.073

[a] Model 1 significant at less than 0.001.
[b] Model 2 significant at less than 0.001.
[c] t-values are in parentheses.
† prob < 0.10; * prob < 0.05; ** prob < 0.001.

most well-known hotels, about 10 percent of the sample, provided very detailed monthly occupancy data. Nonetheless, the majority of hotels only provided six-month estimates of average occupancy levels.

Research limitations and implications for future research

Before elaborating on the conclusions, it is necessary to highlight the limited and preliminary nature of the assessment discussed in this chapter. First, the use of cross-sectional data prevents the analysis of any causal relationships between the variables of interest. Future research needs to overcome this limitation by collecting longitudinal information so that causal relationships can be tested. For example, it is important to determine if hotels obtaining high environmental scores in the CST increase their room prices and/or occupancy as more information about the program is diffused among international tourists.

Second, the sample included only hotels operating in Costa Rica, a middle-income developing country that has obtained a worldwide reputation for its leadership in the management of its national parks. This attracts a significant segment of environmentally aware visitors from industrialized nations. Hence, these findings cannot be generalized to other countries and other voluntary initiatives. Future research needs to collect data from voluntary initiatives established in other developing countries to improve the generalizability of these findings. Third, the sample size was small and the number of CST-audited hotels (n = 52) is even smaller. In the future, as the number of hotels in each CST rating category continues to grow, it may be possible to arrive at more conclusive results. Finally, the use of survey methodology to obtain data on hotel basic characteristics introduced problems of common method variance and social desirability bias intrinsic to survey instruments. Archival information available in Costa Rica helped to reduce these problems by allowing verification of a significant proportion of the self-reported information. Nevertheless, further research should focus on developing and maintaining a reliable database on hotel basic characteristics.

Conclusions

The public policy and management literature has paid little attention to assessing the ability of voluntary environmental programs to generate economic benefits for firms (Andrews, 1998; Khanna, 2001). Yet, because of their voluntary nature, provision of these benefits is a necessary condition for these programs to become effective environmental policy instruments. Given the weak regulatory environment in developing countries, the ability of voluntary initiatives to generate business benefits is even more important to guaranteeing their environmental effectiveness.

The analysis discussed in this chapter provides some of the first cross-sectional empirical evidence about the relationship between participation in voluntary environmental programs and differentiation advantage benefits such as firm prices and sales. It identifies key conditions that have to be met by voluntary initiatives in order to generate these benefits. As in the case of Chapters 7 and 8, data were gathered from hotel participation in the Costa Rican Certification for Sustainable Tourism. This program is being used by the World Tourism Organization as a model for developing its voluntary environmental initiative for hotels. Thus, despite its limitations, this assessment can provide important insights to policymakers designing similar voluntary environmental programs.

CST program and differentiation advantage benefits

Results show that participation in the CST program alone is not significantly related to differentiation advantages that yield higher prices or higher sales. Only CST-affiliated hotels with higher levels of environmental performance show a significant association with higher room prices. These findings suggest that the CST program is taking advantage of market incentives in the form of price premiums to promote superior environmental performance. Firms that enrolled in the CST with "free-riding" purposes are not gaining significant price premiums. Under the relatively weak regulatory context of Costa Rica, this is a basic condition that has to be fulfilled by the CST to be used as an effective environmental policy instrument.

According to the resource-based theory, voluntary initiatives have to fulfill specific necessary conditions to avoid "free-riding" behavior and differentially grant price premium benefits to firms with the best environmental performance. First, they have to be controlled by an independent third party. Second, using performance-based standards, they have to provide a clear indication of a firm's superior environmental performance. Finally, they have to target industries that have a significant segment of "green" consumers.

These necessary conditions are met in Costa Rica where: (1) the CST program is controlled by an independent National Accreditation Commission; (2) green leaves of environmental excellence are granted based on adherence to performance-based standards; and (3) the hotel industry has a significant segment of "green" consumers. Yet, the conditions met in Costa Rica suggest important limitations for the use of the CST program in other developing countries. For instance, the presence of a significant segment of "green" tourists is critical for voluntary programs like the CST to succeed in generating price premiums.

Finally, it is also important to emphasize that – as discussed in Chapter 7 – government monitoring, trade association membership, and hotel focus on "green" consumers are significantly related to higher participation in the CST program. These findings point out how the CST program is complemented by the general regulatory environment, the system of interest representation, and the competitive dynamic prevailing in the Costa Rican hotel industry. Lack of general government monitoring would likely reduce participation. Therefore, traditional mandatory pressures should be seen as a key ingredient to encourage voluntary behavior by firms (Cashore and Vertinsky, 2000; Henriques and Sadorsky, 1996; Khanna *et al.*, 1998). A neo-corporatist system of interest representation characterized by a history of cooperation between the government, the private sector, and other civil society organizations has encouraged the proactive role of the Chamber of Tourism in promoting the CST program. Most importantly, these regulatory and industry association pressures are exerted in the context of a market with a significant segment of environmentally aware tourists ("green" consumers). The absence of this segment of "green" consumers would significantly reduce incentives for participation in the CST program. Hence, it is not surprising that large international chain hotels that serve less environmentally conscious business travelers are less likely to enroll in the program.

It is also important to note that despite the positive reinforcement of these factors in Costa Rica, less that 10 percent of hotels operating in the country have decided to enroll in the CST program. Additionally, the majority of enrolled hotels show low levels of beyond-compliance environmental performance. Although these results cannot be generalized beyond Costa Rica, promoters of the CST program in other countries can learn from this evidence. For instance, lower levels of enrollment and environmental performance can be expected in countries that have one or more of the following: (1) lack a significant segment of "green" consumers; (2) fail to show minimum government oversight; (3) have less cooperative systems of interest representation; and/or (4) lack organized hotel industry associations.

Notes

1. This chapter is an expanded and modified version of portions of: Rivera (2002), reproduced with kind permission of Springer Science and Business Media.
2. Minimum sample size. Results of a power analysis indicated that a sample of at least 138 observations was necessary to have an 80 percent chance of rejecting a false null hypothesis at 95 percent confidence (Cohen and Cohen, 1983: 59). This was assuming that environmental performance, the independent variable of interest, had a "small" effect size on the regression model (about 5 percent unique variance of the dependent variable explained).
3. Probit model of participation (see Table 9.3). Three observations had missing data for the variables involved in the model and were excluded from the analysis. Regression diagnostic tests and index plots (see note 5 below) revealed the best model fit resulted after eliminating influential outlier observations 103 and 65. Additional regression diagnostic tests did not show more influential observations.
4. Price linear regression model: ten observations had missing data and were excluded from the analysis. Condition index and variance inflation measures for OLS Model 1 were not greater than the critical values suggested in the literature. This indicates that "harmful multicollinearity" did not affect this model (Belsley *et al.*, 1980: 105). White's chi-square test for heteroscedasticity was also insignificant indicating the lack of nonconstant error variance (White, 1980). Regression diagnostics: tests and index plots developed by Pregibon (1981) and by Belsley *et al.* (1980) respectively were used to identify influential and/or ill-fitted observations on the probit and ordinary least-squares models, they included: (1) hat matrix diagonal to detect observations with extreme values in the independent variables; (2) outlier points were detected using studentized residual measures. Dffits and dfbetas were used to estimate the extent to which the omission of an individual case caused a change in the fitted regression equation.
5. Occupancy linear regression model: due to missing data, ten observations were excluded from this model. Condition index tests showed a lack of serious multicollinearity problems. Similarly, the lack of heteroskedasticity problems was confirmed by an insignificant White's chi-square test. Regression diagnostics were also performed (see endnote 4 above).

10 Conclusion[1]

The argument that the external context plays a significant role in shaping the behavior and choices of individuals and organizations is the subject of very little controversy in the social sciences. Different streams of neo-institutional scholarship have indeed produced a vast literature emphasizing and explaining how external pressures, factors, and events affect decisionmaking and behavior. There is also little disagreement about the existence of stark differences between developing country contexts and those of industrialized nations. For instance, consider the large discrepancy between the total number of US Environmental Protection Agency (EPA) employees and its equivalent federal government agency in China. In 2005, the Chinese State Environmental Protection Administration had just 300 workers in Beijing and 100 more for the rest of the country, compared to 17,645 employees at the US EPA during the same year (Balfour, 2005: 122; US Office of Management and Budget, 2009). To be sure, these country disparities may be evident not only to social scientists examining regulatory agencies but also to ordinary travelers during a short stopover in a developing country airport.

Yet, most neo-institutional work has been focused on industrialized nations, particularly the US. Thus, it assumes compliance as the taken-for-granted business response to environmental and social protection policies and regulations (called "protective" public policies and regulations throughout this book). A similar focus and assumption can be observed in the corporate political activity and corporate social responsibility scholarship examining business responses to protective public policies. The main contribution of this book to the literature is to develop a framework of analysis that explains how variations in specific country context characteristics – that tend to prevail in developing countries – moderate the protective policy process–business response relationship. In general terms, my framework posits that higher levels of business resistance to different stages of the protective policy process are more likely in countries with lower levels of democracy, state-corporatist interest representation systems (as opposed to pluralistic and neo-corporatist ones), command-and-control regulatory instruments (as opposed to incentive-based ones), more stringent regulations, or lower economic income per capita (see Figure 3.1 in Chapter 3).

In addition to considering how country context variations moderate the protective policy process–business response relationship, it is also important to point out the book's emphasis on taking a policy process perspective. In stressing a policy process view, the book draws ideas from the policy sciences literature and from recent work on institutional process from the organizational sociology literature (Hoffman, 1997; 1999; Hirsch, 1997; Seo and Creed, 2002; Brewer and deLeon, 1983; Lasswell, 1956; 1971). Thus, instead of assuming compliance as the taken-for-granted business response to protective policies and regulations, my framework of analysis follows others in highlighting the intense political dynamic involved in the long-lasting process of institutionalization of these policies (Hoffman, 1999; Oliver, 1991). The book adds to the literature by discussing the underlying logic that explains the nature of business responses to the protective policy process. In particular, I propose that the protective policy process–business response relationship in the US is likely to follow an inverted U-shaped pattern in which business tends to show increasing political opposition as the public policy process moves from initiation to selection and thereafter declining resistance that turns into growing cooperation in mid-implementation (see Figure 2.1, Chapter 2). The main rationale underpinning the proposed nature of the protective policy process–business response relationship in the US and how it is moderated by country contextual variations is discussed in the next few pages.

Protective policy process–business response relationship in the US

During the initiation stage of the policy process, business in the US is more likely to show lower levels of resistance than in the formulation-selection and early implementation stages because most firms are unaware of the existence of nascent conditions that may erode the legitimacy of institutionalized governmental policies and regulations and thus highlight contradictions within the established socio-political order (Hoffman, 1997; Jepperson, 1991; Seo and Creed, 2002). Additionally, at the initiation stage, the inherent complexity and ambiguity of environmental or social phenomena make it very difficult to understand the causes and trends linked to perceived emerging problems that may not receive the attention of policymakers. Accordingly, business managers tend to rely on cognitive simplification processes to focus on narrower problems that are more immediate, simpler, and consistent with already institutionalized expectations in the US (Schwenk, 1984; Tversky and Kahneman, 1974).

On the other hand, during formulation-selection, business tends to display the highest levels of resistance compared to other stages of the policy process. Most firms, given their managers' extensive socialization and internalization of the pre-existing protective public policy order, are spurred to most actively defend its shared logic, values, and symbols, as well as its prescribed structures, routines, regulations, and standards (Barley and Tolbert, 1997; Pettigrew, 1987; Scott, 2001). Business' utmost resistance arises for multiple reasons. First, potential changes to already institutionalized protective policies and norms challenge the issue-specific political accommodation that favors the interests of (powerful) incumbent groups and individuals such as business and top policymakers (Fligstein, 1996; Brewer and deLeon, 1983). Second, managers usually have a strong preference for stable government policies and regulations that reduce risks and allow them to maintain legitimacy and a sense of control over the regulatory environment (Fligstein, 1996; George *et al.*, 2006). Third, business managers rely on multiple decisionmaking simplifications that are likely to negatively bias their perception of the appropriateness and financial implications of new protective policy alternatives.

In early-implementation most companies in the US are still likely to offer high levels of resistance, although probably not as high as during the formulation-adoption stage as they try to shape, challenge, and/or altogether stop the regulations, enforcement styles, standards, and budgets adopted to implement new protective policies (Hoffman, 1997; Suchman and Edelman, 1997). Despite the adoption of new policies, old institutionalized business practices and forms consistent with previous environmental and social protection policies are pervasive among most firms. During mid-implementation as government monitoring and coercion begins, business cooperation with the politically contested regulatory standards and enforcement practices is likely to increase. This is because these standards and enforcement practices progressively become part of the accepted patterns and knowledge shared by business managers, policymakers, and stakeholders (Berger and Luckmann, 1967; Tolbert and Zucker, 1996). The gradual increase of business cooperation is also spurred by the actions of other companies that seek to be recognized as environmental and social responsibility leaders.

Finally, if the process of institutionalization persists over a long period of time, in late implementation the highest levels of business cooperation are likely to be observed as the collective internalized understanding of appropriate social and environmental responsibility becomes part of the objective reality of business (Berger and Luckmann, 1967; Tolbert and Zucker, 1996). During late implementation, aggressive coercion is seldom required and most businesses, independently of their characteristics, have adopted institutionalized social and environmental protection practices and structures prescribed by politically bargained protective public policies and regulations (Hawkins and Thomas, 1984; Tolbert and Zucker, 1996). Resistance to sedimented taken-for-granted practices is seen as highly illegitimate not only by policymakers and stakeholders but also by other members of industry and peer managers (Hoffman, 1997; Tolbert and Zucker, 1996).

Moderating effect of country context

As mentioned at the beginning of this conclusion chapter, the main contribution of this book is to clarify how variations in political and economic contexts typical of developing countries affect the responses offered by business during the different stages of enactment and implementation of protective public policies. The moderating effect of the level of democracy on the protective public policy process–business response relationship arises from traditional democratic rights and liberties. Freedom of the press, speech, association, participation, and the unhindered right to vote are core rights taken-for-granted in democratic systems. These rights open information and advocacy channels to multiple grassroots actors that in authoritarian regimes are traditionally, and almost exclusively, enjoyed by business, military, and political elites (Ascher, 1999; Grindle and Thomas, 1991). Yet, most studies examining business behavior and political context have focused on variations in the distinct systems of interest representation in industrialized countries and thus assume higher levels of democratic traditions as given (Hillman and Keim, 1995; Murtha and Lenway, 1994; Spencer *et al.*, 2005).

Institutionalized freedom of the press and speech allows citizens, scientists, interest groups, the media, and interested government officials to be more informed and to monitor the causes and effects of social and environmental problems produced by business activities (Neumayer, 2001; Payne, 1995). Free speech traditions also make it easier to publicly and timely convey concerns and demands to the media, policymakers, and business managers about the detrimental consequences of problematic social and environmental protection routines that may be pursued by business (deLeon, 1997; Fischer and Hajer, 1999; Payne, 1995). Well-established freedom of association mechanisms inherent in democratic nations expedite the organization of social and environmental protection advocacy groups and coalitions that are better able to debate, promote, and sustain demands for protective policies and enforcement aimed at improving business social and environmental responsibility (Diamond, 1999; Lybecker and Horan, 2005; Payne, 1995). The increased resources, connections, administrative capacities, and legitimacy attained by organized groups significantly reduce their vulnerability to retaliation and/or manipulation and enhance their bargaining power relative to business and the government (Kim *et al.*, 2007). Additionally, freedom of political participation and the right to vote also play a key role in constraining the level of resistance that can be offered by firms during the different stages of the protective policy process. This is because citizens and groups that advocate social and environmental protection can support the election of like-minded politicians that are more likely to promote the adoption and effective enforcement of protective policies perceived as costly by the business sector (Diamond, 1999; Lim and Tang, 2002; Payne, 1995).

Besides stressing the degree of democratization, political science's neo-institutional theory also highlights the importance of identifying the system of interest representation to characterize a country's political context (March and Olsen, 1989; Schmitter, 1974). The extant literature has focused on neo-corporatist/pluralistic variations across systems of interest representation to predict firm responses but has given scant consideration to state-corporatist systems more typical of developing countries (Jepperson and Meyer, 1991; Streeck and Kenworthy, 2005). The moderating effect of different systems of interest representation on the protective policy process–business response relationship arises first, from the variations in the levels of business participation; and second from the distinct emphasis on policymaking consensus inherent in pluralistic, neo-corporatist, and state-corporatist countries.

Compared to pluralistic countries, in a state-corporatist country businesses' likely monopolistic access to policymaking and implementation increases their capacity for using higher levels of resistance in the form of manipulation tactics, often allowing them to capture the policy process. In contrast, business resistance is likely to be lower in neo-corporatist countries compared to pluralistic countries because of shared participation with labor and other environmental/social protection peak associations capable of effectively excluding issues from the public policy agenda. The lower levels of business resistance observed in neo-corporatist countries are also the result of sedimented traditions, routines, and structures that emphasize consensus and collective rights in policymaking over pluralism's priority on political competition and individual rights, and over state-corporatism's emphasis on the exclusion of social protection groups from policymaking (Crepaz, 1995; Scruggs, 1999).

Other key factors that moderate the public policy process–business response relationship are the stringency and the type of regulatory instruments considered, enacted, and implemented to promote social and environmental protection by business. The combination of higher costs and restricted compliance choices associated with more stringent regulations and command-and-control instruments enhances the conflict between institutionalized profit-seeking business traditions and protective policy demands. Accordingly, it can be expected that firms are more likely to offer higher resistance during the different stages of the protective policy process when confronting more stringent regulatory requirements or/and command-and-control instruments (Gunningham *et al.*, 2003; Henriques and Sadorsky, 1996; Winter and May, 2001).

Finally, a large body of the economics and organizational theory literatures details the logic explaining why firms operating in poor countries (below upper-middle gross national income – GNI – per capita) are more likely to offer higher resistance during the different stages of the protective policy process than those operating in wealthier countries. In poor countries demands for social and environmental protection are more likely to be considered incompatible with legitimate subsistence practices of large numbers of barely surviving businesses (Blackman and Bannister, 1998; O'Rourke, 2004; Rivera, 2004). Moreover, it is not only that social and environmental protection demands may be perceived as trivial and illegitimate when faced with the struggle for survival; but also these issues are usually dismissed because it is taken for granted that poor developing country governments lack the capacity and/or the will to enforce "on-paper" protective regulations (Ames and Keck, 1997; O'Rourke, 2004; Rivera, 2004; Stuligross, 1999). Additionally, many business owner-managers rarely have the basic education required to understand complex social and environmental protection requirements (Rivera and deLeon, 2005).

Evidence from empirical research: the Costa Rican hotel industry and the US ski industry

The theoretical framework developed in this book has its main roots in the empirical studies detailed in Chapters 5–9. These chapters present the findings of over a decade of work examining the environmental protection strategies and behavior of the Costa Rican hotel industry and the US ski industry.[2] Accordingly, it is important to stress that these studies are not intended as proof of the conceptual framework proposed. These studies do, however, provide limited and preliminary evidence for a few of the ideas offered by the conceptual framework developed in the first part of the book. For instance, returning to the initial question posited in the introduction: why is it that the Costa Rican hotel industry appears to have shown more cooperation with environmental policy process demands than the US ski industry? This book suggests some of the factors that may explain this difference.

If we consider country income per capita alone, hotels in Costa Rica should be displaying higher levels of resistance to environmental policy demands than ski resorts in the US, since Costa Rica's GNI per capita is much lower than that of the US – $10,950 versus $46,970 respectively in 2008; corrected for purchasing power parity (World Bank, 2009). Yet, per-capita income levels in Costa Rica are not so low as to impose urgent survival needs on the country and its businesses. Both countries also have long and well-established traditions of democracy. Thus, other contextual factors may be at play. First, Costa Rica has a neo-corporatist system of interest representation as opposed to a pluralistic system, as is prevalent in the US. As suggested by the book's framework of analysis, less business resistance to environmental policy process demands is more likely in neo-corporatist countries than in pluralistic countries. This is because in neo-corporatist countries environmentalist groups are less likely to be excluded from policymaking and because of an enhanced emphasis on consensus and collective rights as opposed to the priority given to political competition and individual rights in pluralistic countries like the US. Second, Costa Rica has relied more on incentive-based environmental policies and programs as opposed to the US focus on command-and-control environmental policies and regulations.

The Certification for Sustainable Tourism (CST) in Costa Rica reflects the influence of these factors. It was established by the government in cooperation with representatives of leading business, environmental, and academic groups. Its standards and audit mechanisms have been governed by a National Accreditation Board with equal representation from these sectors. Thus, from its inception, the CST has involved environmental performance-based standards, third-party certification, and public records (available on the Internet) of the environmental performance of its participants. The assessments of the CST discussed in detail in this book suggest that these governance mechanisms may have helped to reduce free-riding behavior by "dirty" hotels and to allow only the hotels with the highest certified environmental performance to show an association with significant price premiums.

On the other hand, the evaluations of the Sustainable Slopes Program (SSP) discussed in the book suggest that this initiative may be characterized as reflecting an aggressive resistance strategy by the US ski industry aimed at pre-empting new environmental regulations and to reduce the enforcement of existing regulations by adopting symbolic "green" practices. Since its inception in 2000, the SSP has been a strictly voluntary initiative with no performance-based standards, no independent certification, and no sanctions/rewards for different levels of environmental performance. Established by the US National Ski Areas Association, the SSP received endorsement from the US EPA and some financial support from the US Forest Service during the George W. Bush administration. However, none of the major environmental conservation organizations, such as the Sierra Club, the Nature Conservancy, and the Natural Resources Defense Council that were initially involved in the design of the SSP, have officially endorsed the program.

Facing SSP's weak institutional mechanisms for preventing opportunistic behavior, it appears that the program tends to attract ski areas with lower environmental performance than non-participant ones. Moreover, once enrolled and compared to non-participants, SSP ski areas do not appear to have higher overall environmental performance or higher scores in the following individual dimensions of environmental protection: expansion management, pollution management, and wildlife and habitat management. SSP participants only appear to show a statistically significant correlation with higher natural resource conservation performance rates.

Future research agenda

Finally, I anticipate that the framework of analysis and initial empirical studies detailed in this book can help guide and spur additional empirical research that focuses on studying the variation in business responses to the protective public policy process in different country contexts. Initially, research may entail in-depth case studies that allow longitudinal examination of the protective policy process and the associated responses adopted by business. An alternative approach involves firm-level, cross-sectional research that collects information about the different levels of resistance/cooperation adopted by businesses during specific stages of the policy process. Other researchers may want to focus on three important topics not discussed in detail in this book. First, they may want to theorize about the business performance implications of adopting different levels resistance to the protective policy process. Second, they may want to develop theoretical arguments explaining how variations in local country conditions moderate the policy process–business response relationship. And third, they may want to theorize about the internal organizational, political, and psychological phenomena that drive firms' responses to the institutionalization dynamic unfolded during the policy process stages.

Notes

1. This chapter includes slightly modified portions of Rivera *et al.* (2009), reprinted with permission.
2. I led this work and had the great fortune of receiving the advice and ideas from multiple co-authors; all duly recognized in the acknowledgment section at the beginning of the book.

References

Adelman, I. and Morris, C. T. 1965. "A factor analysis of the interrelationship between social and political variables and per capita gross national product," *The Quarterly Journal of Economics* 79 (4): 555–78.

Aden, J., Kyu-Hong, A., and Rock, M. 1999. "What is driving pollution abatement expenditure behavior of manufacturing plants in Korea?" *World Development* 27 (7): 1203–14.

Aeschylus 458 BC. *The Oresteia*. Translated by Fagles, R. New York: Penguin Classics, 1979.

Aldrich, J. and Nelson, F. 1984. *Linear Probability, Logic, and Probit Models*. London, UK: Sage Publications.

Alvarez, M., Cheibub, J. A., Limongi, F., and Prezeworski, A. 1996. "Classifying political regimes," *Studies in Comparative International Development* 31: 3–36.

Amenta, E., Dunleavy, K., and Berstein, M. 1994. "Stolen thunder? Huey Long's 'share our wealth,' political mediation, and the second new deal," *American Sociological Review* 59: 678–702.

Ames, B. and Keck, M. E. 1997. "The politics of sustainable development: environmental policy making in four Brazilian states," *Journal of Interamerican Studies and World Affairs* 3: 1–40.

Andonova, L. 2003. "Openness and the environment in Central and Eastern Europe: can trade and foreign investment stimulate better environmental management in enterprises?" *Journal of Environment and Development* 12 (2): 177–204.

Andrews, R. 1998. "Environmental regulation and business self-regulation," *Policy Sciences* 31: 177–97.

Aplin, J. C. and Hegarty, W. H. 1980. "Political influence: strategies employed by organizations to impact legislation in business and economic matters," *Academy of Management Journal* 23 (3): 438–50.

Arnould, R. and Grabowski, H. 1981. "Auto safety regulation: an analysis of market failure," *Bell Journal of Economics* 12 (1): 27–48.

Arora, S. and Cason, T. 1996. "Why do firms volunteer to exceed environmental regulations? Understanding participation in EPA's 33/50 program," *Land Economics* 72: 413–32.

Ascher, W. 1999. *Why Governments Waste Natural Resources: Policy Failures in Developing Countries.* Baltimore: Johns Hopkins University Press.

Bacharach, P. and Baratz, M. 1962. "Two faces of power," *American Political Science Review* **56** (4): 947–52.

Baird, J. 2004. "Utah ski areas rated low on environment," *The Salt Lake Tribune* September 12, B1.

Balfour, F. 2005. "A big, dirty growth engine; pollution still chokes China, but green technology is starting to emerge," *Business Week* **3,948** (22): 122.

Bansal, T. and Roth, K. 2000. "Why companies go green: a model of ecological responsiveness," *Academy of Management Journal* **43** (4): 717–36.

Barbosa, D. 2008. "105 killed in China mine explosion." *The New York Times* December 7. Accessed October 14, 2008: www.nytimes.com/2007/12/07/world/asia/07mine.html?scp=1&sq=Linfen+mine&st=nyt.

Bardach, E. C. 1977. *The Implementation Game.* Cambridge, MA: MIT Press.

Barley, S. and Tolbert, T. 1997. "Institutionalization and structuration: studying the links between action and institutions," *Organization Studies* **18**: 93–117.

Barney, J. 1991. "Firm resources and sustained competitive advantage," *Journal of Management* **17**: 99–120.

Barney, J. and Hesterley, W. 1996. "Organizational economics: understanding the relationships between organizations and economic analysis," in Clegg, S., Hardy, C. and Nord, W. (eds.) *Handbook of Organization Studies.* London: Sage, 115–47.

Baron, D. 2005. *Business and its Environment* (5th edn.). Upper Saddle River, NJ: Pearson Education Inc.

Baron, J., Dobbin, F., and Jennings, P. 1986. "War and peace: the evolution of modern personnel administration in the US industry," *American Journal of Sociology* **92**: 250–83.

Bartel, A. and Thomas, L. 1985. "Direct and indirect effects of regulation: a new look at OSHA's impact," *Journal of Law and Economics* **28**: 1–25.

Bartley, T. and Schneiberg, M. 2002. "Rationality and institutional contingency: the varying politics of economic regulation in the fire insurance industry," *Sociological Perspectives* **45** (1): 47–79.

Baumgartner, F. and Jones, B. 1993. *Agendas and Instability in American Politics.* Chicago: University of Chicago Press.

Baysinger, B. 1984. "Domain maintenance as an objective of business political activity: an expanded typology," *Academy of Management Review* **9**: 248–58.

Bazerman, M. and Hoffman, A. 1999. "Sources of environmentally destructive behavior: individual, organizational, and institutional perspectives," in Sutton, R. (ed.) *Research in Organizational Behavior.* Stanford: Jai Press Inc., 39–79.

Bazerman, M., Messick, D., Tenbrusel, A., and Wade-Benzoni, K. (eds.) 1997. *Environment, Ethics, and Behavior: the Psychology of Environmental Valuation and Degradation.* San Francisco: New Lexington Press.

Beck, T., Demirguc-Kunt, A., and Levine, R. 2005. "SMEs, growth and poverty: cross-country evidence," *Journal of Economic Growth* **10**: 199–229.

Belsley, D., Kuh, E., and Welsch, R. 1980. *Regression Diagnostics: Identifying Influential Data and Sources of Collinearity.* New York: John Willey and Sons.

Berchicci, L. and King, A. 2007. "Postcards from the edge: a review of the business and environment literature," *Academy of Management Annals* **1**: 513–47.

Berger, P. L. and Luckmann, T. 1967. *The Social Construction of Reality: a Treatise in the Sociology of Knowledge.* New York: Anchor Books.

Berry, W. D. 1984. "Utility regulation in the States: the policy effects of professionalism and salience to the consumer," *American Journal of Political Science* **23** (2): 263–77.

Bien, A. 2000. Director: Costa Rican Association of Private Reserves, San Jose, Costa Rica. *Interview by author.*

Birnbaum, P. H. 1985. "Political strategies of regulated organizations as functions of context and fear," *Strategic Management Journal* **6**: 135–50.

Blackman, A. 2000. "Informal sector pollution control: what policy options do we have?" *World Development* **28**: 2,067–82.

Blackman, A. and Bannister, G. 1998. "Community pressure and clean technology in the informal sector: an econometric analysis of the adoption of propane by traditional Mexican brickmakers," *Journal of Environmental Economics and Management* **35**: 1–21.

Blackman, A. and Sisto, N. 2005. "Muddling through while environmental regulatory capacity evolves: what role for voluntary agreements?" *Resources for the Future,* Washington, DC. Working paper.

Blake, B. and Becker, A. 1998. *The New Key to Costa Rica.* Berkeley, CA: Ulysses Press.

Blevins, J. 2004. "It's not easy being green: ski areas dispute analysis of their environmental records," *Denver Post* August 30.

Blondel, J. 1997. "Political opposition in the contemporary world," *Government and Opposition* **32** (4): 462–86.

Boddewyn, J. J. and Brewer, T. L. 1994. "International-business political behavior: new theoretical directions," *The Academy of Management Review* 19 (1): 119–43.

Bollen, K. 1980. "Issues in the comparative measurement of political democracy," *American Sociological Review* 45: 370–90.

1986. "Political rights and political liberties in nations: an evaluation of human rights measures, 1950 to 1984," *Human Rights Quarterly* 8: 567–91.

1993. "Liberal democracy: validity and method factors in cross-national measures," *American Journal of Political Science* 37 (4): 1,207–30.

Bonardi, J. and Keim, G. 2005. "Corporate political strategies for widely salient issues," *Academy of Management Review* 30 (3): 555–76.

Bonardi, J., Hillman, A., and Keim, G. 2005. "The attractiveness of political markets: implications for firm strategy," *Academy of Management Review* 30 (2): 397–413.

Boo, E. 1990. *Ecotourism: The Potential and Pitfalls.* Washington, DC: World Wildlife Fund, 25–37.

Bourdieu, P. and Wacquant, L. C. 1992. *An Invitation Toward Reflexive Sociology.* Chicago: University of Chicago Press.

Bowen, F. 2002. "Organizational slack and corporate greening: broadening the debate," *British Journal of Management* 13 (4): 305–16.

Brack, D. 1996. *International Trade and the Montreal Protocol.* London: Chatham House.

Bray, D., Sanchez, J., and Murphy, E. 2002. "Social dimensions of organic coffee production in Mexico: lessons for eco-labeling initiatives," *Society and Natural Resources* 15: 429–46.

Brewer, G. D. 1978. "Termination: hard choices, harder questions," *Public Administration Review* 38: 338–44.

Brewer, G. D. and deLeon, P. 1983. *The Foundations of Policy Analysis.* Monterey, CA: Brooks/Cole.

Briggs, J. 2000. "Ski resorts and national forests: rethinking forest service management practices for recreational use," *Boston College Environmental Affairs Law Review* 28: 79–118.

Burns, S. 2005. "Bringing down the mountains: the impact of mountaintop removal surface coal mining on southern West Virginia communities, 1970–2004," unpublished doctoral dissertation, West Virginia University.

Carmin, J., Darnall, N., and Homens, J. 2003. "Stakeholder involvement in the design of US voluntary environmental initiatives: does sponsorship matter?" *Policy Studies Journal* 31 (4): 527–43.

Carpenter, D. 2001. *The Forging of Bureaucratic Autonomy: Reputation, Networks, and Policy Innovation in Executive Agencies, 1862–1928.* Princeton: Princeton University Press.

Cashore, B. and Vertinsky, I. 2000. "Policy networks and firm behaviors: governance systems and firm responses to external demands for sustainable forest management," *Policy Sciences* **33**: 1–30.

Castrogiovanni, G. J. 1991. "Environmental munificence: a theoretical assessment," *Academy of Management Review* **16** (3): 542–65.

Cavazos, D. 2005. "Organizations and the state: an interactive view," unpublished dissertation, Texas Tech University.

Chen, M. and Hambrick, D. 1995. "Speed, stealth, and selective attack: how small firms differ from large firms in competitive behavior," *Academy of Management Journal* **38**: 453–82.

Chivers, C. J. 2008. "Gorbachev, rebuking Putin, criticizes Russian elections," *The New York Times* January 29. Accessed February 18, 2008: www.nytimes.com/2008/01/29/world/europe/29russia.html.

Christensen, C., Craig, T., and Hart, S. 2001. "The great disruption," *Foreign Affairs* **80** (2): 80–95.

Christmann, P. 1997. "Environmental strategies of multinational companies: determinants and effects on competitive advantage," unpublished doctoral dissertation, University of California, Los Angeles.

Christmann, P. and Taylor, G. 2001. "Globalization and the environment: determinants of firm self-regulation in China," *Journal of International Business Studies* **32**: 439–58.

Clark, T. 2002. *The Policy Process: a Practical Guide for Natural Resource Professionals*. New Haven, CT: Yale University Press.

Clawson, D., Neustadtl, A., and Bearden, J. 1986. "The logic of business unity: corporate contributions to the 1980 congressional elections," *American Sociological Review* **51**: 797–811.

Clegg, S. R., Courpasson, D., and Phillips, N. 2006. *Power and Organizations*. London: Sage Publications.

Clemens, E. S. and Cook, J. M. 1999. "Politics and institutionalism: explaining durability and change," *Annual Review of Sociology* **25**: 441–66.

Clifford, H. 2002. *Downhill Slide: Why the Corporate Ski Industry is Bad for Skiing, Ski Towns, and the Environment*. San Francisco: Sierra Club Books.

Cody, E. 2008. "Safety subverted in China's mines: corruption comes to the surface after disaster that halted production," *The Washington Post* February 18, A10.

Cohen, A. and Einav, L. 2003. "The effects of mandatory seat belt laws on driving behavior and traffic fatalities," *Review of Economics and Statistics* **85** (4): 828–43.

Cohen, J. and Cohen, P. 1983. *Applied Multiple Regression: Correlation Analysis for the Behavioral Sciences*. Hillsdale, NJ: Lawrence Erlbaum Associates.

Conner, K. 1991. "A historical comparison of resource-based theory and five schools of thought within industrial organization economics: do we have a new theory of the firm?" *Journal of Management* 17: 121–54.

Constable, P. and Rondeaux, C. 2008. "Desiring a fair vote, doubting it will be: Pakistanis expect rigging by government," *The Washington Post* February 18, A13.

Cordano, M. and Frieze, I. 2000. "Pollution reduction preferences of US environmental managers: applying Ajzen's theory of planned behavior," *Academy of Management Journal* 43: 627–41.

Cottrell, S. 2003. "Influence of sociodemographics and environmental attitudes on general responsible environmental behavior among recreational boaters," *Environment and Behavior* 35: 347–75.

Crepaz, M. M. L. 1995. "Explaining national variations of air pollution levels: political institutions and their impact on environmental policy-making," *Environmental Politics* 4 (3): 391–414.

Crepaz, M. M. L. and Lijphart, A. 1995. "Linking and integrating corporatism and consensus democracy: theory, concepts and evidence," *British Journal of Political Science* 25 (2): 281–8.

Culhane, P. 1981. *Public Lands Politics*. Baltimore: Johns Hopkins University Press.

Dacin, T., Goodstein, J., and Scott, R. 2002. "Institutional theory and institutional change: introduction to the special research forum," *Academy of Management Journal* 45 (2): 45–57.

Dahl, R. A. 1971. *Polyarchy: Participation and Opposition*. New Haven, CT: Yale University Press.

(ed.) 1973. *Regimes and Oppositions*. New Haven, CT: Yale University Press.

Darnall, N. 2001. *To Signal or Not to Signal: Green!* Washington DC: Academy of Management Conference.

2002. "Why firms signal 'green': environmental management system certification in the United States," doctoral dissertation, University of North Carolina, Chapel Hill.

2003a. "Motivations for participating in a voluntary environmental initiative: the multi-state working group and EPA's EMS pilot program," in Sharma, S. and Starik, M. (eds.) 2003. *Research in Corporate Sustainability: the Evolving Theory and Practice of Organizations in the Natural Environment*. Boston: Edward Elgar Publishing, 123–54.

2003b. "Why firms certify to ISO 14001: an institutional and resource based view," *Academy of Management Conference's Best Paper Proceedings*. Seattle, Washington, B1–6.

2009. "Environmental regulations, green production offsets and organizations' financial performance," *Public Administration Review* **69** (3), 418–34.

Darnall, N. and Edwards Jr., D. 2006. "Predicting the cost of environmental management system adoption: the role of capabilities, resources and ownership structure," *Strategic Management Journal* **27** (2): 301–20.

Darnall, N. and Sides, S. 2008. "Assessing the performance of voluntary environmental programs: does certification matter?" *Policy Studies Journal* **36**: 95–117.

Dasgupta, N. 2000. "Environmental enforcement and small industries in India: reworking the problem in the poverty context," *World Development* **28**: 945–67.

Dasgupta, S., Hettige, H., and Wheeler, D. 2000. "What improves environmental compliance? Evidence from Mexican industry," *Journal of Environmental Economics and Management* **39**: 39–66.

Dasgupta, S., Laplante, B., Wang, H., and Wheeler, D. 2002. "Confronting the environmental Kuznets curve," *Journal of Economic Perspectives* **16**: 147–68.

Davies, J. and Smith, T. 1996. *General Social Surveys, 1972–1996: Cumulative Codebook*. Chicago: National Opinion Research Center.

deLeon, P. 1997. *Democracy and the Policy Sciences*. Albany, NY: SUNY Press.

deLeon, P. and deLeon, L. 2002. "What ever happened to policy implementation? An alternative approach," *Journal of Public Administration Research and Theory* **12**: 467–92.

deLeon, P. and Rivera, J. (eds.) 2009. *Voluntary Environmental Programs: A Policy Perspective*. Maryland: Lexington Books for the Policy Studies Organization.

DeSharzo, J. R. and Vega, L. 1999. *The Importance of Public Protected Areas in the Development of Tourism in Costa Rica: An Analysis of Visit*. Cambridge, MA: Harvard Institute for International Development.

De Soto, H. 2000. *The Mystery of Capital*. New York: Basic Books.

Delmas, M. 2002. "The diffusion of environmental management standards in Europe and in the United States: an institutional perspective," *Policy Sciences* **35** (1): 91–119.

Delmas, M. and Keller, A. 2005. "Strategic free riding in voluntary programs: the case of the US EPA Wastewise Program," *Policy Sciences* **38**: 91–106.

Delmas, M. and Marcus, A. 2004. "Firms' choice of regulatory instruments to reduce pollution: a transaction cost approach," *Business and Politics* **6**: 1–20.

Delmas, M. and Toffel, M. 2004. "Stakeholders and environmental management practices: an institutional framework," *Business Strategy and the Environment* **13** (4): 209–22.

Delmas, M. and Terlaak, A. 2001. "A framework for analyzing environmental voluntary agreements," *California Management Review* **43** (3): 44–63.

De Young, R. 1996. "Some psychological aspects of reduced consumption behavior: the role of intrinsic satisfaction and competence motivation," *Environment and Behavior* **28**: 358–409.

Diamond, L. 1999. *Developing Democracy.* Baltimore, MD: Johns Hopkins University Press.

Dierickx, I. and Cool, K. 1989. "Asset stock accumulation and sustainability of competitive advantage," *Management Science* **35**: 1,504–11.

Dietz, T. and Stern, P. 2002. *New Tools for Environmental Protection.* Washington DC: National Academy Press.

Dillman, D. A. 1978. *Mail and Telephone Surveys: The Total Design Method.* New York: John Wiley.

DiMaggio, P. and Powell, W. 1983. "The iron cage revisited: institutional isomorphism and collective rationality in organizational fields," *American Sociological Review* **48**: 147–60.

Dingell, J. and Stupak, B. 2008a. Letter to EPA Administrator Johnson in regard to industry use of Bisphenol A. US House of Representatives, Committee on Energy and Commerce, March 12.

2008b. Letter to American Chemistry Council President and CEO Gerard in regard to the use of consulting firms to manipulate public opinion related to the use of Bisphenol A and other chemicals. US House of Representatives, Committee on Energy and Commerce, April 2.

Dombeck, M. 2000. "*Letter of resignation as Chief of the US Forest Service*," Washington, DC: United States Forest Service.

Dorsey, J. 2004. "Debunking the SACC scorecard," *NSAA Journal* **Oct./Nov.**: 11–13.

Dowell, G., Hart, S., and Young, B. 2000. "Do corporate global environmental standards create or destroy market value?" *Management Science* **46** (8): 1,059–74.

Downs, A. 1957. "An economic theory of political action in a democracy," *The Journal of Political Economy* **65** (2): 135–50.

Dunlap, R. and van Liere, K. 1978. "The new environmental paradigm: a proposed measuring instrument and preliminary results," *Journal of Environmental Education* **9**: 1–19.

Eccles, R., Nohria, N., and Berkley, J. 1992. *Beyond the Hype: Rediscovering the Essence of Management.* Boston: Harvard Business School Press.

Edelman, L. 1992. "Legal ambiguity and symbolic structures: organizational mediation of civil rights law," *The American Journal of Sociology* 97 (6): 1,531–76.

Egri, C. and Herman, S. 2000. "Leadership in the North American environmental sector: values, leadership styles, and contexts of environmental leaders and their organizations," *Academy of Management Journal* 43: 571–604.

Elkins, Z. 2000. "Gradations of democracy? Empirical tests of alternative conceptualizations," *American Journal of Political Science* 44 (2): 293–300.

Estrada, F. 2008. "Luis Ferrate: 'Debo proteger la vida de dodos'," *Prensa Libre* August 3. Accessed August 6, 2008: www.prensalibre.com/pl/2008/agosto/03/253102.html.

Evans, P. 1995. *Embedded Autonomy*. Princeton, NJ: Princeton University Press.

Evans, P., Rueschemeyer, D., and Skocpol, T. (eds.) 1985. *Bringing the State back in*. Cambridge: Cambridge University Press.

Ewert, A. and Baker, D. 2001. "Standing for where you sit: an exploratory analysis of the relationship between academic major and environment beliefs," *Environment and Behavior* 33: 687–707.

Fahrenthold, D. 2008. "Mining giant to pay $20 million EPA fine," *The Washington Post* January 18, A16.

Farrell, T. and Marion, J. 2001. "Identifying and assessing ecotourism visitor impacts at eight protected areas in Costa Rica and Belize," *Environmental Conservation* 28 (3): 215–25.

Fischer, D. W. 1983. "Strategies toward political pressures: a typology of firm responses," *Academy of Management Review* 8 (1): 71–8.

Fischer, F. and Hajer, M. (eds.) 1999. *Living with Nature*. Oxford, UK: Oxford University Press.

Flannery, B. and May, D. 2000. "Environmental ethical decision making in the US metal-finishing industry," *Academy of Management Journal* 43: 642–62.

Fleming, P. and Spicer, A. 2007. *Contesting the Corporation: Struggle, Power and Resistance in Organization*. Cambridge, UK: Cambridge University Press.

Fligstein, N. 1996. "Markets as politics: a political-cultural approach to market institutions," *American Sociological Review* 61: 656–73.

Fligstein, N. and McAdam, D. 1993. "A political-cultural approach to the problem of strategic action," working paper originally presented at the Annual Meetings of the American Sociological Association, Washington DC, 1990.

Friedland, R. and Alford, R. 1991. "Bringing society back in: symbols, practices, and institutional conditions", in Powell, W. W. and DiMaggio, P. J. (eds.) *The New Institutionalism in Organizational Analysis*. Chicago, IL: University of Chicago Press, 232–63.

Friedman, M. 1970. "The social responsibility of business is to increase profits," *The New York Times Magazine* September 13 (32–33): 122–6.

Fukuyama, F. 1992. *The End of History and the Last Man*. New York: Free Press.

Gall, C. 2007. "Bhutto assassination ignites disarray," *The New York Times* December 28. Accessed February 18, 2008: www.nytimes.com/2007/12/28/world/asia/28pakistan.html#.

Garcia-Johnson, R. 2000. *Exporting Environmentalism: US Multinational Chemical Corporations in Brazil and Mexico*. Cambridge, MA: MIT Press.

Gentry, B. 1998. *Private Capital Flows and the Environment: Lessons from Latin America*. Cheltenham, UK: Edward Elgar.

George, E., Chattopadhyay, P., Sitkin, S. B., and Barden, J. 2006. "Cognitive underpinnings of institutional persistence and change: a framing perspective," *Academy of Management Review* **31** (2): 347–65.

Gerber, B. and Teske, P. 2000. "Field essay: regulatory policymaking in the American states: a review of theories and evidence," *Political Research Quarterly* (4): 849–86.

Giddens, A. 1984. *The Constitution of Society*. Berkeley: University of California Press.

Goodmann, L. and Kruskal, W. 1972. "Measures of association for cross-classification IV," *Journal of the American Statistical Association* **67**: 415–21.

Gorte, R. 2000. *RS20178: Forest Service Receipt-Sharing Payments: Proposal for Change*. Washington, DC: Congressional Research Service Report to Congress.

Gorte, R. and Corn, L. 1995. *The Forest Service Budget: Trust Funds and Special Accounts*. Washington, DC: Congressional Research Service Report to Congress, 96–604 ENR.

Granovetter, M. 1983. "The strength of weak ties," *Sociological Theory* **1**: 201–33.

1985. "Economic action and social structure: the problem of embeddedness," *American Journal of Sociology* **91**: 481–510.

Grasmick, H., Burski, R. J. and Kimsey, K. A. 1991. "Shame and embarrassment as determinants to noncompliance with the law: the case of an antilittering campaign," *Environment and Behavior* **23**: 233–51.

Gray, W. and Jones, C. 1991. "Longitudinal patterns of compliance with occupational safety and health administration health and safety regulations in the manufacturing sector," *Journal of Human Resources* **36**: 623–53.

Greene, W. H. 2000. *Econometric Analysis* (4th edn.). New Jersey: Prentice-Hall, Inc.

Griffin, J. and Koerber, C. 2006. "Does industry matter when managing stakeholder relations?" *Proceedings of the Best Papers of the Annual Academy of Management Conference.*

Griffiths, A. and Zammuto, R. F. 2005. "Institutional governance systems and variations in national competitive advantage: an integrative framework," *Academy of Management Review* **30** (4): 823–42.

Grindle, M. and Thomas, J. 1991. *Public Choices and Policy Change: The Political Economy of Reform in Developing Countries.* Baltimore, MD: Johns Hopkins University Press.

Grossman, G. and Krueger, A. 1991. "Environmental impacts of the North American Free Trade Agreement," working paper, National Bureau of Economic Research, Cambridge, MA.

Gunningham, N., Kagan, R. and Thornton, D. 2003. *Shades of Green: Business, Regulation, and Environment.* Stanford, CA: Stanford University Press.

Hall, P. 1986. *Governing the Economy: the Politics of State Intervention in Britain and France.* New York: Oxford University Press.

Hall, B. and Kerr, M. 1991. *1991–1992 Green Index.* Washington DC: Island Press.

Hall, P. and Taylor, R. 1996. "Political science and the three new institutionalisms," *Political Studies* **44**: 936–57.

Hambrick, D. and Abrahamson, E. 1995. "Assessing managerial discretion across industries: a multimethod approach," *Academy of Management Journal* **38**: 1,427–42.

Hambrick, D. and Mason, P. 1984. "Upper echelons: the organization as a reflection of its top managers," *Academy of Management Review* **9**: 193–206.

Hardin, G. 1968. "The tragedy of the commons," *Science* **162**: 1,243–8.

Harrison, K. 1999. "Talking with the donkey: cooperative approaches to environmental protection," *Journal of Industrial Ecology* **2** (3): 51–72.

Hart, S. 1995. "A natural resource based view of the firm," *Academy of Management Review* **20**: 986–1,014.

Hart, S. and Sharma, S. 2004. "Engaging fringe stakeholders for competitive imagination," *Academy of Management Executive* **18** (1): 7–18.

Hartman, R. S. 1988. "Self-selection bias in the evaluation of voluntary energy conservation programs," *Review of Economics and Statistics* 70: 448–58.

Hartman, B. and Zalaznick, M. 2003. "Impeccable peaks or sloppy slopes?" *Vail Daily* February 23. Accessed May 18, 2005: www.eaglevalleyalliance.org/sloppy_slopes.htm.

Hawkins, K. and Thomas, J. M. (eds.) 1984. *Enforcing Regulation.* Boston, MA: Kluwer-Nijhoff.

Heckman, J. 1978. "Dummy endogenous variables in a simultaneous equation system," *Econometrica* 46 (6): 931–59.

1979. "Sample selection bias as a specification error," *Econometrica* 47 (1): 153–61.

Henriques, I. and Sadorsky, P. 1996. "The determinants of an environmental responsive firm: an empirical approach," *Journal of Environmental Economics and Management* 30: 381–95.

Hettige, H., Huq, Q., Pargal, S., and Wheeler, D. 1996. "Determinants of pollution abatement in developing countries: evidence from South and Southeast Asia," *World Development* 24: 1,891–904.

Higgins, M. and Williamson, J. 1999. "Explaining inequality the world round: cohort size, Kuznets curves, and openness," working paper 7224, National Bureau of Economic Research.

Highley, C. J. and Leveque, F. (eds.) 2001. *Environmental Voluntary Approaches: Research Insights for Policy-Makers.* Italy: Fundazione Eni Enrico Mattei.

Hillman, A. 2003. "Determinants of political strategies in US multinationals," *Business and Society* 42 (4): 455–84.

Hillman, A. and Hitt, M. 1999. "Corporate political strategy formulation: a model of approach, participation, and strategy decision," *Academy of Management Review* 24 (4): 825–42.

Hillman, A. and Keim, G. 1995. "International variation in the business-government interface: institutional and organizational considerations," *Academy of Management Review* 20 (1): 193–214.

Hillman, A., Keim, G., and Schuler, D. 2004. "Corporate political activity: a review and research agenda," *Journal of Management* 30 (6): 837–57.

Hines, J., Hungeford, H., and Tomere, A. 1987. "Analysis and synthesis or research on responsible pro-environmental behavior: a meta analysis," *The Journal of Environmental Education* 18: 1–8.

Hirsch, P. 1997. "Sociology without social structure: neoinstitutional theory meets brave new world," *American Journal of Sociology* 102 (6): 1,702–23.

Hirsch, P. and Lounsbury, M. 1997. "Ending the family quarrel: toward reconciliation of 'old' and 'new' institutionalism," *American Behavioral Scientist* 40 (4): 406–18.

Hoffman, A. 1997. *From Heresy to Dogma: An Institutional History of Corporate Environmentalism*. San Francisco, CA: New Lexington Press.

1999. "Institutional evolution and change: environmentalism and the US chemical industry," *Academy of Management Journal* **42**: 351–71.

2000. *Competitive Environmental Strategy: A Guide to the Changing Business Landscape*. Washington, DC: Island Press.

Holm, P. 1995. "The dynamics of institutionalization: transformation processes in Norwegian fisheries," *Administrative Science Quarterly* **40**: 398–422.

Honey, M. 1999. *Ecotourism and Sustainable Development*. Washington DC: Island Press.

Horowitz, D. L. 1989. "Is there a third world policy process?" *Policy Sciences* **22**: 197–212.

Howlett, M. and Ramesh, M. 1995. *Studying Public Policy: Policy Cycles and Policy Subsystems*. New York: Oxford University Press.

Hsiao, C. 1986. *Analysis of Panel Data*. New York: Cambridge University Press.

Hudson, S. 2000. *Snow Business: A study of the International Ski Industry*. New York: Cassell.

Huntington, S. 1952. "The marasmus of the ICC," *Yale Law Journal* **6**: 467–509.

Husted, B. 1999. "Wealth, culture and corruption," *Journal of International Business* **30**: 339–59.

Huxley, T. 1880. "The coming of age of The Origin of Species," *Science* **1** (2): 15–20.

Instituto Centroamericano de Administración de Empresas (INCAE) 2002. *Tourism in Costa Rica: A Competitive Challenge*. San Jose, Costa Rica: INCAE.

Instituto Costarricense de Turismo (ICT) 1995. *Strategic Sustainable Development Plan for the Costa Rican Tourism Sector, 1995–1999*. San Jose, Costa Rica: ICT.

1999. *Costa Rican Institute of Tourism: Annual Report of Statistics, 1998*. San Jose, Costa Rica: ICT.

2002. *Costa Rican Institute of Tourism: Annual Report of Statistics, 2001*. San Jose, Costa Rica: ICT.

2009. *Costa Rican Institute of Tourism: Annual Report of Statistics, 2008*. San Jose, Costa Rica: ICT.

Isham, J., Kaufmann, D., and Pritchett, L. H. 1997. "Civil liberties, democracy, and the performance of government projects," *The World Bank Economic Review* **11** (2): 219–42.

Issac, L. and Griffin, L. 1989. "Ahistoricism in time-series analysis of historical process: critique, redirection, and illustration from US labor history," *American Sociological Review* **54**: 873–90.

Jaffe, A. B., Peterson, S. R., and Portney, P. 1995. "Environmental regulation and competitiveness of US manufacturing," *Journal of Economic Literature* 33: 132–63.

Janis, I. L. 1982. *Groupthink: Psychological Studies of Policy Decisions and Fiascoes*. New York: Houghton Mifflin.

Janofsky, M. 2000. "Environment groups' ratings rile ski industry," *The New York Times* December 3, 46.

Jennings, P. D. and Zandbergen, P. A. 1995. "Ecologically sustainable organizations: an institutional approach," *Academy of Management Review* 20(4): 1,015–52.

Jepperson, R. L. 1991. "Institutions, institutional effects, and institutionalism," in Powell, W. W. and DiMaggio, P. J. (eds.) *The New Institutionalism in Organizational Analysis*. Chicago, IL: University of Chicago Press, 143–63.

2002. "Political modernities: disentangling two underlying dimensions of institutional differentiation," *Sociological Theory* 20 (1): 61–85.

Jepperson, R. L. and Meyer, J. W. 1991. "The public order and the construction of formal organizations," in Powell, W. W. and DiMaggio, P. J. (eds.) *The New Institutionalism in Organizational Analysis*. Chicago, IL: University of Chicago Press, 204–31.

Jermier, J., Knights, D., and Nord, W. (eds.) 1994. *Resistance and Power in Organizations*. London: Sage.

Jones, C., Inman, C., Pratt, L., Mesa, N., and Rivera, J. 2001. "Issues in the design of a green certification program for tourism," in Panayotou, T. (ed.) *Environment for Growth in Central America*. Cambridge, MA: Harvard University Press, 292–321.

Kagan, R. A. 1984. "On regulatory inspectorates and police," in Hawkins, K. and Thomas, J. M. (eds.) *Enforcing Regulation*. Boston, MA: Kluwer-Nijhoff, 37–64.

Kaiser, K. 1980. "The new regulation of health and safety," *Political Science Quarterly* 95 (fall): 479–91.

Kamieniecki, S. 2006. *Corporate America and Environmental Policy: How Often does Business get its Way?* Stanford, CA: Stanford University Press.

Katz, D. and Kahn, R. 1966. *The Social Psychology of Organizations*. New York: Wiley.

Katzenstein, P. 1994. *Corporatism and Change: Austria, Switzerland, and the Politics of Industry*. Ithaca, NY: Cornell University Press.

Keim, G. and Baysinger, B. 1988. "The efficacy of business political activity: competitive considerations in a principal agent context," *Journal of Management* 14 (2): 163–80.

Kellert, S. 1996. *The Value of Life: Biological Diversity and Human Society*. Washington, DC: Island Press.

Kessler, D. *et al.* 1996. "The Food and Drug Administration's regulation of tobacco products," *New England Journal of Medicine* **335**: 988–94.

Khan, J. and Yardley, J. 2007. "As China roars, pollution reaches deadly extremes," *The New York Times* August 26, 1A and 6–7A.

Khanna, M. 2001. "Non-mandatory approaches to environmental protection," *Journal of Economic Surveys* **15** (3): 291–324.

Khanna, M. and Damon, L. 1999. "EPA's voluntary 33/50 program: impact on toxic releases and economic performance of firms," *Journal of Environmental Economics and Management* **37**: 1–25.

Khanna, M., Quimio, W., and Bojilova, D. 1998. "Toxics release information: a policy tool or environmental protection?" *Journal of Environmental Economics and Management* **36**: 243–66.

Kim, T., Shin, D., Oh, H., and Jeong, Y. 2007. "Inside the iron cage: organizational political dynamics and institutional changes in presidential selection systems in Korean universities, 1985–2002," *Administrative Science Quarterly* **52**: 286–323.

King, A. and Lenox, M. 2000. "Industry self-regulation without sanctions: the chemical industry responsible care program," *Academy of Management Journal* **43**: 698–716.

King, A. and Shaver, M. 2001. "Are aliens green? Assessing foreign establishments' environmental conduct in the US," *Strategic Management Journal* **22** (11): 244–56.

Kingdon, J. 1995. *Agendas, Alternatives, and Public Policies* (2nd edn.). New York: Longman.

Klassen, R. D. and McLaughlin, C. 1996. "The impact of environmental management on firm performance," *Management Science* **42**: 1,199–214.

Kollmuss, A. and Agyeman, J. 2002. "Mind the gap: why do people act environmentally and what are the barriers to pro-environmental behavior?" *Environmental Education Research* **8**: 239–60.

Kostova, T. and Roth, K. 2002. "Adoption of an organizational practice by subsidiaries of multinational corporations: institutional and relational effects," *Academy of Management Journal* **45**: 215–33.

Kraft, M. and Kaminiecki, S. (eds.) 2007. *Business and Environmental Policy*. Cambridge, MA: MIT Press.

Kuhn, T. S. 1962. *The Structure of Scientific Revolutions*. Chicago: University of Chicago Press.

Langeland, T. 2002. "Green room or greenwash?" *Colorado Springs Independent* February 14. Accessed May 18, 2005: www.csindy.com/csindy/2002–02–14/news3.html.

Lasswell, H. 1948. *Power and Personality*. New York: Norton.
1956. *The Decision Process*. College Park, MD: University of Maryland Press.
1971. *A Pre-view of Policy Sciences*. New York: American Elsevier.
Layton, P. 2008. "Chemical industry's influence at EPA probed," *The Washington Post*, April 4, A4.
Lee, L. and Trost, R. 1978. "Estimation of some limited dependent variable models with application to housing demand," *Journal of Econometrics* 8: 357–82.
Levine, M. E. and Forrence, J. L. 1990. "Regulatory capture, public interest, and the public agenda: toward a synthesis," *Journal of Law, Economics, and Organization* **6**: 167–98.
Levison, A. 1996. "Environmental regulations and manufacturers' location choices: evidence from census manufacturers," *Journal of Public Economics* **62**: 5–29.
Levy, C. 2008. "Putin's iron grip on Russia suffocates his opponents," *The New York Times* February 24, A1.
Levy, D. and Kolk, A. 2002. "Strategic responses to global climate change: conflicting pressures on multinationals in the oil industry," *Business and Politics* **4**: 275–300.
Levy, D. and Newell, P. 2000. "Oceans apart? Business responses to the environment in Europe and North America," *Environment* **42** (9): 8–20.
Lieberman, R. 2002. "Ideas, institutions, and political change," *American Political Science Review* **96** (4): 697–712.
Lijphart, A. 1984. *Democracies: Patterns of Majoritarian and Consensus Government in Twenty-one Countries*. New Haven: Yale University Press.
Lim, J. H. and Tang, S. 2002. "Democratization and environmental policy-making in Korea," *Governance* **15**: 561–82.
Lindblom, C. and Woodhouse, E. 1993. *The Policy-Making Process*. New Jersey: Prentice Hall.
Link, G. 2005. Director of Public Policy, National Ski Areas Association, Lakewood. *Interview by author*, March 29.
Little, R. 1995. "Modeling the drop-out mechanism in repeated-measures studies," *Journal of the American Statistical Association* **90**: 1,112–21.
Lizano, R. 2001. Director, Certification for Sustainable Tourism, San Jose, Costa Rica. *Interview by author.*
Lo, C. W. H. and Leung, S. W. 2000. "Environmental agency and public opinion in Guangzhou: the limits of a popular approach to environmental governance," *The China Quarterly* **163**: 677–704.

Lowi, T. 1964. "Review: American business, public policy, case-studies, and political theory," *World Politics* **16** (4): 677–715. (Reviewed work: Bauer, R., Pool, I. and Dexter, L. 1963. *American Business and Public Policy: The Politics of Foreign Trade*. Baltimore: Johns Hopkins University Press.)

Lukes, S. 1974. *Power: A Radical View*. London: Palgrave.

Lybecker, D. L. and Horan, J. E. 2005. "Multi-party environmental negotiations: perspectives from democratizing nations in Latin America," *International Journal of Organization Theory and Behavior* **8**: 210–36.

Lyon, T. P. and Maxwell, J. 2002. "Voluntary approaches to environmental regulation: an overview," in Franzini, M. and Nicita, A. (eds.) *Economic Institutions and Environmental Policy*. Aldershot, UK: Ashgate Publishing Ltd.

2004. *Corporate Environmentalism and Public Policy*. Cambridge: Cambridge University Press.

Maddala, G. S. 1986. *Limited-Dependent and Qualitative Variables in Econometrics*. New York: Cambridge University Press.

Mahon, J. 1993. "Shaping issues/manufacturing agents: corporate political sculpting," in B. Mitnick (ed.) *Corporate Political Agency*. Newbury Park, CA: Sage, 22–39.

Makino, S., Isobe, T., and Chan, C. M. 2004. "Does country matter?" *Strategic Management Journal* **25**: 1,027–43.

March, J. G. and Olsen, J. 1989. *Rediscovering Institutions: The Organizational Basis of Politics*. New York: The Free Press.

Marcus, A. A. 1984. *The Adversary Economy: Business Responses to Changing Government Requirements*. Westport, CT: Quorum Books.

Margolis, J. and Walsh, J. 2001. *People and profits? The search for a link between company's social and financial performance*. Mahwah, NJ: Lawrence Erlbaum Associates.

2003. "Misery loves companies: rethinking social initiatives by business," *Administrative Science Quarterly* **48**: 268–305.

Mason, S. 2008. "Letter to the chairman of the House Committee on Energy and Commerce in regards to FDA rationale for safety of Bishphenol A," US Food and Drug Administration, Office of Acting Assistant Commissioner for Legislation, February 25.

Mazur, A. and Welch, E. 1999. "The geography of American environmentalism," *Environmental Science and Policy* **2**: 389–96.

Meier, K. 1988. *The Political Economy of Regulation: The Case of Insurance*. Albany, NY: SUNY Press.

Mesa, N. and Inman, C. 1999. *Tourism in Costa Rica: A Competitive Challenge*. Costa Rica: Instituto Centroamericano de Administración de Empresas.

Meyer, J. 1980. "The world polity and the authority of the nation-state," in Bergeson, A. (ed.) *Studies of the Modern World-System.* New York: Academic Press, Inc., 109–37.

Meyer, J. and Rowan, B. 1977. "Institutional organizations: formal structure as myth and ceremony," *American Journal of Sociology* 80: 340–63.

Meyer, J. and Scott, W. 1983. *Organizational Environment: Ritual and Rationality.* Beverly Hills, CA: Sage.

Meyer, J., Boli, J., Thomas, M., and Ramírez, F. 1997. "World society and nation state," *American Journal of Sociology* 103: 144–81.

Meznar, M. and Nigh, D. 1995. "Buffer or bridge? Environmental and organizational determinants of public affairs activities in American firms," *Academy of Management Journal* 38 (4): 975–96.

Milanovic, B. 2005. "Can we discern the effect of globalization on income distribution? Evidence from household surveys," *The World Bank Economic Review* 19: 21–44.

Milstein, M., Hart, S., and York, A. 2002. "Coercion breeds variation: the differential impact of isomorphic pressures on environmental strategies," in Hoffman, A. and Ventresca, M. (eds.) *Organizations, Policy, and the Natural Environment.* Stanford, CA: Stanford University Press.

Mitchell, N. 1997. *The Conspicuous Corporation: Business, Public Policy, and Representative Democracy.* Ann Arbor, MI: University of Michigan Press.

Mizruchi, M. 1992. *The Structure of Corporate Political Action.* Cambridge, MA: Harvard University Press.

Mizruchi, M. and Bey, D. 2005. "Corporate control, interfirm relations, and corporate power," in Janoski, T., Alford, R., Alexander, H., and Schwartz, M. *The Handbook of Political Sociology.* Cambridge, UK: Cambridge University Press.

Moldan, B. *et al.* 2006. "Choosing environmental policy responses," in *Millennium Ecosystem Assessment Synthesis Report.* New York: United Nations.

Montrie, C. 2003. *To Save the Land and the People: a History of Opposition to Surface Coal Mining in Appalachia.* Chapel Hill, NC: University of North Carolina Press.

Moon, S. 2005. "Contexts, timing, and corporate voluntary environmental behavior: a new look at voluntary participation in the Environmental Protection Agency's Green Lights Program," Doctoral dissertation, University of Colorado.

Mui, Y. 2008. "Wal-Mart to pull bottles made with chemical BPA," *The Washington Post* April 18, 1B.

Murtha, T. P. and Lenway, S. A. 1994. "Country capabilities and the strategic state: how national political institutions affect multinational corporations' strategies," *Strategic Management Journal* 15: 113–29.

National Ski Areas Association (NSAA) 2000. *Sustainable Slopes: The Environmental Charter for Ski Areas*. Denver, CO: NSAA.

2001. *Sustainable Slopes: Annual Report 2001*. Denver, CO: NSAA.

2002. *Sustainable Slopes: Annual Report 2002*. Denver, CO: NSAA.

2003a. *Kottke National End of Season Survey 2002/03: Preliminary Results*. Denver, CO: NSAA.

2003b. *Kottke National End of Season Survey 2003/04: Preliminary Results*. Denver, CO: NSAA.

2003c. *Sustainable Slopes: Annual Report 2003*. Denver, CO: NSAA.

2004a. "Estimated US ski industry skier visits by region," NSAA. Accessed May 18, 2005: www.nsaa.org/nsaa/press/2004/skiervisits.pdf.

2004b. "494 US ski resorts in operation during 2003–2004 season," *NSAA*. Accessed May 18, 2005: www.nsaa.org/nsaa/press/2004/03-04-sa-number-history.pdf.

2005a. *Sustainable Slopes: Annual Report 2005*. Denver, CO: NSAA.

2005b. "Preliminary report indicates 2004/05 season as fourth best on record," NSAA. Accessed May 20, 2005: www.nsaa.org/nsaa/press/2005/nc-05-prelim-kottke.asp.

Neumayer, E. 2001. "Pollution havens: an analysis of policy options for dealing with an elusive phenomenon," *Journal of Environment and Development* 10 (2): 147–77.

Nordlinger, E. 1981. *On the Autonomy of the Democratic State*. Cambridge, MA: Harvard University Press.

North, D. N. 1990. *Institutions, Institutional Change and Economic Performance*. New York: Cambridge University Press.

Nystrom, A. D. and Smith, W. 1996. *The Berkeley Guide for Central America* (2nd edn.). New York: Fodors Travel Publications, Inc.

Oetzel, J. 2005. "Smaller may be beautiful but is it more risky? Assessing and managing political and economic risk in Costa Rica," *International Business Review* 14 (6): 765–90.

Office of Technology Assessment (OTA) 1995. *Environmental Policy Tools: A User's Guide*. Washington, DC: US Congress, OTA.

Oliver, C. 1991. "Strategic responses to institutional processes," *Academy of Management Review* 16: 145–79.

1992. "The antecedents of deinstitutionalization," *Organization Studies* 13 (4): 563–88.

Olson, M. 1965. *The Logic of Collective Action: Public Goods and the Theory of Groups*. Cambridge, MA: Harvard University Press.

Olsen, R. 1980. "A least squares correction for selectivity bias," *Econometrica* 48 (7): 1,815–20.

O'Day, R. 1974. "Intimidation rituals, reactions to reform," *The Journal of Applied Behavioral Science* 10 (3): 373–86.

O'Rourke, D. 2003. "Outsourcing regulations: analyzing nongovernmental systems of labor standards and monitoring," *Policy Studies Journal* 31 (1): 1–29.

2004. *Community-driven Regulation: Balancing Development and the Environment in Vietnam.* London: MIT Press.

Ostrom, E. 1990. *Governing the Commons: The Evolution of Institutions for Collective Action.* New York: Cambridge University Press.

Palmer, K., Oates, W. E., and Portney, P. R. 1995. "Tightening environmental standards: the benefit-cost or the no-cost paradigm?" *Journal of Economic Perspectives* 9: 119–32.

Palmeri, C. 2003. "An uphill battle on the slippery slopes: can cheap tickets and snowboard 'terrain' save the ski resorts?" *Business Week* 3815: 44.

Panayotou, T. 1997. "Demystifying the environmental Kuznets curve: turning a black box into a policy tool," *Environment and Development Economics* 2: 465–84.

Pargal, S. and Wheeler, D. 1996. "Informal regulation of industrial pollution in developing countries. Evidence from Indonesia," *Journal of Political Economy* 104: 1,314–27.

Payne, R. A. 1995. "Freedom and the environment," *Journal of Democracy* 6: 41–55.

Pedhazur, E. J. and Schmelkin, L. 1991. *Measurement, Design, and Analysis: An Integral Approach.* Hillsdale, NJ: Lawrence Erlbaum Associates.

Peltzman, S. 1976. "Toward a more general theory of regulation," *Journal of Law and Economics* 19 (2): 211–40.

Peters, G. and Pierre, J. 1998. "Institutions and time: problems of conceptualization and explanation," *Journal of Public Administration Research and Theory* 8 (4): 565–83.

Pettigrew, A. 1987. "Context and action in the transformation of the firm," *Journal of Management Studies* 24: 649–70.

Pfeffer, J. and Salancik, G. 1978. *The External Control of Organizations: A Resource Dependence Perspective.* New York: Harper and Row.

Popper, K. 2002. *The Logic of Scientific Discovery.* London: Routledge.

Porter, M. E. and van der Linde, C. 1995. "Green and competitive," *Harvard Business Review* Sep/Oct: 149–63.

Posner, R. 1974. "Theories of economic regulation," *Bell Journal of Economics and Management Science*: 335–58.

Potoski, M. and Prakash, A. 2005. "Green clubs and voluntary governance: ISO 14001 and firms' regulatory compliance," *American Journal of Political Science* **49** (2): 235–48.

Powell, W. W. and DiMaggio, P. J. 1991. *The New Institutionalism in Organizational Analysis.* Chicago, IL: University of Chicago Press.

Powell, W., Poput, K. W., and Smith-Doerr, L. 1996. "Interorganizational collaboration and the locus of innovation: networks of learning in biotechnology," *Administrative Science Quarterly* **46**: 116–45.

Pregibon, D. 1981. "Logistic regression diagnostics," *The Annals of Statistics* **9**: 705–24.

Pressman, J. and Wildavsky, A. 1984. *Implementation.* Berkeley, CA: University of California Press.

Preti, A. 2002. "Guatemala: violence in peacetime – a critical analysis of the armed conflict and the peace process," *Disasters* **26** (2): 99–119.

Procassini, A. 1995. *Competitors in Alliance.* Westport, CT: Quorum Books.

Puhani, P. 2000. "The Heckman correction for sample selection and its critique," *Journal of Economic Surveys* **14** (1): 53–68.

Quirk, P. J. 1988. "In defense of the politics of ideas," *The Journal of Politics* **50** (1): 31–41.

Rachowiecki, R. 1997. *The Lonely Planet Guide: Costa Rica* (3rd edn.). Hong Kong, China: Lonely Planet Publications.

Reed, R. and DeFillippi, R. 1990. "Causal ambiguity, barriers to imitation, and sustained competitive advantage," *Academy of Management Review* **15**: 88–102.

Reinhardt, F. L. 1998. "Environmental product differentiation: implications for corporate strategy," *California Management Review* **40** (4): 43–73.

Reinhardt, F. L. and Vietor, R. H. K. 1989. *Du Pont Freon Products Division, Case Study (A).* Cambridge, MA: Harvard Business School.

1996. *Business Management and the Natural Environment: Cases and Text.* Cincinnati, OH: Southwestern Publishing Company.

Rey, M. 2005. "Congressional Testimony before the Subcommittee on Public Lands and Forests by Mark Rey, Under Secretary of Natural Resources and Environment, USDA," February 8. Accessed April 4, 2006: www.fs.fed.us/congress/109/senate/oversight/rey/020805.html.

Rivera, J. 1998. "Public private partnerships: the tourism industry in Costa Rica," in Gentry, B. *Private Capital flows and the Environment: Lessons from Latin America.* Cheltenham, UK: Edward Elgar Press, 223–40.

2001. *Does it Pay to be Green in the Developing World? Participation in a Costa Rican Voluntary Environmental Program and its Impact on Hotels' Competitive Advantage.* Washington DC: Academy of Management Best Paper Proceedings.

2002. "Assessing a voluntary environmental initiative in the developing world: the Costa Rican certification for sustainable tourism," *Policy Sciences* **35**: 333–60.

2004. "Institutional pressures and voluntary environmental behavior in developing countries: evidence from Costa Rica," *Society and Natural Resources* **17**: 779–97.

Rivera, J. and deLeon, P. 2004. "Is greener whiter? The Sustainable Slopes Program and the voluntary environmental performance of western ski areas," *Policy Studies Journal* **32** (3): 417–37.

2005. "Chief executive officers and voluntary environmental performance: Costa Rica's Certification for Sustainable Tourism," *Policy Sciences* **38**: 107–27.

In press. "Concluding opinion, voluntary environmental programs: are carrots without sticks enough for effective environmental protection policy?" in deLeon, P. and Rivera, J.

In press. *Voluntary Environmental Programs: A Policy Perspective.* Maryland: Lexington Press.

Rivera, J., de Leon, P., and Koerber, C. 2006. "Is greener whiter yet? The Sustainable Slopes Program after five years," *Policy Studies Journal* **34** (2): 195–224.

Rivera, J. and Delmas, M. 2004. "Business and environmental policy: an introduction," *Human Ecology Review* **11** (3): 230–4.

Rivera, J., Oetzel, J., deLeon, P., and Starik, M. 2009. "Business responses to environmental and social protection policies: towards a framework for analysis," *Policy Sciences* **42**: 3–32.

Robertson, L. S. 1975. "Factors associated with safety belt use in 1974 starter-interlock equipped cars," *Journal of Health and Social Behavior* **16** (2): 173–7.

1976. "The great seat belt campaign flop," *Journal of Communication* **26**: 41–5.

Rockwood, C. 1998. *Fodor's 99: Costa Rica Travel Guide.* New York: Fodor's Travel Publications.

Rogers, P. 2002. "Cold cash: ski resorts profit on cheap US land," *San Jose Mercury News* April 7.

2003. "Forest service to review rents paid by ski resorts," *Knight Ridder Tribune Business News* January 10.

Romero, S. 2007. "Chavez's move against critic highlights shift in media," *The New York Times* May 27. Accessed February 27, 2008: www.nytimes.com/2007/05/27/world/americas/27venez.html?scp=2&sq=venezuela+and+RCtv&st=nyt.

Roome, N. 1992. "Developing environmental management strategies," *Business Strategy and the Environment* **1**: 11–24.

Rowley, T. 1997. "Moving beyond dyadic ties: a network theory of stakeholder influences," *Academy of Management Review* **22** (4): 887–910.

Rubin, D. 1976. "Inference and missing data," *Biometrika* **63**: 581–92.

Russo, M. and Fouts, P. 1997. "A resource-based perspective on corporate environmental performance and profitability," *Academy of Management Journal* **40**: 534–59.

Rust, S. and Kissinger, M. 2008a. "Gift to center headed by FDA panel raises questions," *The Washington Post* October 13, A11.

2008. "Donation raises questions for head of FDA's bisphenol A panel," *The Milwakee Journal Sentinel* October 12. Accessed October 16, 2008: www.jsonline.com/story/index.aspx?id=805074.

Sabatier, P. A. (ed.) 1975. "Social movements and regulatory agencies: toward a more adequate – and less pessimistic – theory of 'clientele capture'," *Policy Sciences* **6**: 301–42.

Sabatier, P. A. 1999. *Theories of the Policy Process*. Boulder, CO: Westview Press.

Sabatier, P. A. 2007. *Theories of the Policy Process*. Boulder, CO: Westview Press.

Sabatier, P. A. and Jenkins-Smith, H. C. 1999. "The advocacy coalition framework: an assessment," in Sabatier, P. A. (ed.) *Theories of the Policy Process*. Boulder, CO: Westview Press, 117–66.

Sachs, B. 2002. "National perspective on mountain resorts and ecology," *Vermont Law Review* **23** (3): 515–42.

Salomon, L. 1981. "Rethinking public management: third-party government and the changing forms of government action," *Public Policy* **29** (3): 255–75.

Schmidt, P. 2002. "Pursuing regulatory relief: strategic participation and litigation in US OSHA rulemaking," *Business and Politics* **4** (1): 71–89.

Schmitter, P. 1974. "Still the century of corporatism," *Review of Politics* **36**: 85–131.

Schuler, D. A. 1996. "Corporate political strategy and foreign competition: the case of the steel industry," *Academy of Management Journal* **39** (3): 720–37.

Schuler, D. A., Rehbein K., and Cramer R. D. 2002. "Pursuing strategic advantage through political means: a multivariate approach," *Academy of Management Journal* **45** (4): 659–72.

Schwenk, C. 1984. "Cognitive simplification processes in strategic decision-making," *Strategic Management Journal* **5**: 111–28.

Scott, R. W. 1991. "Unpacking institutional arguments," in Powell, W.W. and DiMaggio, P. J. (eds.) *The New Institutionalism in Organizational Analysis*. Chicago, IL: University of Chicago Press, 164–82.

2001. *Institutions and Organizations* (2nd edn.). Thousand Oaks, CA: Sage Publications.

Scruggs, L. A. 1999. "Institutions and environmental performance in seventeen western democracies," *British Journal of Political Science* 29 (1): 1–31.

Sen, S. and Bhattacharya, C. 2001. "Does doing good always lead to doing better? Consumer reactions to corporate social responsibility," *Journal of Marketing Research* 38: 225–43.

Seo, M. and Creed, W. E. D. 2002. "Institutional contradictions, praxis, and institutional change: a dialectical perspective," *Academy of Management Review* 27 (2): 222–47.

Shah, K. and Rivera, J. 2007. "Export processing zones and corporate environmental performance in emerging economies: the case of the oil, gas, and chemical sectors of Trinidad and Tobago," *Policy Sciences* 40 (4): 265–85.

Sharma, S. and Vredenburg, H. 1998. "Proactive corporate environmental strategy and the development of competitively valuable organizational capabilities," *Strategic Management Journal* 19: 729–53.

Simon, H. 1947. *Administrative Behavior: A Study of Decision Making Processes in Administrative Organizations.* New York: MacMillan.

Ski Areas Citizens' Coalition (SAAC) 2002. "Environmental Score Card Reports," SAAC. Accessed November 30, 2002: www.coloradowild.org/sacc.html.

2005. "How are ski areas graded?" SAAC. Accessed May 15, 2005: www.skiareacitizens.com/criteria.html.

Smith, K. 1995. "Does education induce people to improve the environment?" *Journal of Public Policy Analysis and Management* 14: 15–29.

Smith, M. 2000. *American Business and Political Power: Public Opinion, Elections, and Democracy.* Chicago: University of Chicago Press.

Solimano, A., Aninat, E., and Birdsall, N. (eds.) 2000. *Distributive Justice and Economic Development: the Case of Chile and Developing Countries.* Ann Arbor, MI: University of Michigan Press.

Spencer, J. W., Murtha, T. P., and Lenway, S. 2005. "How governments matter to new industry creation," *Academy of Management Review* 30 (2): 321–37.

Starik, M. and Rands, G. P. 1995. "Weaving an integrated web: multilevel and multisystem perspectives of ecologically sustainable organizations," *Academy of Management Review* 20 (4): 908–35.

Staw, B. M. and Szwajkowski, E. 1975. "The scarcity-munificence component of organizational environments and the commission of illegal acts," *Administrative Science Quarterly* 20 (3): 345–54.

Steelman, T. and Rivera, J. 2006. "Voluntary environmental programs in the United States: whose interests are served?" *Organization and Environment* 19 (4): 505–26.

Steinberg, P. 2001. *Environmental Leadership in Developing Countries: Transnational Relations and Biodiversity Policy in Costa Rica and Bolivia*. Cambridge, MA: MIT Press.

Steiner, G. A. and Steiner, J. F. 2006. *Business, Government, and Society* (11th edn.). New York: McGraw-Hill.

Steinmo, S., Thelen, K., and Longstreth, F. 1992. *Structuring Politics: Historical Institutionalism in Comparative Analysis*. New York: Cambridge University Press.

Stem, C., Lassole, J., Lee, D., and Deshler, D. 2003. "How 'eco' is ecotourism? A comparative case study of ecotourism in Costa Rica," *Journal of Sustainable Tourism* **11** (4): 322–47.

Stern, D. 2004. "The rise and fall of the environmental Kuznets curve," *World Development* **32**: 1,419–39.

Stern, P., Kalof, L., and Guagnano, G. 1995. "Values, beliefs, and proenvironmental action: attitude formation toward emergent attitude objects," *Journal of Applied Social Psychology* **25**: 1,611–36.

Stigler, G. 1971. "The theory of economic regulation," *Bell Journal of Economics* **2**: 3–21.

Stiglitz, G. 2006. *Making Globalization Work*. New York: W. W. Norton and Company.

Streeck, W. and Kenworthy, L. 2005. "Theories and practices of neocorporatism," in Janoski, T., Alford, R., Hicks, A. M., and Schwartz, M. (eds.) *The Handbook of Political Sociology*. Cambridge, UK: Cambridge University Press, 441–60.

Stuligross, D. 1999. "The political economy of environmental regulation in India," *Pacific Affairs* **72**: 392–406.

Suchman, M. 1995. "Managing legitimacy: strategic and institutional approaches," *Academy of Management Review* **20**: 571–610.

Suchman, M. and Edelman, L. 1997. "Legal rational myths: the new institutionalism and the law and society tradition," *Law and Social Inquiry* **21**:903–41.

Sutton, J. R. and Dobbin, F. 1996. "The two faces of governance: responses to legal uncertainty in US firms, 1955–1985," *American Sociological Review* **61** (Oct): 794–811.

Tashman, P. and Rivera, J. 2008. *Business Association and Corporate Social Performance: The Case of Business for Social Responsibility*. Anaheim, CA: Academy of Management Best Paper Proceedings, Social Issues in Management Division.

Teske, P. 2001. "Interests and institutions in state regulation," *American Journal of Political Science* **35** (1): 139–54.

2003. "State regulation: captured Victorian-era anachronism or 're-enforcing' autonomous structure?" *Perspectives on Politics* **1** (2): 291–306.

Tiwana, A. 2008. "Do bridging ties complement strong ties? An empirical examination of alliance ambidexterity," *Strategic Management Journal* **29** (3): 251–72.

Toffel, M. 2005. "Voluntary environmental management initiatives: smoke signals or smoke screens?" Doctoral dissertation, University of California, Berkeley.

Toffel, M. and Marshall, J. 2004. "Improving environmental performance assessment: a comparative analysis of weighing methods used to evaluate chemical release inventories," *Journal of Industrial Ecology* **8** (1–2): 143–72.

Tolbert, P. S. and Zucker, L. G. 1983. "Institutional sources of change in the formal structure of organizations: the diffusion of civil service reform, 1880–1935," *Administrative Science Quarterly* **28**: 22–39.

1996. "The institutionalization of institutional theory," in Clegg, S., Hardy, C., and Nord, W. R. (eds.) *Handbook of Organization Studies.* Thousand Oaks, CA: Sage Publications, 175–90.

Tversky, A. and Kahneman, D. 1974. "Judgment under uncertainty: heuristics and biases," *Science* **185**: 1,124–31.

Tyler, T. 1990. *Why People Obey the Law.* New Haven: Yale University Press.

United States Code 2003. Section 497c. Accessed May 15, 2005: frwebgate.access.gpo.gov/cgi-bin/getdoc.cgi?dbname=browse_usc&docid=Cite:+16USC497c.

Urbina, I. 2006. "Senators have strong words for mine safety officials," *The New York Times* January 24. Accessed November 28, 2006: www.nytimes.com/2006/01/24/national/24mine.html.

US Forest Service (USFS) 2002. *Record of Decision for the Land and Resource Management Plan – 2002 Revision, White River National Forest.* Washington, DC: USFS.

US Office of Management and Budget. 2009. "EPA Budget and Activities Summary, 2005." Accessed August 14, 2009: www.whitehouse.gov/omb/rewrite/budget/fy2005/epa.html.

Utting, P. 2002. *The Greening of Business in Developing Countries.* London: United Nations Research Institute for Social Development and Zed Books.

Vasudeva, G. 2005. "How national institutions influence firms' knowledge-building alliance strategies: a longitudinal study of fuel cell technology development," unpublished doctoral dissertation, George Washington University.

Videras, J. and Alberini, A. 2000. "The appeal of voluntary environmental programs: which firms participate and why?" *Corporate Economic Policy* **8**: 449–61.

Vig, N. J. and Kraft, M. E. 2006. *Environmental Policy, 6th edition: new Directions for the Twenty-first Century*. Washington, DC: CQ Press.

Vogel, D. 1986. *National Styles of Regulation: Environmental Policy in Great Britain and the United States*. Ithaca, NY: Cornell University Press.

Waddock, S. 2003. "Myths and realities of social investing," *Organization and Environment* **16** (3): 369–80.

Walley, N. and Whitehead, B. 1994. "It's not easy being green," *Harvard Business Review* May–Jun: 46–52.

Wathne, K. and Heide, J. 2000. "Opportunism in interfirm relationships: forms, outcomes, and solutions," *Journal of Marketing* **64**: 36–51.

Weeks, J. 2003. "The fox guarding the chicken coop: monitoring exposure to respirable coal mine dust, 1969–2000," *American Journal of Public Health* **93** (8): 1,236–44.

Wehrmeyer, W. and Mulugetta, Y. 1999. *Growing Pains: Environmental Management in Developing Countries*. Sheffield, UK: Greenleaf Publishing Limited.

Weidenbaum, M. and DeFina, R. 1978. *The Cost of Federal Regulation of Economic Activity*. Washington, DC: American Enterprise Institute Reprints, No. 88.

Weil, D. 1996. "If OSHA is so bad, why is compliance so good?" *Rand Journal of Economics* **27** (3): 618–40.

Weinberg, A., Bellows, S., and Ekster, D. 2002. "Sustaining ecotourism: insights and implications from two successful case studies," *Society and Natural Resources* **15**: 371–80.

Welch, E., Mazur, A., and Bretschneider, S. 2000. "Voluntary behavior by electric utilities: levels of adoption and contribution of the Climate Challenge Program to the reduction of carbon dioxide," *Journal of Policy Analysis and Management* **19** (3): 407–25.

Wernerfelt, B. 1984. "A resource-based view of the firm," *Strategic Management Journal* **5**: 171–80.

Wharton, T. 1997a. "Recreation bumps logging as top use of America"s forests," *The Salt Lake Tribune* December 4.

1997b. "Forests' overseer promotes public lands partnerships," *The Salt Lake Tribune* December 6.

Wheeler, D. 1999. *Greening Industry: New Roles for Communities, Markets, and Governments*. New York: Oxford University Press/ World Bank.

2001. "Racing to the bottom? Foreign investment and air pollution in developing countries," *Journal of Environment and Development* **10** (3): 225–45.

White, H. A. 1980. "Heteroskedasticity-consistent covariance matrix estimator and direct test for heteroskedasticity," *Econometrica* **48**: 817–38.

Whitley, R. 1999. *Divergent Capitalisms: The Social Structuring and Change of Business Systems*. Oxford, UK: Oxford University Press.

Wiersema, M. and Bantel, K. 1992. "Top management team demography and corporate strategic change," *Academy of Management Journal* **35**: 91–121.

Wikle, T. 1995. "Geographical patterns of membership in US environmental organizations," *Professional Geographer* **47**: 41–8.

Wildes, F. T. 1998. "Influence of ecotourism on conservation policy for sustainable development: the case of Costa Rica," doctoral dissertation, University of California, Santa Barbara.

Williamson, O. 1975. *Markets and Hierarchies: Analysis and Antitrust Implications*. New York: The Free Press.

1985. *The Economic Institutions of Capitalism*. New York: The Free Press.

Williamson, P. 1989. *Corporatism in Perspective. An Introductory Guide to Corporatist Theory*. London: Sage.

Wilson, J. 1980. *The Politics of Regulation*. New York: Basic Books.

Windolf, P. 2002. *Corporate Networks in Europe and the United States*. Oxford, UK: Oxford University Press.

Winston, C. 1993. "Economic deregulation: days of reckoning for macroeconomists," *Journal of Economic Literature* **31** (3): 1,263–89.

Winter, S. and May, P. 2001. "Motivation for compliance with environmental regulations," *Journal of Policy Analysis and Management* **20**: 675–98.

World Bank 2006. *World Development Indicators Database*. Washington, DC: World Bank.

2009. *World Development Indicators Database*. Washington, DC: World Bank.

Yardley, J. and Barbosa, D. 2008. "Despite warnings, China's regulators failed to stop tainted milk," *The New York Times* September 27, A1 and A10.

Zucker, L. G. 1987. "Institutional theories of organization," *Annual Review of Sociology* **13**: 443–64.

Index

tates
ısher Services